PICTURA

Essays on the Works of
Roy Kiyooka

Essential Writers Series 53

Canada Council **Conseil des Arts**
for the Arts **du Canada**

ONTARIO ARTS COUNCIL
CONSEIL DES ARTS DE L'ONTARIO
an Ontario government agency
un organisme du gouvernement de l'Ontario

Canada

Guernica Editions Inc. acknowledges the support of the Canada Council
for the Arts and the Ontario Arts Council. The Ontario Arts Council
is an agency of the Government of Ontario.

We acknowledge the financial support of the Government of Canada.

PICTURA

Essays on the Works of
Roy Kiyooka

Edited by
Juliana Pivato

GUERNICA
EDITIONS
TORONTO · CHICAGO · BUFFALO · LANCASTER (U.K.)
2020

Juliana Pivato, editor
Michael Mirolla, general editor
Joseph Pivato, series editor
David Moratto, cover and interior design
Cover image: Michael de Courcy
Guernica Editions Inc.
287 Templemead Drive, Hamilton (ON), Canada L8W 2W4
2250 Military Road, Tonawanda, N.Y. 14150-6000 U.S.A.
www.guernicaeditions.com

Distributors:
Independent Publishers Group (IPG)
600 North Pulaski Road, Chicago IL 60624
University of Toronto Press Distribution,
5201 Dufferin Street, Toronto (ON), Canada M3H 5T8
Gazelle Book Services, White Cross Mills
High Town, Lancaster LA1 4XS U.K.

First edition.
Printed in Canada.

Legal Deposit—First Quarter
Library of Congress Catalog Card Number: 2019947114
Library and Archives Canada Cataloguing in Publication
Title: Pictura : essays on the works of Roy Kiyooka / edited by Juliana Pivato
Names: Pivato, Juliana, editor.
Series: Essential writers series ; 53.
Description: Series statement: Essential writers series ; 53
Identifiers: Canadiana (print) 20190166142 | Canadiana (ebook) 20190166177 |
ISBN 9781771834940 (softcover)
| ISBN 9781771834957 (EPUB) | ISBN 9781771834964 (Kindle)
Subjects: LCSH: Kiyooka, Roy—Criticism and interpretation.
Classification: LCC NX513.Z9 K59 2020 | DDC 700.92—dc23

title/s are difficult: they
want to be a haiku of the whole book's content/s
they want to prognosticate, but,
we both know, the best ones, simply, ring, true

inflections
—felicitous—
reflections

—(Kiyooka, "Notes Toward a Book of Photoglyphs," 91)

a table of contents:
an entablature of contentlessness
breath's tracing/s

— (Kiyooka, "Notes," 78)

Introduction:
Notes Toward a Book on Roy Kiyooka

Juliana Pivato

> It was Jean Arp I believe that said, painting and poetry go together. The one activity complements the other and both together give me a context for articulation more than either discipline per se ... that's all and I feel that way about it. Painting ... Poetry ... *Art is where you're in it*.
> (Kiyooka, interview with Sheila Watson, "With Roy Kiyooka," 18)

Roy Kenzie Kiyooka made it difficult to know what kind of artist he was because such a question would have been absurd to him. He readily experimented with legibility through form and possessed an intensity that was activated by complexity, density and excess. His audio and photo documentation and diaristic correspondence clearly render his generous diffusion into the various aesthetico-social worlds he worked within. He was immanent to many important developments in the Canadian vanguard (Lowry, 370), which at the time made it quite unnecessary to define himself as an artist—everyone knew who he was. Roy Kiyooka refused to settle into a nameable profile that could be readily anthologized. He preferred to *unsettle*.

How do you write about an artist who would not be contained? Widely published and celebrated, Roy Kiyooka was an influential Canadian artist and writer who gifted an extensive body of work that unfolded in nearly every dimension of media. Throughout his life, he continued to redefine his context for articulation. His early success and recognition as a painter and poet expanded to include a practice in photography, sculpture, film, performance and music improvisation.

But his compulsion for articulation also manifested as a resistance towards resolution and an embracing of its provisionality: "... I always think of clarity as provisional anyhow. It's clear at this moment but if I talk (sic) away from it and come back three months from now?" (Kiyooka qtd. in Miki, "Inter-face" 54).

Ideas of legibility and articulation emerge repeatedly in Kiyooka's poetry, letters and conversations. In an interview with Roy Miki published in *Inalienable Rice*, Kiyooka discusses how he came to writing after recognizing himself as an intuitive learner:

> "... there was no way I could analytically grasp what it was because it had to undergo some very complex kind of metamorphosis ... It's as though you found yourself, despite yourself, having to do everything the most difficult way imaginable because you had to explore the whole terrain before you got a purchase on it." (61)

Although this statement describes his meticulous attention to detail and the exhaustiveness of his process, it is actually a disclosure about Kiyooka's sense of fragmented positioning and "the resilience of his imagination" (Miki, *InFlux*, 24).

Kiyooka's art activism, his infiltration of language, of disciplines, of institutions, was itself an artwork. He was well aware of the force of identification: that hectoring reflex to name and herd invention into its most predictable forms, and abandon the beauty and pain of the remainders. His comfort in working across multiple media throughout his practice relied on endurance at its core. Encountering the pull between individual and discursive experiences of self, he leveraged his tools (speech, sight, sound). His works were acts of inflection: performing relations, always in flux—always in process. This book attempts to track Roy Kiyooka through the generous revelations of his work. This introduction aims to provide a context for his unique approach to process.

picture this thing; picture it in this exacting
light. the narrative i am questing, indeed
veering, towards, will only reveal itself after
many dumbfound hours in the darkroom. each
time i return from a long walk in the snow bound
winter light and re-enter the darkroom i re-
learn the alchemy of clandestine images ...

each time i sit down to my IBM
    i'm nonetheless at Language's behest

    listen! can you hear the snow—
    pelting, these slant/ january/ cadences ...
(Kiyooka, "Notes," 87)

Kiyooka's "Notes Toward a Book of Photoglyphs" was published in 1990 in *The Capilano Review*. An 18-page letter to the editors, it narrates his working process for putting together a text and photo work that would compose an entire issue of the magazine later that same year. Eventually titled *Pacific Windows*, the work was cultivated from a compilation of his photographic practice and writings. This description of process, of IBM-typed "cadences" "pelted" with snow, speaks to Kiyooka's habitual folding in of the autobiographical. Each sensory detail animates, reminding us of the body that observes and feels even as it composes the text we read, an effect that primes our experience of it. Indeed, "Notes" is a particularly acute example of the way in which Kiyooka manages his simultaneous relationships as author and artist to reader and viewer. Alternating between poet and correspondent, he clearly delights in his playful deviation from second to first person.

a hitherto, un-bidden Interleaving
of Photos and Texts unfolding, page-by-page
(fan-wise) like a pleated Renga Scroll

such are my immediate thoughts; have a listen
tell me your parameters for TCR #3
bark, loudly, if you want me to do a summersault

i would daub this grey november pallor
all over these clandestine filmic faces if the
weather didn't already posit their rune
(Kiyooka, "Notes," 77)

"Notes" is prescient for how it anticipates much of what will come to be discussed about Roy Kiyooka's work as writer and artist in the decades that followed his passing. The personal reflectiveness of his address creates a space for earnest speculation. To "daub" (smear) his images with "this grey november pallor," suggests the possible application of a pale appearance; an obscuring of visible identity with one paler, greyer. He then elaborates that this would only be possible "if the weather didn't already posit their rune." A reference to letters of alphabets in use prior to the standard Latin alphabet, *rune* is easily misread as *ruin*—destruction. One interpretation might imagine the phrase as connecting weather/conditions with image/document defacement or erasure. The suggestion of damage done by language, specifically proto-English letters, could be measured by the metric of nature personified. Is this play of rune against ruin code for the destruction of any image by language? Is this almost throwaway line in Kiyooka's text a critique of the mind's urge to summarize—reduce—confine an image to nameable, definable terms, specifically those images that do not conform to a particular "pallor"?

Kiyooka used a density of meanings in his poetry in much the same way that he used photography, destabilizing interpretations with an "accuracy of perception" (Bowering, n.p.). Having grown up experiencing the world through two languages, his approach to writing was also a construction of context, "Art is where you're in it." His use of *inglish* existed as its own autonomous, parallel mode of invention: the Kochi-ben of his parents' home and the street slang learned as a child

in a culturally diverse Calgary neighbourhood fitted over with an as-
similating application of "the Language of the Anglo mainstream"
("Inter-Face" 42). It was a language that Donald C. Goellnicht described
as being able to "represent his unique lived experience and resist the
hegemony of the dominant culture" (Goellnicht, 11). In all his writing,
Kiyooka invented and hybridized words and interpolated unusual
grammar. It was a playful weaponization of self against linguistic rei-
fication and a blurring of meaning in a manner that also disturbed and
complicated the visual.

> . . . . My painting's silences.
> should we not use words w/utmost discretion viz
> painting/s lest they get in the way. words as step
> ping-stones-a hop skip and a jump over/into the
> painting ... (the stones forgotten . etc.
> (Kiyooka, qtd. in Townsend-Gault, 11).

In "Light Speaking: Notes on Poetry and Photography," V. Penelope
Pelizzon describes her process of coming to an understanding of the
relationship of photography to poetry. Beginning with the argument
that *ekphrastic*[2] writing, any written description of the exclusively
visual, "often positions itself as a controlling voice that must speak for
the silent art object," (151) she argues that the same cannot be said for
any writing that might aim to describe photography. Ekphrasis, the act
of describing a work of art "as vividly as possible in order to 'bring it
before the eye' of the listener" (Robillard and Jongeneel, ix), presumes an
equivalence of image to text. It asserts that the subject, rendered through
the affordances of the visual—historically, painting—can be equally
apprehended by way of language "without remainder" (Bann, 28).
    The origins of ekphrasis can be traced to *Ars poetica* (19BC) and
Horace's Ut pictura poesis, which in translation reads "as is painting
so is poetry"(qtd. in Lee, 3) and offered that although painting and
poetry differed in medium and form they might be "considered almost
identical in fundamental nature, in content, and in purpose." (Lee, 3)
Pelizzon reviews the binary comparison put forward by scholars like

W.J.T. Mitchell, situating poetry as time-based and dependent on duration for its apprehension, and painting and sculpture as spatial and static
(150). However, she argues that although they exist in space, photographs are more like poems for their dependence on time (151) and the
way in which they make time visible (159): "a photo's essence is that
millisecond caught by the shutter, an instant that often gains power and
meaning the further we move away from it" (151). Pelizzon proceeds
to coin the term "luciphrasis" to describe "a verbal representation of
a photograph that emphasizes the photo's time-filled status" (152).

Kiyooka's description in "Notes" of the processing of photographs
in the darkroom pairs the visual and the written as entirely dependent
on each other for actualization. The course of narrative revealing itself
concurrently to the images that it will describe when they materialize
certainly constitutes a luciphrastic portal impervious to standard temporal reality. It is an incidental nod to the grandfather paradox[3] with
the poem performing as a time-machine that can sync the past, present, and future. (Gallagher qtd. in Pellizon, 155). For Kiyooka, text is
in no way subordinate to image here. The narrative can only emerge
from "the alchemy of clandestine images" and yet the images exist first
by way of their description in the text.

In "With Roy Kiyooka" an interview with Sheila Watson[4] in *White
Pelican* (1971) (republished in this volume), Kiyooka touches briefly on
the simultaneous emergence of text and image in his celebrated series
StoneDGloves (1971), suggesting an organic progression in which
"photos and words grew apart together" (18). Kiyooka explains the
accumulation of content for *StoneDGloves* in Osaka: shooting photographs on site while working on a commissioned sculpture, making
notes when he returned home, dropping off the film at the lab and
picking up the previous day's prints. He establishes that *StoneDGloves*
was not initially a combined text and image work, but that it grew out
of the collecting of material, without premeditated form (18).

A dis-inhibition regarding form is evident both in Kiyooka's
own statements on his works and in his published writing. In a 1975
conversation with Alvin Balkind and Gerry Gilbert published in *artscanada*[5] (concurrent to *Roy K. Kiyooka: 25 Years*, a touring retrospective of his work), Kiyooka admits:

> The dilemma that I've come to in terms of art is simply that I no longer know the form of anything. There isn't a form, a container, a structure, *per se*, that is given, that has been given to me, incrementally through all of the past, that at this moment I can say of, "I'm going to use that as the form of what I'm going to do." In that sense I've come to a most curious place, and that is: everything I'm going to make will have to find its form. (Kiyooka qtd. in Gilbert, 12).

Kiyooka generated a relational discourse around his practice: dialogue was his primary method for the routing of form. There is a fearlessness in his work that can be tied to his evolving understanding of identification and positioning throughout his life, a primary topic for discussion on the artist in existing criticism (*In Flux*, 14). But this fearlessness is also revealed in his oscillation between methods of filtration[6] and mediation and in his unique approach to collaboration. His work with text and music improvisation often included collaboration. Many performances of reading and sound that Kiyooka created in private, in sessions with collaborators and/or for audiences were documented in audio recordings[7] or in film/video footage. Examples of performance collaborations were excerpted in both *Reed*, a film by his daughter Fumiko Kiyooka (2012) and *Voice*, a film by Michael de Courcy (1998).

Among Kiyooka's lesser-known contributions exploring collaboration and appropriation is *artscanada / afloat* (1971). A site-specific performance-installation that was disseminated as photographic documentation,[8] *artscanada / afloat* was published as a single page in the Fall 1971 issue of *artscanada*. The header of the page reads "letter's cont'd," and informs the reader that the work is neither ad nor artist feature, but has been submitted as a letter to the editor. Scott Watson describes *artscanada / afloat* as "a rebuke, albeit a playful one" of the Gary Lee-Nova's *artscanada* article that had been published earlier that year (Watson, 15). Lee-Nova's "Our Beautiful West-Coast Thing" (1971) was a celebration of the "life-style" of seven British Columbia land and nature-based artists who for the most part had little recognition in the mainstream Canadian art-world at that time (O'Brian et al, 15).

"Our Beautiful West-Coast Thing" begins with a quote from Jack

Spicer, "We are a coast people. There is nothing but ocean out beyond us" (Spicer, 421). *artscanada / afloat* performs a literal interpretation of the quote. Kiyooka along with Krisy van Eyk, Gerry Gilbert and Carole Itter "took the magazine apart page by page and set it floating off a wilderness beach" (Watson, 15). Images of the group holding the collected pieces of the waterlogged magazine suggest the intervention as an irreverent treatment of the artist feature with its own "back-to-nature" medicine. The "letter" in *artscanada* appears as 64 small images laid-out on the last page of the magazine captioned in all caps as follows:

READING THE WEST COAST ISSUE OF ARTSCANADA MAGAZINE

AT SCHOONER COVE—LONG BEACH—VANCOUVER ISLAND

ON A SILVER DAY IN JULY 1971—BC.

COPACIFIC
WASH—OUT—THERE
BOX 8884. STATION H. VANCOUVER

PHOTOS: CANADAS NATIONAL MAGAZINE

Although no artists' names are listed or credited with the work, the esoteric captions give some hint to intention, nested within inside jokes, including the reference to "CANADAS NATIONAL MAGAZINE" and a post office box, the moniker and address used by the poetry magazine, *B.C. Monthly* and its editor Gerry Gilbert.[9] Indeed the work also appeared as a single issue of *BC Monthly* in 1974.[10] In this version all 125 images of the work are accessible in a larger scale, permitting a more careful viewing than the tiny images provided in *artscanada*. Migrating from its initial evasion of credit however, here a clearer articulation of authorship is in evidence. In the caption on the last page, all four artists are credited for "performing" the work, followed by a sentence that identifies Kiyooka as both editor of the issue and author of the photographs.[11]

In its initial letter-form, *artscanada / afloat* presents as a single, cheeky gesture towards the publication it was intended for and the particular way in which the Lee-Nova article had grouped and contextualized these west-coast artists. Emerging from a collaborative approach to conception and production,[12] *artscanada / afloat* is a performative reframing of appropriated content—a levelling or grounding of rhetorical nuance through its personification in form and time. At 125 images however, the later incarnations in BC Monthly and museum collections[13] reveal a more elaborate literalization. In a typical example of Kiyooka's play with density and excess—it seems to take the idea of levelling well beyond its initial limits—where actions of parody are performed through an earnest exploration of what they mock.

Another fascinating example of collaborative material exploration by Kiyooka is his contribution to Robert Filliou's *Teaching & Learning as Performing Arts, Part II,* (1979, 32')[14] created during Filliou's 1979 residency at Western Front, Vancouver.[15] At the time of this publication the work was accessible on the Western Front online archive,[16] where Filliou's *Video Breakfasting Together, If You Wish* (1979) is followed at 12:47' with *October 19th footnote to footnote A VIDEO-BREAK-FAST with Roy KIYOOKA* (1979). [17]

In *Video Breakfasting Together,* Filliou sits alone at a table reading the want ads and offering commentary (to an imagined partner) on how each advertised position might be suitable for an artist. He pours tea from a Dobin teapot into a white coffee cup, sipping periodically, and at 6 minutes, extracts and smokes a cigarette from a white paper pack. *October 19th footnote to footnote* begins with a view of Kiyooka from behind turning on the monitor to view Filliou's segment. He banters with the video, playing the imaginary partner. He pours tea from the same pot into the same cup and lights a cigarette from a matching white pack when Filliou begins to smoke: "I like these. Robert, I only smoke them when you come to town." The atmosphere of joviality offered by Filliou is echoed in Kiyooka's play with the language and phrasing of the advertisments. Kiyooka's mode of participation with the work seems to invest heavily in Filliou's articulated philosophies,[18] and a subtle interrogation is underscored by the repeated pausing of Filliou's video throughout *October 19th footnote to footnote.*

In his 1970 text *Teaching & Learning as Performing Arts*, Filliou suggests that the difficulties of teaching and learning can be improved — "through an application of the participation techniques developed by artists" (12). Sharla Sava argues that also in this text, Filliou "repositions Art in relation to an alternative theory of value, positing an *enhanced* economy where abstract labour, instead of being defined through the relative exchange value of the commodity, could be evaluated in relation to the "innocence," "imagination," or "freedom it was worth" (Sava, 22). *October 19th footnote to footnote* provides an obliging counterpoint to Filliou's playfully pedantic *Video Breakfasting Together*. As Kiyooka watches Filliou explaining why each ad might be a real opportunity for an artist, he improvises free-style deviations, removing the words to a space of experimental analysis, where each line becomes a puzzle piece, to be inspected and rediscovered:

> [17:27]
> Filliou: Here they want: "... a dependable personable person."
>
> F: "Hours, 9am to 5pm."
> Kiyooka: [simultaneous] a dependable personable person.
>
> F: That's want a (sic) "Experienced secretary"... wanted by
>   White Caps." Whatever that is.
> K: [simultaneous] a dependable personable person.
>
> F: Now, are artists dependable? (smiles, shrugs with hands, pauses)
> K: [simultaneous] a dependable personable person.
>
> K: A. Dependable. B. Personable. C Perso-nage. (Kiyooka stares
>   at the screen, pauses). Hey Robert, ain't that us?"

Following an opening section of direct interaction in real time, edits between front views and rear views of Kiyooka responding to the monitor show him stop/starting the tape to provide more elaborate responses than the gaps in Filliou's speech allow, allotting Filliou the role of captive audience. Kiyooka's play between interaction and di-version activates underlying sites of friction between the two perfor-mances and performers. He entertains Filliou's argument for an artist's universal employability in the primarily blue-collar jobs advertised. But, having lived through years of unforgiving manual labour follow-ing his family's difficult move to Opal, Alberta, the repercussions of Pearl Harbour and the R.C.M.P.'s fingerprinting of all issei and nisei[19] (then classified as enemy aliens in Canada) (Kiyooka, *Pacific Windows*, 304), Kiyooka's responses at times seem to drop into absent agreement —a kind of numb tolerance that resists Filliou's discussion regarding the employability of artists.[20] The fact that Filliou can neither hear nor react to Kiyooka or acknowledge what he brings to the dialogue adds an additional element of tension. *October 19th footnote to footnote* concludes with Kiyooka reciprocating Robert's "bye-bye now" at which point the titles from the video complete the segment ("copyright Robert Filliou, 1979") with Kiyooka not listed in these end credits.

Viewing the work, I recognized a quality of "forced collaboration" in evidence. The term was coined by Montreal artist Thérèse Mas-troiacovo in describing her work *Hello Fellow Artists* (2000–2002),[21] a series of videos "that appropriates, or somehow re-orients, the work of other video artists in a way that acknowledges the source but re-ar-ranges the outcome." (Tousignant, 29). Mastroiacovo's work offers some comparison to Kiyooka's contribution for its playful and reverent treatment of William Wegman's *Crooked Finger, Crooked Stick* (39 sec, b/w, 1972–73).[22] Her camaraderie with Wegman's signature style of jesting didacticism creates a space for the cultivation of relation with a chosen art ancestry as primary practice. Forced collaboration was a strategy used by Mastroiacovo for active viewership that permitted a unique encounter with and through form, framing action beyond the acknowledgement or approval of the quoted artist. By mediating the work through her own actions, Mastroiacovo engaged in a dialogue with the material: acting as a presence that attended to the work as it remained outside it (Mastroiacovo, n.p.).

Although he was an invited participant in the series, Kiyooka's treatment of Filliou's *Video Breakfasting Together* actively explores the margins of this participation. His actions acknowledge Filliou's primary content but they also serve to re-orient the work and draw attention to his own erasure as participant. Like Mastroiacovo, Kiyooka is conscious of the connection of form to place. A common tension in collaboration of this kind is an awareness that the viewer prefers to respond to the solo artist as a primary source of information (Mastroiacovo, n.p.). Mastrociacovo describes her own erasure when using the intact work of another artist, even with the positioning of herself through its selection and her interaction: "There is no additional place —and so no recognition of form. Form is place." (Mastroiacovo, n.p.). Kiyooka's contribution in *Video Breakfasting Together*, a performance by Filliou that remains one-sided, even as it acts to acknowledge participation, speaks to Kiyooka's own unique capacity for navigating Filliou's "alternative theory of value." But evident in his mode of interaction, beneath the play and the banter, there is a consciousness of tone: one that understands the cost, even as it celebrates this experiment in negotiation.

> : if the propensity
> of Language is not a veering
> towards, 'fiction' —
> it's surely a slide down the old
> translation-trough ...
>
> : 'i' suspect i am
> a sheer-product of all all such
> linguistic-transaction/s:
> an intransitive 'noun' at best—
> 'i' translate my 'self'
> (Kiyooka, *October's Piebald Skies & Other Lacunae*, n.p.)[23]

Accounting for Kiyooka's entire oeuvre of solo, collaborative and contributed work is a project well beyond the scope of this modest volume.[24] Without confining his practice to the list of available categories, it is possible to describe Kiyooka as an artist who explored the innate properties of mediation and the limits of legibility (Lowry, 371) by routing dialogue through practice. Charlotte Townsend-Gault suggests that preceding Kiyooka's appointment at UBC, the restlessness suffusing years of nomadic employment and fragmented social context sedimented[25] into a unique strain of resourcefulness: "It is a history where as an individual, moved by inclination or by coincidence, he has been able to perceive himself as free to build a life from dissonance" (Townsend-Gault, 10). *Transcanada Letters*[26] offers brief glimpses of the intensities Kiyooka faced during this period; rapid adaptation to shifts in artistic milieu where, as Townsend-Gault succinctly puts it, "articulating self, finding speech, has been tantamount to articulating art, finding discourse" (10). In essence, language was Kiyooka's means of transport.

Kiyooka's years of transition and movement facilitated a momentum of intense participation in artistic communities. His involvement with Vancouver's Intermedia (Douglas, 51); his participation in the Emma Lake Workshops (Varley, n.p.); his facilitation of the Vancouver-Halifax Exchange (*Transcanada Letters*, 183); his organization of poetry readings at Emily Carr (including one of the earliest public readings of members of the TISH group) ("Inter-Face," 46); his Blue Mule studio/gallery on Powell street (Kamboureli, 39); his co-curation of "The Medium is the Message," a two-day series of happenings during the 1965 Festival of Contemporary Arts in Vancouver (Schmalz, 39) and numerous other readings and performances in Vancouver and Montreal, all speak to an altruistic nurturing of his peers.

Transcanada Letters is filled with examples of invitations to poets and artists as Kiyooka continually sought out ways to bridge his communities. In his 1976 critique in *NeWest Review*, Wilfred Watson praises Kiyooka's efforts: "When he writes, as he often does, trying to explain what's going on in one place to someone in another place, the reader because of Kiyooka's sheer joy in making this sort of verbal transaction has the sense of being translated from milieu to milieu." (Watson, 8). The impulse to support and cultivate the work of his peers by whatever strategy was within his power was a means through which he found much clarity for both his practice and his own sense of identification. Letter writing played a central role in Kiyooka's poetic practice. He describes his letters as "the mode of discourse I liked best, was most moved by" (Townsend-Gault, 9). In his conversation with Alvin Balkind about the editing of *Transcanada Letters*, he summarizes the way in which his almost daily habit of correspondence was central to his work as a writer and how this discovery figured in the construction of the book: "For me, the letters in some actual sense supercede my poetry. Addressed on each occasion to a particular human being, and gathering the recipient's energy into the letter, enabled me to speak at levels my poems left out." (Kiyooka, qtd. in Gilbert, 12).

Kiyooka's correspondence was a mode of diffusion but it was also a tool for ideation: a means of completing a circuit. Filtration serves as an apt metaphor as each letter clearly anticipated for Kiyooka a particular absorption or reflection: an aid for locating focus inside a complex shape of thought. Having recognized that through the performance of conversation his words could flow more easily, Kiyooka seems to have spent a considerable amount of time crafting a route through an idea or story acutely attentive to each recipient. In his afterward for *Transcanada Letters,* Glenn Lowry asserts that the everyday components of Kiyooka's life, "provide a critical aspect of what drives his work." He offers that Kiyooka's own statements in "Notes" celebrate the "mundane" as the channel by which meaning is made legible (375). This embracing of the mundane extends to his disclosures of a more diaristic nature: "My poems are notable for what they leave out. They don't include much of the actual events of my life, which my letters hopefully do ..." (Gilbert, 12).

Douglas Barbour offers a comparative analysis of *Transcanada Letters* and the role of letter writing in poetic practice. He refers to Barbara Herrnstein Smith's *On the Margins of Discourse,* wherein she suggests that unlike the "natural" discourse of a letter that relies on its particular context (Barbour, 15), a poem is "fictive discourse," acting as an instruction or score "for the performance of a purely verbal act"(14). "Historically indeterminate"(14), it engages through this suggestion of performance. Barbour argues that Kiyooka's *Transcanada Letters* sits "between reflection and creation, history 'outside' and artifice 'within'" (16). Kiyooka's style of articulation along this continuum of fiction/non-fiction for Barbour has the effect of destabilizing readers (16) but achieves a particular end in how it "maps a possible autobiography." Barbour frames this continuum of diaristic to fictive in Kiyooka's letters as a "multiplex form" inhabiting an ambiguous status, much like the utanikki (16), a Japanese genre of poem-diary dating back to the 9th Century (Hood Chambers, 94).

Kiyooka's engagement with the interstitial space between the real and the possible also extends to his visual works. In "Is a Door A Word?" Fred Wah reflects on "The Accidental Tourist," a 2003 exhibition of Kiyooka's photo, sound and video work.[27] He describes a slide-projection in the exhibition with images from a series he recognizes — a photograph from the same vantage point as had been used for the cover of Daphné Marlatt's[28] *Net Work* (1980) edited by Wah. He relates a particular moment in the exhibition when, standing before the projected slides he discovers himself as a cast silhouette: "The series in the slide carousel records the shots across the street, mostly to Save-On-Meats. Roy hidden in the dark of the stairwell, trying different lenses, a voyeur, tourist. I walk in front of the slide projector and see my shadow on the wall, then, as part of the image. I raised my digital camera and photographed myself into Roy's photos." (Wah, 43). For Wah, these seconds of rupture articulate a "condition in negotiation" (45) and an internalization of a spatial and temporal hyphenation. He describes the sensation of being captured between image and source as one of being "replaced in a scene from my own memory's making" (43). Wah outlines the discrete experiences of site shared by both himself and Kiyooka: "Not just the explicit twoness in the shadow, Plato's cave, not the real but the 'actually' and the projected, the imagined, the imago, the magic" (Wah, 45).

For Wah, Kiyooka's work also "belies the diaristic" (42). Like Barbour, he offers a comparison with the *utanikki*, that according to Earl Minor "is at once related to fact and freed by art; it is like a balloon that whips about high in the air while still attached to firm ground by a cable" (Minor, 10). Kiyooka's movement between poetic, diaristic and documentary modes across media, enables a simultaneity of vulnerability and circumvention with his reader and viewer. At once grounded in relation while arching out in a radiance of iteration, it actively hyphenates the space between the real and the still fictive possible.

The word "photoglyph" in Kiyooka's "Notes Toward a Book of Photoglyphs," also suggests a condition of negotiation. Fred Wah speculates on Kiyooka's coining of the term. Exploring the etymology of *photoglyph*—an inscribed photograph (Wah, 46), Wah's approach to the word frames it first in terms of the Greek origin *glypho*, "to carve," (Nuttall, 168) before invoking the Proto-Indo-European root of *gleubh* to cut out (Mallory, et al, 143): "We can think of hieroglyphic incisions into clay, or petroglyph, the chipped, scraped, and carved line drawings on rock. But this CUT, what he sometimes calls in (sic) INFLECTION (i.e. the type or typos, that Olsonian poetic of an imprint or face planted on the world) is not a clean and silent place" (Wah, 46). Wah's comparison of prehistoric mark making with coded modernist detachment directs attention to the variable motivations of mark-making altogether and Kiyooka's own origins in painting, drawing and sculpture. To this end, following from Wah's impressions of the term, a quick search reveals two additional records for *photoglyph* that perform in compelling counterpoint to Kiyooka's own application.

In 1958 Otto John Munz of Annapolis filed a patent for an apparatus that employs photographic techniques for "photo-glyph recording" (Munz, n.p.). It is a proposal that anticipates rapid prototyping technologies developed a half a century later. Munz suggests that photosensitive material might also serve to capture a "three-dimensional record," and that photo technology could write "the shape of physical bodies" in space (Munz, n.p.). In 1973, Gordon Matta-Clark composed a work entitled *Graffiti Photoglyph*, which consists of two hand-coloured prints, each a horizontal line of collaged black and white photographs of graffiti-covered, "artistically reclaimed" New York City subway cars (Lee, 164). The graffiti has been traced over by Matta-Clark, recolorized by hand such that it reframes the graffiti text, reorienting clandestine street art as "objects that emphasize their materiality as much as the social field from which they were derived" (Thompson, 101). The artist Jack Stewart argued for a direct line between subway graffiti and art's prehistory, stating that "drawing probably preceded every other form of art, and what we call 'graffiti' was in fact the beginning of art" (Duncan, 45).

> i'd hazard the guess that photography is
> nothing if not the phenomenologist's dream-of-
> the irrefutable thing-ness of things/s: all
> comprising the retinal-world. what the eye can
> plainly clasp in all its rotundness posits
> photography's occulate terrain. each thing visible
> a permeable 'text' by which we measure our own
> sentience, conceit and recognition/s...
> (Kiyooka, "Notes," 89–90)

Kiyooka's contribution to the term *photoglyph* is apparent in the above excerpt. In it, he acknowledges the negotiation of thingness that is both retinal and measured as our sensory faculties shift between the ever "permeable text" and the plain "clasp" of the lens (both "occulate" (sic) and photographic). Inferring an understanding of process as the only surface on which one might safely alight while stewarding the unformed idea, the text describing what will eventually be *Pacific Windows* performs an almost mythical elaboration on a work not yet formed: perhaps a means of navigating the discomfort of its development (a frequent reality of pure invention). This phenomenological twitching between disconnecting modes of articulation captures and performs the relationship of being between media, and the recognition that resolution guarantees no relief.

In his brief statement for his 1991 solo exhibition hosted by Artspeak and Or Galleries, Kiyooka writes: "It may well be cellular or genetic but there's a substance in us that secretes our untidy forensic skills. I've never been able to finger where the 'mind' is located in us but I suspect it has its coruscations in our abdomen ... To find the logos of rapture, accord and dissonances buried in your own guts: locate its bodily instrumentation." (*Roy Kiyooka*, 7). Exquisite for its concision in summarizing the blind probing of creative process, Kiyooka's artist statement describes a submission to one's own body as a container of unknown quantity. The image is wholly absorbing in its conflation of logic, abjection and navigation. His grouping of *dissonance, guts* and *instrumentation* performs in surrender, according the navigation of 'mind' as a tracking of sudden flashes or a finger tracing a specter of transitory insight. Here discovery is a durational action requiring gradations of immersion and detachment.

Kiyooka acknowledges that having honed his craft exclusively through practice he is conscious of the mode of attention that was essential for his awareness as a painter and advantageous for sustaining his unorthodox approach to writing: "being concentrated, open, and not too self-censorious in the beginning, you have to give yourself a chance ..." (Kiyooka qtd. in "Inter-Face," 52). He also remained open to the associations that emerged from the chance proximity of content. Mark Nakada in his 1995 honors thesis begins his text with a summary of his process of cataloguing the Roy Kiyooka Papers for the Kiyooka estate over a six-month period following Kiyooka's sudden passing. He describes his navigation of Kiyooka's office/studio, moving with incredible care and respect and with full awareness of the vulnerability of such spaces:

> In some cases, as with correspondence and certain chapbooks, Kiyooka had established a loose order by boxing items by their approximate chronology. Many of the manuscripts, typescripts, loose poems, and miscellaneous materials were piled on the shelves and tables without an apparent structure. Some or all of the papers may have been moved from Kiyooka's original positioning, but there was no evidence that his scrupulous storage or accounting methodology was disrupted. I felt it necessary, however, to create the archive akin to archaeological methods of "seriation." Using the methodology of seriation, I recorded the physical placement of objects as they were discovered in relation to each other. In this way I had hoped to

avoid the risk of destroying a spatial relationship between
"pieces" of writing through my own categorization. If Kiyooka
had stored letters, articles, images, etc., alongside a manuscript,
it may be that these were source materials, or were intended to
be appended to the text. To separate those materials, or to throw
out apparently "irrelevant" material (i.e. material that did not
adhere to conventional expectations of what might be found)
could have done great violence to that work. (Nakada, 5)

Nakada's statements about Kiyooka's office/studio are startling for their
revelation of the careful coding of space by the artist. His text renders a
subtle ecology that even the most careful observer might not recognize
in person. Prepared by this information, it is amusing then to come
across a passage in the 1991 Artspeak and Or Galleries catalogue, *Roy
Kiyooka*. When asked by Roy Miki how he knew a text was over, he
simply replied: "I abandon it. That's what I do, really ... or it abandons
me." (Kiyooka qtd. in "Inter-Face", 53–54). Perhaps this refers to the loss
of interest in a work when other, more pressing ideas or obligations take
hold. Or possibly, it refers to the loss of a work in a room with such
activity that Kiyooka remained always on the edge of distraction.

   Accretion of material over a life practice implies unavoidable density: the sedimentation of projects with overlapping priority, where
each new movement or displacement affects the entirety of the ecology.
In visualizing Kiyooka's workspace as a system, through the lens of
archeological technique or geological metaphor, one grasps the orientation of the space as critical to Kiyooka's methodologies and opinions
regarding relations of process and its living form in social parallel.

   a
   sustaining vision of
   the intricate palimpsest-of-relationships
   supporting every living/dying
   thing ought to inform an enlightened polis:
   to imagine oneself interacting
   with everything (imaginable) at a strategic

> moment: pen, brush, spear to hand
> is simply what it's always been about
>
> lascaux painter/hunters haunt the precincts
> of these commotions
> (Kiyooka, "Notes," 80)

The title of this volume is *Pictura*, a reference to the invigorating pull that endures between acts of sight and acts of speech. The authors have each given critical attention to a particular text or series of texts by Roy Kiyooka, but many also place emphasis on his work as a visual artist with specific focus on the manner in which his unbounded disciplinary practice allowed for a unique activation of media. A lot has been written about Roy Kiyooka's creative agility and his movement between material and formal strategies. This agility is in evidence in his nearly daily employment of documentation. His abundance of original letters,[29] photographs and audio recordings[30] reveals Kiyooka's interest in the slow articulation of the ephemeral and the everyday, and the density of minutiae that build stories over decades. This evidence of a discipline of regular observation speaks to his belief that total immersion and investment are essential to a creative practice.

> "That's part of being *watchful*, I think. It's a word which in
> some ways I use interchangeably with the word "witness." I think
> that to be watchful is a true aspect of an artist's vocation ...
> The watchful ones are those who can see how perverse we are
> or can be. How we can go on making the same mistakes over
> and over again." (Kiyooka qtd. in Gilbert, 21)

We begin this volume with Deanna Fong's "'*I love you* is a vocal variable': Everyday Life and Collective Self-articulation in the Roy Kiyooka Audio Archive." This chapter is a careful overview of the accomplishments of Kiyooka's audio recordings and their historical value in the mapping of his own artistic community. Archived in the Special Collections of Simon Fraser University are 404 audio recordings created from 1963 to 1988 in reel-to-reel and cassette formats. Kiyooka used recording to document readings, improvisations and conversations, take verbal notes, improvise text for later composition and capture the sound of his environment in field recordings. Most of these recordings are not yet accessible to the general public but are gradually being digitized. In an audio assemblage created for the Spring 2015 *The Capilano Review,* to serve as an accompaniment to the "Pacific Windows" issue of *The Capilano Review,* Fong offers the following summary: "In translating from visual to auditory media, the 'windows' of image-text become durational rather than spatial—an event framed between pause buttons." (Fong, n.p.)

Fong ends her chapter in this volume with a discussion of the solo and collective forms of production that reveal themselves throughout these recordings and specifically "make the production of sociality legible," including the production of physical and symbolic spaces, time freely given for the generation of community and the work of daily life in the creation of art and self. It is a careful analysis of the role that these recordings played in Kiyooka's rigorous approach to writing and making. It also illustrates his commitment to his community of artists and writers and his recognition of their contributions and labour.

Felicity Tayler's "Serial Positionings: Roy K. Kiyooka's 'Conceptual Art Trips'" reframes Kiyooka's *Transcanada Letters* as a conceptual bookwork in which letters serve as coordinates that map Kiyooka's travel from east to west along both a metaphorical and literal Trans-Canada Highway. The work reveals Kiyooka's enduring capacity to reach out and maintain relationships with community through correspondence despite nomadic movement for employment and the chronic impermanence of home during this nine-year period (1966–1975). Tayler suggests that the principles of projective verse (the scoring of text to reflect the poet's breath or pulse of speech) in evidence throughout the text are mirrored in the mapping of landscape within the photo-work (Long Beach BC to Peggy's Cove Nova Scotia, 1971) that sits at the centre of the text in a structuralist grid form. In addition to this, Tayler outlines the way in which Kiyooka's instinctive shifting between image and text and his playful reworking of established tropes of Canadian nationhood within the text introduce a welcome complexity to both the "idea of locality" and the "politics of localism." She argues that this relationship between text and image echoes the pull between individual experience and the discursive invention of self through and within multiple territories. These components of the work interact as a mapping of locus, creating space and place as something that can and should exist beyond a sanctioned imaginary, "the geopolitical entity" that was/is Canadian nationhood.

Veronica J. Austen's "The Pivot of Athwartedness: Roy Kiyooka's 'Pacific Windows'" is a detailed analysis of the publication "Pacific Windows" as a work with text and image. Although the original 94-page publication of text paired with image comprised an entire issue of *The Capilano Review*, it is not available except in libraries that have TCR among their archived periodicals. The poem "Pacific Windows" is more widely available in a text-only version in *Pacific Windows: Collected Poems of Roy K. Kiyooka* (1997).

For Austen, the text and image version of the work serves to measure and compare the relative expression of verbal to visual in the navigation of "cultural inheritances and positions." She describes the way in which the narrator speaking the text eventually moves from being a character in the story to being a viewer of his own experience. Kiyooka's own descriptions of his "struggle to communicate" manifested through an 'inglish' of playfully unconventional spelling, punctuation and word choice that recognized the potentiality of incidental meaning-making is only possible through iterative combination. The layout of "Pacific Windows" (images captioned with text) might connote the defaulting of image as support for text and text as description of image. However, Austen argues that as the images repeat in reverse halfway through the text, by way of turning the publication upside down and continuing to read it back to front, the layout fosters resistance to any direct, mutual description. There is a destabilizing and resettling that is "kaleidoscopic": a shifting of component parts that enables new patterns to emerge out of each iteration of paired material, something that a more discrete pairing could not accomplish.

Austen argues that the fluctuation of confidence in the meaning of the photographs experienced by the viewer speaks both to photography's inability to take us to the place and time that they depict, and to their powerlessness to preserve what they frame. The visual cues of misaligned images and disrupted vectors caused by the pairing of the same two images oriented 180 degrees from one another on the page (with a few exceptions), suggests to Austen a failure to connect in the very act of stabilizing a story. It is a compositional action that she argues is itself a visual manifestation of Kiyooka's frequent application of the word "athwarted" where the friction of inclusion and exclusion in the context of more than one identification (the Japanese ancestry of a Canadian Nisei) worry a fissure in the privileging of one identity at the expense of another.

Max Karpinski's "Diddling the Archive: The Crooked Speech of Roy Kiyooka's *The Artist and the Moose*" is a careful study of a work that Kiyooka had been writing and revising since the late 1960s but was only published after his death. Karpinski sees the work evolving alongside the narrative of Canadian literary nationalism but presenting an "alternate genealogy" to the one typified by Northrup Frye's "Conclusion."[31] Through an application of critical parameters found in the writings of contemporary critical theorists (Moten, Latour, Rancière, Berlant), Karpinski presents an analysis of the way in which the text operates as a recalcitrant reimagining of Canadian nationalism, one in which opportunities for speech are redistributed among an atypical community of human and non-human characters.

To provide a bit of context for this work, it is important to note that the protagonist in the story is hired by The Royal Commission to generate a "White Paper" on a "Genuine Multi-Cultural Aesthetic for Canadians in the 21st Century." It is a mandate for which he is given official documents that reinforce a dominant cultural paradigm, one in which landscape is voided of Indigenous populations and framed as empty, hostile and uninhabitable but for the imposition of force and purpose that is brought to it by way of colonization. The protagonist struggles with the task and ultimately finds that he cannot comply with this request once he recognizes its role in the preservation and

consolidation of state power. He ultimately signs off, though not before
providing playful clues for what might constitute suitable, provisional
repairs to the broken Canadian trope that was founded on white supremacy, exclusion and a considerable share of violence. Karpinski recognizes *The Artist and the Moose* as performing an agitating counterpoint
to Canada's history of tropes. He argues that the text activates a space
of complexity inside the negations of Cultural Nationalism; a rendering
of the possible beyond a designated and mandated "common world."

Tavleen Purewal's "The Imaginary of the Masculine 'Northland':
Asian-Canadian and Indigenous Kinships in Roy Kenzie Kiyooka's *The
Artist and the Moose*" recognizes the motif of palimpsest in the structure of Kiyooka's narrative and its literary allusion both to the erasure
of representation and the power relations between visibility and invis-
ibility. Beginning with references to the burial imagery throughout
Kiyooka's *StoneDGloves*, Purewal organizes her analysis of *The Artist
and the Moose* around repeated images of sedimentation[32] that absorb
and erase one subject to instantiate and stabilize another, referring to
this as a cycle of inverse proportionality. Purewal understands the
layering and sedimenting of the text as reflecting and inscribing colonial and settler colonial politics, specifically the choice of diaspora
populations to be complicit in the perpetuation of a "buried Indigenous presence" established and maintained by the written histories of
Canadian nation formation. This erasure is what is exchanged for an
invitation to labour as a means of claiming entitlement to land and the
recognition of personhood by the state. Purewal observes that Kiyooka
crafts the story through "difficult language" (a density of polysemy and
polyvalency in character naming and storyline), establishing sedimentation as the essential framework for the story where meaning is accessible only through a layered saturation that simultaneously obscures
as it reveals. This density of signification is a performance of resistance
where easy summaries of nationhood and patriotism are upended to
reveal the complexity of relations sublimated below.

Purewal discusses kinship, specifically male kinship, within *The
Artist and the Moose*, through Daniel Heath Justice's formulation of
its performance as a verb: rather than functioning as the descriptor of

a relation, she argues that kinship is an active and activating process of relation that fosters encounters between racialized beings within the state. The story of the "nameless protagonist" is revealed through a series of overlapping fables, each one relating interactions between a series of male characters: Pipe, the avuncular Ol'Moose, Algonquin man's skeleton, Tom Aplomb (Tom Thomson), along with a succession of tertiary female characters. Purewal has also dedicated a section of her analysis to the "reductive and limited representations of the women" in the narrative, instrumentalized solely to facilitate further complexity in the depiction of male characters and perpetuate the established trope of the north as a site of initiation and development of masculinity.

Referring to the work of Jeannette Armstrong, Purewal's analysis alludes to land's extra linguistic force. Land is an organizing principle for Indigenous knowledge and belief and for subsistence through generalized reciprocity. The paradigm of land is a triangulating agent. Land teaches and guides. Not to learn this language is to disappear. The Moose in *The Artist* invokes a kind of land-language and cautions the protagonist to be wary of the oppressive potentials of the mandate. Unearthing the myth of Canadian authenticity, the entanglement of these two characters establishes the import of Indigenous presence, and the centrality of collaboration between racialized subjects for paradigm shifts in relations to render kinship as a viable process within the land, one that the state cannot capture or control.

In Roy Miki's "English with an 'i': Imagining Japan in the Poetry of Roy K. Kiyooka," the author describes Kiyooka's developing relationship to Japan through the filter of languages learned and created. His mother tongue had been Kochi-ben but "inglish" was Kiyooka's description of his own articulation. This inglish was to force a bond between the two languages: a Japanese that would reveal itself in his turns of phrase but never manifest in fluency and an English that Kiyooka would acutely master early in life for his own "survival." It was English that would filter his experience of his ancestry throughout his life. And it was English that would serve as his rhetorical tool for holding his country of birth accountable for the prejudice experienced by his family during and after WWII. Although Kiyooka would emerge as a force in progressive art circles from the mid fifties onward, Miki argues that this formative experience cast him as an outsider to main-stream culture.

Miki's brief biographical overview of Kiyooka's formative years and this "athwarted" relationship to belonging in his country of birth is followed by a description of Kiyooka's emerging relationship to Japan as his country of ancestry, depicted in three works of poetry. In *Kyoto Airs*, *Wheels* and *Gotenyama*, Miki argues that a very clear journey of catharsis is in evidence. Here language leads Kiyooka through congestion and alienation towards an awareness and celebration of his own unique relationship to his origins, closing the gap between the abstract Japan that he'd grown up imagining through his mother's stories and the community of individuals that would become so important to him.

Marisa Lewis' "Strands of Autoethnography: Roy Kiyooka's Poetics of Locality in *Mothertalk*" is a meticulous analysis of belonging that examines the dialogic relationship between Kiyooka's poetry and biographical entries that relate the story of his mother, Mary Kiyoshi Kiyooka. *Mothertalk* is a work of plural authorship and 'serial' collaboration composed of interviews with Mary Kiyooka conducted by her son and Matsuki Masutani that were later reworked by Kiyooka and, following his passing, edited into a publishable form by Daphne Marlatt. Lewis' text focuses on the insertion of Kiyooka's poetry alongside Mary Kiyooka's narrative and the way in which their presence acknowledges the complexity of locality that is experienced by both Roy and Mary Kiyooka.

Lewis uses autoethnography as the medium through which to understand the collective function of the component parts of this work in the articulation of place, community and individual. She cites Kiyooka's descriptions of an inheritance of silence shared by issei and nisei[33] alike, pointing to the tensions between belonging and not belonging that are prevalent in communities subject to intergenerational trauma and institutionalized racism. This silence, argues Lewis, is also a space of potentiality addressed within the work. She presents Mary Kiyooka's story-telling as locating her at the centre of language and meaning-making in the text, supported by Kiyooka's poetry which frames story-telling as central to cultural knowledge. Lewis addresses displacement as a key component of the autoethnographic text. The difficulty of articulation shared by both Kiyooka and his mother is echoed by creative and unstable sites of recognition and belonging. Lewis describes Kiyooka's witnessing of locality as routed through the dialogic and embodied by a constellation of descriptors, exploring the interplay of proximity and distance in both the narrative and the poetry. For Lewis there is an aphasic deferral of meaning that underscores the entirety of this work, allowing one to experience articulation as fluid and forever open to the possible.

Sergiy Yakovenko's "Man Dwells on Burial Ground: Roy Kiyooka and Martin Heidegger," is a reading of Roy Kiyooka's *StoneDGloves* by way of Heideggerian language and strategy. *StoneDGloves* is a work of text and poetry that Kiyooka began while on site in Osaka, Japan. Invited to represent Canada at Expo 70, he was there to install a large sculpture entitled *Abu Ben Adam's Vinyl Dream*. During this time he began to photograph hundreds of gloves that were strewn around the Expo site, discarded by workers installing the pavilions and commissioned works. *StoneDGloves* would later be published as a catalogue (Coach House Press, 1970) and exhibited throughout Canada, Japan and France. Yakovenko's text outlines the way in which *StoneDGloves* operates in dialogue with and in defiance of Heidegger's writings.

Yakovenko begins his argument with the physical context of the gloves estranged from the body, half-submerged in the ground and acquiring an ontology discrete from their association with the world. Referring to Heidegger's "Building Dwelling Thinking" Yakovenko applies the concept of dwelling in space to the particular relationship between the buildings on the Expo site and the discarded gloves. He suggests that the gloves, as objects, inhabit a space of permanent transition regarded as both indexes of the hands that used them and as things now separate from their former function. Legible in the images and in their personification in the texts, this transitional status affords the gloves a simultaneous relationship to human and ground. Yakovenko argues that Kiyooka's serial work of collected gloves is performing "an act of aesthetic rebellion." The gloves acquire the status of art objects independent of their service to the construction of the site, the pavilions and commissioned works that were positioned to be the real art.

A central focus of the text is the proposition that language is an agent, active beyond its discursive utility. Yakovenko refers to the "automatic textualization of reality" to suggest that Kiyooka's anecdote of the text for *StoneDGloves* had written itself. He frames Kiyooka's process as an illustration of "dialectical synthesis" in which there is an accretion or palimpsest of mediation: the glove overwritten by its image and then by a text that performs as its speech. For Yakovenko, what is implied by Kiyooka's text is an equivalent accounting of the words and gloves as abandoned, belonging to no one and then found and acquired through their capture and emergence as a work of art.

Jason Wien's "Revisionings: Form and History in Roy Kiyooka's 'the 4ᵗʰ avenue poems'" is an analysis of the implications of revision on interpretation. Wiens focuses much of his critique on the shifts between found drafts that differ significantly from each of the two published versions of the poems (*Imago*, 1969 and *Pacific Windows*, 1997). Referencing Ferrer's genetic critical approach, Wiens' comparison is not occupied with Kiyooka's fluctuating motives between drafts but with the social and material conditions of the poems' production. Multiple iterations of the work embody an "aesthetic continuum," where shifts between versions describe the social history of the forms, styles, and strategies explored by the west coast poetry scene over 25 years along with the changing conditions and social networks that formed Kiyooka's daily context.

The counterpoint between letter and diaristic address found in Kiyooka's poems enable plural angles of focus and reflection on the residues of his daily experiences. However, there exists no official sequence to the drafts that have been collected and no way to verify their ordering. Wiens argues that revision does not necessarily serve to improve the work and in fact has the potential to reveal the meticulous construction of the poem as an "aesthetic object" destabilizing sincerity or authenticity in the work. He argues that the poem lies by ongoing contradiction: an index of revisions with no stable timeline infers perpetual process without resolution. However, he points to Kiyooka's attention to and incorporation of the quotidian throughout these revisions, which served to sustain the production of new texts. He refers to DF McKenzie's description of the "contained" text as an "illusion" indebted to revision, and suggests that Kiyooka's apparent unwillingness to abandon these poems to a default final form renders him open and available to their further generosity of invention.

Pictura concludes with the 1970 interview "With Roy Kiyooka" originally published in the inaugural issue of *White Pelican* (1971). The interview was conducted by Sheila Watson at the University of Alberta. Both the issue of *White Pelican* and the interview were edited by Watson, who chose to revise the interview questions into headings for each response. Watson conducted her PhD research on the work of Wyndham Lewis, an English writer, painter and critic. This sensitivity to interdisciplinary practice is evident in the questions that were asked. The resulting text provides a generous overview of Kiyooka's observations on career, poetry, visual art and contemporary culture. A portion of the interview took place in the student union building at the University of Alberta where students were invited to ask questions of the artist, his current work and his opinions on such things as photographic processing, talent, the relationship between painting and poetry, pop lyrics, Frank Zappa and parenting the creative child. These questions are also reframed as headings for the text.

Evident throughout the texts in *Pictura* is Roy Kiyooka's capacity for capturing, articulating and inventing the possible even inside a context of conflicted identification and struggle. He accomplished all that he did through his embracing of the dialogic, and his atypical endurance for exploring modes of articulation, shifts between media and the balancing of a potent plurality of social contexts. Chance proximity to fascinating individuals, movements and moments is coupled with his own careful nurturing of relationships and their source as a space of creativity that sustained him as a working artist. Visionary and fearless, Roy Kenzie Kiyooka held himself to account for all that he could see, feel, hear and say and made the rendering of these things through a multiplicity of forms his life's work, again and again and again.

Works Cited

Balkind, Alvin. Interview with Roy Kiyooka. "Laughter: Five Conversations with Roy Kiyooka." Edited by Gerry Gilbert. *Artscanada*, XXXII, no. 202–3, 1975–76, p. 12.

Bann, Stephen. *The True Vine: On Visual Representation and the Western Tradition*. Cambridge University Press, 1989.

Barbour, Douglas. "Roy Kiyooka: Writing the 'Trans' in Transcanada Letters." *West Coast Line: A Journal of Contemporary Writing and Criticism*. Edited by Roy Miki, 29.1, 1995, pp. 11–23.

Douglas, Stan. "Daring Documents: The Practical Aesthetics of Early Vancouver Video." *Vancouver Anthology: a Project of the Or Gallery*. Talonbooks, 2011, pp. 47–83.

Duncan, Charles H. "Graffiti's Vasari: Jack Stewart and Mass Transit Art." *Archives of America Art Journal*, 49.3/4, 2010, pp. 40–49., www.jstor.org/stable/23025810.

Filliou, Robert. *Teaching & Learning as Performing Arts*. Edited by Kasper König. Verlag Gebr, Köln—New York, 1970.

Filliou, Robert et al. *The Filliou Tapes: From Political to Poetical Economy*. Morris and Helen Belkin Art Gallery/University of British Columbia, 1995.

Fong, Deanna. "The Roy Kiyooka Audio Assemblage," *The Capilano Review* (blog), Web. https://www.thecapilanoreview.ca/roy-kiyooka-audio-assemblage/.

Gilbert, Gerry. "Laughter: Five Conversations with Roy Kiyooka." Edited by Anne Trueblood Brodzky. *Artscanada*, 202/203, 1975, pp. 11–21.

Goellnicht, Donald C. "Asian-Canadian, Eh?" *Canadian Literature*, no. 199, 2008, pp. 71–99, doi:218786842.

Hood Chambers, Anthony H. *The Secret Window: Ideal Worlds in Tanizaki's Fiction*. Council on East Asian Studies, Harvard East Asian Monographs. Harvard University, 1994.

Jeffries, Catriona, Catriona Jeffries (Gallery). Email correspondence with the editor, November 15, 2016.

Herrnstein Smith, Barbara. *On the Margins of Discourse: Relation of Literature to Language*. University of Chicago Press, 1979.

Kamboureli, Smaro. *Making a Difference: Canadian Multicultural Literatures in English.* Oxford Univ. Press, 2007.

Kiyooka, Roy. "artscanada/afloat." *BC Monthly*, 2.1, January 1974.

----. "COPACIFIC, wash-out-there." *Artscanada*, no. 158–9, August / September 1971, p. 72.

----. *October's Piebald Skies & Other Lacunae.* Self-published, edition of 40, 648 Keefer Street, Vancouver. 1988.

----. *Roy Kiyooka*, edited by William Wood. Artspeak Gallery / Or Gallery, 1991, pp. 7. Print.

----. "Notes Toward a Book of Photoglyphs." *The Capilano Review*, 2.2 1990, pp. 76–94.

----. and Roy Miki, ed. *Pacific Windows: Collected Poems of Roy K. Kiyooka.* Talonbooks, 1997.

----. et al. *Transcanada Letters.* NeWest Press, 2005.

----. and Bowering, George. *Roy K. Kiyooka: 25 Years.* Vancouver Art Gallery, 1975.

Lowry, Glen. "Afterword." *Transcanada Letters.* NeWest Press, 2005, pp. 370–377.

Lee, Rensselaer W. *Ut Pictura Poesis: the Humanist Theory of Painting.* Norton, 1967.

Mastroiacovo, Thérèse. Multiple telephone conversations with the editor in March, April and May 2018.

Miki, Roy. *In Flux: Transnational Shifts in Asian Canadian Writing.* Edited by Smaro Kamboureli, NeWest Press, 2011.

----. *In Flux Transnational Signs of Asian Canadian Writing.* NeWest Press, 2011.

----. "Inter-Face: Roy Kiyooka's Writing, A Commentary/Interview." *Roy Kiyooka*, edited by William Wood. Artspeak Gallery / Or Gallery, 1991, pp. 41–54.

----. "Roy Kiyooka: An Interview." *Inalienable Rice: A Chinese and Japanese Canadian Anthology*, 1979, issuu.com/ricepaper/docs/inalienable_rice_compiled.

Minor, Earl. *Japanese Poetic Diaries.* Berkeley and Los Angeles University of California Press, 1969.

Munz, Otto John. *Photo-Glyph Recording.* Patent Application. 25 Dec. 1956. https://patents.google.com/patent/US2775758

Nakada, Mark Tadao. "The 'Multiform Aesthetic: Reading the Poetry of Roy K. Kiyooka, Catalogue of the Kiyooka Papers." English 494 Honors Thesis, Supervisor, George Bowering, Second Reader, Roy Miki. *Simon Fraser University,* Simon Fraser University, 1995.

O'Brian, John, Naomi Sawada and Scott Watson, editors. *All Amazed for Roy Kiyooka,* Arsenal Pulp / Morris & Helen Belkin Art Gallery / Collapse, 2002.

Pelizzon, V. Penelope. "Light Speaking: Notes on Poetry and Photography." *Poetry,* 202.2, May 2013, pp. 144–165., www.jstor.org/stable/ 23561732.

Robillard, Valerie K., and Else Jongeneel. *Pictures into Words: Theoretical and Descriptive Approaches to Ekphrasis.* VU University Press, 1998.

Schmaltz, Eric. "The Language Revolution: Borderblur Poetics in Canada, 1963–1988." PhD Dissertation, Graduate Program in English. *York University,* 2018, pp. 1–374.

Spicer, Jack. *My Vocabulary Did This to Me: the Collected Poetry of Jack Spicer.* Edited by Peter Gizzi and Kevin Killian. Wesleyan University Press, 2010. Print.

Thompson, Jeffrey. "Split Definitive." *Art Journal,* 63.3, 2004, pp. 110–113.

Townsend-Gault, Charlotte. "The Living of Modern Life—In Canada," *Roy Kiyooka.* Edited by William Wood. Artspeak Gallery / Or Gallery, 1991, pp. 9–17. Print.

Varley, Chris. "Intersections: the cassette tape interviews between Chris Varley and Roy Kiyooka edited at the intersection of conversation and writing by the artist." *Roy Kiyooka 25 Years.* Edited by Kiyooka, Roy K. and Bowering, George. Vancouver Art Gallery, 1975.

Wah, Fred. "Is a Door a Word?" *Mosaic: An Interdisciplinary Critical Journal,* 37.4, Dec. 2004, pp. 39–70.

Watson, Sheila. "With Roy Kiyooka." *White Pelican,* 1.1, 1971, pp. 18–35.

Watson, Wilfred. "Born in Moosejaw: The Letters of Roy Kiyooka." *NeWest Review,* vol. 1, 10 May 1976, p. 8.

"I love you is a vocal variable": Everyday Life and Collective Self-articulation in the Roy Kiyooka Audio Archive

Deanna Fong

The Roy Kiyooka Audio Archive is a collection of 404 recordings made between 1963 and 1991, housed at Simon Fraser University's W.A.C. Bennett Special Collections. Inscribed on a variety of formats, including cassettes, reel-to-reel tapes and mini-cassettes, these recordings offer a unique autobiographical perspective on one of Canada's foremost artistic and literary figures, creating a rich soundscape of genres, textures, voices, and locales. More than this, the tapes also provide vital insight into Vancouver's burgeoning arts and literary scenes during an intense period of cultural production. They capture the voices of TISH-affiliated poets and scholars such as George Bowering, [Gladys] Maria Hindmarch, Daphne Marlatt, Warren Tallman, and Fred Wah; "downtown poets" Judith Copithorne, Maxine Gadd, and Gerry Gilbert; visual artists and curators such as Alvin Balkind, Taki Bluesinger, Carole Itter, Rhoda Rosenfeld and Trudy Rubenfeld; and musicians Lindsay Kenyon and Al Neil, among many others.

Kiyooka brought his recorder with him nearly everywhere he went, capturing sounds indiscriminately: dinner with friends, a poetry reading at the Vancouver Art Gallery, the background hum of CBC radio playing in his living room, traffic speeding down the No. 5 highway, white-noise chatter at a café in Kyoto. There are conversations, audio letters, stream-of-consciousness monologues, readings, performances, field recordings, and ambient sounds.

While the tapes vary in their subject matter, participants, audience

and purpose, they share the common quality of inscribing the spontaneous, the improvisational, and the everyday. This chapter interrogates
the significance of these recordings from an aesthetic, political, and
ethical vantage, asking: What would it mean to approach art and literary history through the medium of sound recording? How might the
social dialogue inscribed on these tapes remap the field of cultural
production to emphasize the *relations* between actors and objects, and
represent the diverse spectrum of activities that contribute to cultural
production and community formation? How can the act of recording
the everyday intervene in the workings of structural power?[34]

Combining the methods of "close listening" (Bernstein 1998) with
theoretical meditations on the everyday by Michel de Certeau, Guy
Debord, and Henri Lefebvre, this chapter situates Kiyooka's tape recording practice alongside and within his oeuvre. It outlines a community-based political aesthetics that is mobilized through careful
attention to, and reverence for, everyday relations, spaces, labours, and
affects. The recordings document the diverse and unevenly distributed
work that supports the twinned ventures of art-making and community-building, placing social relations at the heart of artistic production. This aesthetic turn toward the everyday has profound political
implications at the level of both the subject and the community.

Sound recording concretizes the everyday as an object of contem-
plation and critique, creating the necessary critical distance to assess
our relations with one another and the world around us. Entering these
works into the institutional art world gives weight to the micropolitical, interpersonal relations that form the basis of social reality. In so
doing, they create the conditions for adapting, however incrementally,
the everyday life of the community they represent by providing a
means for collective self-articulation—the ability to define the parameters of space, time, labour, and value in their own terms.

Crucially, Kiyooka's tape recording practice cannot be read as a
documentary endeavour separate from his artistic practice—indeed,
all artistic representations are based in real life, and real life is in turn
shaped by the representations that give it its symbolic meaning. Rather,
it opens up a minimal, irreducible gap between the empirical facts of

everyday life and the artistic modes that represent those facts, creating a limit case that probes the relation between reality and its representation.

In her article for the 1991 retrospective of Kiyooka's work at Artspeak and the Or Gallery, "The Living of Modern Life—in Canada," Charlotte Townsend-Gault insists that Kiyooka's interest in the everyday is based on a "struggle for the articulation of language, in essence to struggle to articulate the self" (9). Examining a number of Kiyooka's works across media, including his 1975 book *Transcanada Letters*, serial photographic works from the 1970s, and films such as *Powell Street Promenade* (c. 1979), Townsend-Gault identifies in Kiyooka's work a context-specific "discourse-history" (10) in which the authoring/speaking subject situates himself in relation to wherever he happens to be, creating a fluid, even stylistically inconsistent sense of self. "In each place," she writes, "he picked up on the circumambient discourse in order to work out who he was, and, importantly, where" (10).

This struggle for self-articulation arises in the context of Kiyooka's alienation from his family roots in Japan as well as his outsider position as a first-generation racial and ethnic minority in Canada. Modes of artistic expression that speak from the position of a universal "literary" subject are of no interest to him because this position is unable to express his experience of being *in relation to* a majority—cultural, racial, aesthetic, and linguistic.[35] Kiyooka carves out space in the canon for his particular experience of the world, against standard notions of aesthetic and linguistic propriety, echoing Roy Miki's statement in *All Amazed for Roy Kiyooka* that he was writing for a future generation of readers that simply did not exist in his time (80).

Townsend-Gault focuses on articulation as an individual rather than collective phenomenon, exploring how Kiyooka's self-documentation is a way of finding his voice as a subject, of speaking himself into existence. While she notes that the "subtext of Kiyooka's work, even at its most egocentric, is the work of others" (11) and concludes with the possibility that self-articulation can also be read as a "cultural voice in a collective sense" (16), the article stops just short of exploring the political potential of these collective modes of articulation. These

historically situated, polyvocal artifacts do not only serve to produce
a subject in the way that Townsend-Gault describes. They also produce
sociality in a particularly legible way, attuning us to the way that everyday life is shaped by our interactions with others. Rather than merely
operate as a site of self-articulation, I want to suggest that Kiyooka's
audio archive also points our attention toward a mode of articulation
that is thickly social, tied to a different kind of production in the
Marxist sense of the term.

Sounding everyday life

What do we mean when we speak of everyday life? What is its substance
and character, the activities in which it is composed? Where does everyday life stop and where do other forms of life (if they can be separated
as such) begin? In his 1971 monograph *Everyday Life in the Modern
World*, Henri Lefebvre outlines the problem that the quotidian poses
to philosophy: it is the object of philosophy precisely because it is non-
philosophical, and yet philosophy cannot be imagined apart from it
because it is the material base against which its abstract principles
must be tested. The everyday takes on a curious liminal status where
it can be thought of as neither inside nor outside the universal realm of
human thought and activity. If it is, as Lefebvre at one point suggests,
the residue of "whatever remains after one has eliminated all specialized
activities" (32) one might think everyday life so particular, so mundane,
that it is ill-suited to make any grand pronouncements about human
existence and society. It is "a compendium of seemingly unimportant
activities ... products and exhibits" (13)—walking and talking, sleep-
ing and waking, cooking and cleaning, opening doors and filling glasses;
fashion, food and furniture. But at the same time precisely because it is
composed in minutiae, everyday life can also be imagined as totalizing
—so all-encompassing as to be incomprehensible—that we cannot
find an outside position to speak about it objectively.

As Guy Debord states in his 1961 "Perspectives for Conscious
Alterations in Everyday Life," everyday life "represents the standpoint

of totality ... Everyday life is not everything—although its osmosis with specialized activities is such that in a sense we are never outside of everyday life ... Everyday life is the measure of all things; of the fulfillment or non-fulfillment of human relations; of the use of lived time; of artistic experimentation; of revolutionary politics" (239).[36] A short-circuit between the singular and the universal, finite and cyclical time, performance and knowledge, the everyday is the site where social transformation can take place from the ground up. It is the common ground subtending the spheres of cultural, political and economic activity; as such, one cannot hope to revolutionize any of these structures without first transforming the way that we live—first and foremost, among each other.

A revisitation of an earlier work, *The Critique of Everyday Life* (1941), Lefebvre's *Everyday Life in the Modern World* is a passionate argument for the need to reclaim everyday life, which he sees as increasingly coopted by the systematic operations of capital. This work seeks to outline a "general theory of society" (66) under late capital in the historical milieu of post-Liberation France, taking into account its social relations, methods of production, and ideological expressions. This period, he claims, is marked by an overarching trend in all spheres of life towards isolation, organization, systematization, and control—what he terms the "Bureaucratic Society of Controlled Consumption" (64).

This regime manifests a number of correlating symptoms: the gradual dissociation of the quotidian and the non-quotidian (art, religion, philosophy); the decline of art as a life-integrated practice and the rise of aestheticism or "art for art's sake"; man's estrangement from nature under the currents of urbanization; the emergence of the individual and the nuclear family as the primary units of sociality; the emergence of leisure as a sphere separate from both working life and the everyday; the devaluation of creative activity in the workplace; and, ultimately, the overall decline of humankind's basic social needs expressed as time, space, and connectivity.

The role of art and culture under this regime is particularly troubling to Lefebvre: before rationalist organization, he insists, labour is still to some extent infused with an essence of creativity and a sense of ethical and practical value. However, as work drifts further and further afield of everyday life (through productivism, the redefinition of non-working life as "leisure," etc.), art increasingly falls under the purview of specialized institutions—the market, the academy, and "culture" writ large. Here, art reinforces alienating tendencies of capitalist society. It becomes a method to escape the spiritual poverty of everyday life, leading to a series of vacuous aesthetic gestures that "make-believe" (90) that a different kind of life is possible and, furthermore, that this fantasy might be realized through a never-ending series of consumer transactions.

Art camouflages the compulsory character of an everyday life that is organized around production and consumption by offering an illusory choice between this or that commodity. Lefebvre's point here resounds with Peter Bürger's analysis in *Theory of the Avant-Garde* (1984), where he explains how, in the late nineteenth century, art emerges as an institution, "a social realm that is set apart from the end-means rationality of daily bourgeois existence" (10). While art's autonomy from the bourgeois public sphere made it a potential vantage for critique, he notes that it had rather the opposite effect: "because art is detached from daily life, [aesthetic] experience remains without tangible effect" (13). In fact, it promotes "the neutralization of critique" (13) as subjects withdraw into aesthetic experience and in the process nullify their desire to change society. "Making-believe" also corresponds to the ideological surplus value of commodity fetishism, whereby a product is not only consumed as a practical object but also as a *sign*—"the act of consuming is as much an act of the imagination (fictitious) as a real act" (Lefebvre 90). Artworks are commodities *par excellence* in this mode of symbolic consumption, invested as they are with the status of cultural capital, exceptionalism and prestige.

Though Lefebvre's critique is grounded in the cultural milieu of post-1960 France, there are a number of striking parallels between the situation he describes and the geo-political milieu of Vancouver in the early 1960s, which suggests that the emergence of the society he describes is a global phenomenon among late-capitalist Western nations—though, of course, with pronounced material and cultural differences. As historian Lawrence Aronsen notes in his 2010 *City of Love and Revolution: Vancouver in the Sixties*, Vancouver in the early 1960s was marked by "a stodgy and repressive middle-class culture that valued consumerism and economic growth over artistic accomplishment" (13). Its booming resource-based economy quickly shifted its status from "frontier town" to growing metropolis, while its scenery and natural beauty made it an attractive site for leisure-seeking elites.

Aronsen notes how, in the midst of this period of rapid economic growth and urbanization, mainstream values were overwhelmingly geared toward expanding the economy and "convert[ing] the masses into middle-class consumers" (15). Many neighbourhoods such as Vancouver's West End saw an unprecedented development of upscale high-rise construction, which resulted in rent increases that displaced many people. By 1965, a youthful counterculture emerged against these currents—a transnational phenomenon running latitudinally from San Francisco to Vancouver, which rejected the "prevailing myths and values in society: the work ethic, repressive sexuality, mainstream religion, technocratic scientism, and the capitalist system itself" (11).

The Vancouver scene was heavily influenced by the countercultural movements that began south of the border. A large number of American draft dodgers sought refuge up north, and there was an exchange of avant-garde cultural figures such as the Beats and Black Mountain poets, who had an extended presence in Vancouver's poetry communities. Countercultural movements in this era sought an alternative to the individualist and consumerist lifestyle of bourgeois society, advocating for communal living, free education, and more equitable social relations. In short, they sought to fundamentally transform the conditions of everyday life. However, as Aronsen notes, the movement's aesthetics and ideals were quickly coopted by mainstream culture, and as such its political objectives were evacuated and displaced into other avenues such as the feminist, queer, antipoverty, and antiracist collectives that emerged in the decades following.

It is in this context that Kiyooka begins his recording practice in the early 1960s, as recording technologies become more portable and affordable. He is one of many figures in Vancouver in this era with an interest in sound recording, among them Fred Wah, who recorded the 1963 Vancouver Poetry Conference and other New American poetics events in San Francisco, Albuquerque, and Buffalo, and Warren Tallman, who produced a series of tapes around Robert Duncan's readings and lectures between 1959 and 1961 in the Vancouver home he shared with his wife, Ellen.

While Kiyooka actively recorded events in the early 1960s, it was only after he rejected painting and the commercial art world in the latter part of the decade that recording became a major part of his artistic practice. As he expresses in a 1981 interview with David Howard, the turn away from painting was in part because of its inability to reflect subjective experience. "Painting ... leaves out so much of one's own life," he says, "the perceptions that they have" (00:05:17.90). For Kiyooka, the impersonality of painting relates to the "bereftness" of capitalist art, in which "there is no discourse that opens up, in the very act of being part of the process, to look at it" (00:16:08.90)—to think of or speak about it critically.

For Kiyooka, other forms and media are necessary to express subjective experience in a more compelling way, which initiates his shift in the late 1960s to an interdisciplinary practice that involves collage, photography, sculpture, music, filmmaking, and poetry in addition to sound recording. In this milieu, Kiyooka's decision to point the tape recorder toward himself and his contemporaries is a significant one that responds to the pressures of the commercial art market, shaped as it is by the larger economic and cultural pressures that Lefebvre outlines in *Everyday Life*. Kiyooka's strategy is to turn away from the public sphere and instead focus his energies on an intimate coterie of friends and contemporaries. As he expresses later on in the interview:

> I've never been a maker of things for a large number of people. If I had been, I would have sold a lot of art. Never have. And these days, I know my community, really. It consists of a couple dozen people in the sense of doing things, making images of all sorts that these two dozen people are continuously a witness to. Now, that's a tangible relationship. I know each one of them. And the

kinetics of that kind of social intercourse is again a complex matter. But as a creative person, I feel that I'm non-sustained by the body politic at large so much as a handful of people. I would really be in a vacuum if I didn't have them. But I've always had them. Always. Through years. And that's tangible to me, see? So in a way, if I'm making things, I'm really making it for them as much as myself. I make images of them. I record their voices. I make poems out of conversations I've had with them. They bring some portion of the world to me that I had neither the time nor the willingness to go out and get for myself. (00:17:45.09)

For Kiyooka, community is both the impetus for writing and that writing's intended audience, the site of an ongoing conversation that emphasizes small-scale communication over mass consumption. This statement accords with his lifelong practice of publishing limited-run print artifacts with small presses such as Takao Tanabe's Periwinkle Press (*Kyoto Airs*, 1963) as well as the reproduction of his personal correspondence in *Transcanada Letters*. Recording partakes in an alternative artistic economy that is based on communal, reciprocal forms of exchange rather than commercial transactions. In this manner, it is a profoundly anticommerical and anticapitalist gesture. However, at a more fundamental level, focusing on the community is also a way of reconnecting art to everyday life, composed as it is in minute interactions with other people, spaces, and objects.

What happens when everyday life becomes the subject of art and not simply its surrounding context? Does a turn to the quotidian not only alter the discourse around artistic production — questions of value and legitimacy — but also the material relations under which these works are produced?

To answer these questions, I would like to turn to a particular recording in Kiyooka's audio archive that takes the intimate and the everyday as its subject. The label on the tape reads (Side A) "No. 5 North / Takahashi's Pomes / & The Kids in Banff", (Side B) "Bus Terminals & The New Era / Thurs P.M. June 29." While the tape is undated, the content suggests that it was recorded in 1972, as Kiyooka talks about his upcoming residency in Banff and the artists' retreat at Emma Lake, Saskatchewan, that will take place later that summer.

Photograph of cassette tape from the Roy Kiyooka Audio Archive.
Reproduced with permission from the estate of Roy Kiyooka and
SFU Special Collections.

The tape begins with the sound of Kiyooka crossing the Canada-US border after he disembarks from a Greyhound bus. We can hear muted conversations and shuffling feet; authorities direct passengers to collect their baggage and proceed through customs. A border guard asks Kiyooka how long he's been out of Canada and if he's acquired any goods; he responds that he's been gone for exactly seven days and bought some books at a value of five or six Canadian dollars. There's a cut in the tape and the next thing we hear is Kiyooka giving a cab driver instructions to a destination on Balaclava and Broadway, an intersection in Vancouver's Kitsilano neighbourhood. He pays the driver and enters his destination, where he is greeted by the exclamations of friends: "Hi, kid!" "There he is!" "Back already?" (00:10:36.24).

There is a buzz of collective activity: in one room, Gerry Gilbert and Bob Amussen are collating an issue of *BC Monthly* quipping, "It'll be collected by all the universities in North America as the magazine of the seventies that, uh, did something." To which Kiyooka responds, laughing, "Showed the greatest promise" (00:12:27.04). In the next room, Taki Bluesinger is jamming with some fellow musicians, setting the fluttering notes of a flute atop brooding, dissonant organ chords. As Kiyooka enters the room, Bluesinger asks, "How does it sound to your ear? Does it sound good with the flute?" (00:15:19.70). A brief discussion ensues between Kiyooka and a friend—the latter owes him twenty-six dollars. They make arrangements for a cheque to be sent when Kiyooka is in Banff later that month. A cut in the tape and we're back to Gilbert and Amussen chatting as they assemble the magazine. "Witchy Woman" by The Eagles plays on the radio in the background. Gilbert asks Kiyooka for a contribution to the next issue of *BC Monthly* and he agrees, replying: "I'll take a selection of my tapes. I'll put together a wild collage of sound" (00:24:21.43).

Another cut in the tape and everyone is convened in the same room. There's a young woman visiting and she and Kiyooka try to figure out where they've met before. She says it must have been at a party at the Cecil Hotel where someone was putting Jell-o in the beer. Everyone laughs. She inquires about a mutual friend of theirs and Kiyooka responds, "I'll never sit at another table with him" "No?" she asks. "No, he died" (00.26:49.35). People take turns imagining what people might say about them at the Cecil Hotel after they die. Everyone laughs again.

The recording is full of details both fascinating and mundane —the routine activity of travelling through the city, conversation with friends and total strangers, non sequiturs that make us pause and laugh, shared memories that make us feel sadness or nostalgia, the unrepeatable sounds of spontaneous music produced here, on this day, in this air, with these people. One gets a palpable sense of the dual character of everydayness that Lefebvre and Debord describe: on the one hand, the tape records the particularity of a non-returning, material situation; on the other, it points us toward the cyclical time that underlies the quotidian, full as it is with recurrence, habit, and practice, and by which everyday life passes from "the relative to the absolute" (Lefebvre 6).

The tape recorder is a mechanism that makes the everyday audible by presenting a discrete slice of life, captured in the 30-minute span of the tape spool. And while everyday life spills over the borders of what the tape can feasibly contain, there is nonetheless an expansive quality to the conversations inscribed there—both a weighted history between individuals, as well as a community ethos that is greater than the sum of its parts. There is a backwards-glancing temporality as speakers reminisce about the things that they've done together, but also an uncanny future-oriented anticipation as speakers imagine the world without them and think about how the social field might re-constellate around their absence. Though on a much smaller scale, the tape gives credence to Lefebvre's pronouncement that "the history of a single day includes the history of the world and civilization" (4) —that is, it folds the cumulative history of the past into the present, but also engages the future as a kind of virtual or potential presence.

Part of the challenge of studying everyday life, then, is attempting to find a vantage from which to understand and critique it, while at the same time realizing that a completely outside perspective is impos-sible. The objective, Lefebvre insists, is to not passively accept the quotidian *qua* quotidian; rather, we must step back and put it into perspective via a certain critical distancing. This is not to adopt the position of authority accorded to the master disciplines (science, phi-losophy, and psychology) that imagine themselves as having dominion over everyday life by virtue of somehow being outside it. Rather, as Michel de Certeau reminds us in *The Practice of Everyday Life*, we must learn to speak *of* the everyday without speaking "in its name" (9); or, in Debord's words, take it as "an object which is itself less to be studied than to be altered" (238).

Tape recording provides an ideal technical method for encounter-ing the everyday without the pretense of stepping outside it or speaking for it: by sampling everyday life as a series of discrete moments or encounters, the tape recorder creates a minimal distance between every-day life as *lived experience* and everyday life as *observable object*. It is, as Kiyooka expresses in another recording, "the ear's equivalent of a mirror" ("Trudi [sic] & I Talking" 00:06:05.52), which one gazes upon for self-affirmation or negation.

This critical space is extended when we consider that Kiyooka intended for these recordings as works of art in their own right, collapsing the space between the context of artistic production and its content. The publication and exhibition of these tapes was a lifelong and multifaceted project. On a 1975 tape ("Roy + Alvin + Gerry"), Kiyooka explains to Alvin Balkind that he and Gilbert are planning to make and exhibit a series of "conversation pieces" that would occur between two or more speakers—at one point, they imagine calling random people on the phone and recording whatever conversation ensued. Kiyooka would be the interviewer, Gilbert would act as a stand-in for the audience or listener, and "the most interesting parts, in human terms" (00:00:47.96) would be transcribed and displayed alongside other visual works.

A series of these conversations were produced for a 1975 exhibition of Kiyooka's visual art titled *Roy Kiyooka: 25 Years*, which showed at the Vancouver Art Gallery and a number of other Canadian galleries.[37] The project yielded an unpublished manuscript called *Laughter* (1975), which consists of a series of recorded, transcribed, and edited conversations with friends on various topics such as love, politics, economics, poetry and music. Kiyooka prefaces the collection with the remark, "Every occasion is its own artifact. It doesn't need to go through an artifice to become something" (11), suggesting that conversation, inscribed on an auditory medium, is one way of getting at the perceptual, subjective elements that he found lacking in painting. Four of the conversations in *Laughter* also appeared in *artscanada* in 1975, prefaced by Gerry Gilbert's statement, "The people present are those friends we found in when we went looking" (par 1).[38]

Another tape made in 1982 ("GG & RK Talking at the CBC") records Gilbert and Kiyooka talking about a radio project with the CBC, which would have been a twenty-five minute segment of Kiyooka and Gilbert in conversation with friends. The program, originally proposed by CBC producer Don Mowatt, seems to have fallen through because of artistic differences; however, these numerous artistic projects that emerge from the practice of recording evidence the fact that they were intended to circulate publically, and that the content recorded therein was of inestimable social and artistic value precisely *because* of its proximity to everyday life.

Sound recording and collective self-articulation

Kiyooka's recordings transmute social context into artistic content, answering Lefebvre's revolutionary call at the end of *Everyday Life* to reintegrate art and life as a countermeasure to the systematic closures of capitalism. Here Lefebvre proclaims:

> Let everyday life become a work of art! Let every technical means be employed for the transformation of everyday life! From an intellectual point of view the word 'creation' will no longer be restricted to works of art but will signify a self-conscious activity, self-conceiving, reproducing its own terms and its own reality (body, desire, time, space), being its own creation; socially, the term will stand for the activity of a collectivity assuming the responsibility of its own social function and destiny—in other words for self-administration. (204)

We can imagine "self-conceiving" or "self-administration" as Townsend-Gault's notion of articulation written *socially*, a process that transforms a collective's shared reality through the creative strategies of art. The concurrence of art and the quotidian enables a more capacious definition of production in a way that attends to the full spectrum of the word's meaning according to Karl Marx. Here, the making of products is only one definition among numerous others. Production also includes: 1) the production of space; 2) the production of time; 3) the production of social relations; 4) the *re*production of daily life and labour; and, ultimately, 5) the "production by a human being of his own existence" (Lefebvre 32)—that is, the production of subjectivity itself. It is important to recognize the ways in which Kiyooka's audio works enable these collective as well as individual forms of production, and so to conclude this chapter I will deal with each form of production in turn, outlining the specific ways that the tapes make the production of sociality legible.

1. The production of space.

Kiyooka's sound recordings encourage us to encounter space in its intimate and particular detail—the local, intimate, and communal spaces that were important to him throughout his lifetime. Tapes record the sound of rainfall from his studio on Powell Street as traffic whips by on the rain-slicked streets; they trace the contours of the spaces in which domestic labour takes place, bringing conversations about literary value, economies of reception, and the avant-garde together with the everyday speech around hosting guests, serving food, doing the dishes; they record the social parole of public gatherings at coffee shops and bars, registering the cultural climate of the era through debates about psychedelic drug culture, birth control, sexual liberation, and the war in Vietnam.

By drawing attention the materiality of these spaces—their physical, acoustic properties but also the materiality of their social situation—these recordings serve as an important reminder that spaces are as much produced by the people who inhabit and move through them as they are by the top-down structures of nationhood, region, and municipality. The ongoing, everyday negotiation of these spaces gives them their meaning; we code and recode them through encounter, dialogue, and movement.

The "No. 5 Highway" recording, described in detail above, compellingly traces the ways that regulated or systematic space always exists in tandem with space as an emergent social site: Kiyooka crosses the border and navigates the civic grid of the city, to arrive in the intimate, space of the collective where the composition of the space is constantly shifting at a micro level. People move from room to room, enter into and exit out of dialogue with one another, take up different shared activities. Putting these many spatial registers side by side in the span of a single recording reminds us that space can never be fully accounted for by top-down structures; there is always a micropolitical sociality that eludes its control. In this manner, the recordings give testimony to the ways that a community can articulate alternative spatial formations simply by being together that exist alongside and sometimes even counter official ones.

2) The production of time.

As discussed previously in this chapter, the everyday asserts a different temporal rhythm that is at odds with the means-end teleological time of capitalism. Debord insists that the accelerated history of our time "is governed by the reign of scarcity: scarcity of free time and scarcity of possible uses of this time" (240). The recordings capture instances of time freely given, in the sense that their speakers labour in the service of producing community rather than commodities and their attendant forms of (financial, cultural) capital. In so doing, they are marked by—and produce—different temporalities: sometimes suspended or interrupted, sometimes protracted and lethargic, sometimes cyclical and repeating.

In her speech for the 1999 Roy Kiyooka Conference (itself a tape recording that was transcribed and printed in *All Amazed for Roy Kiyooka*), Sarah Sheard notes that Kiyooka's "greatest art—of conversation" was marked by "picking up precisely where we'd left off last time" (40), positioning the temporality of conversation as simultaneously intermittent and continuous. Similarly, Kiyooka notes on a 1970 tape made at the Cecil Hotel that he can record and erase sections of the evening's dialogue at random because "the nature of what occurs as conversation is *that thing*. It is not discriminatory, it never stops, and it is totally impartial to what is uttered or said" ("At the Cecil," 00:12:54.00).

There is a social continuity that flows beneath the cassette's modular format, a temporal fluidity that marks the experience of everyday life. Speakers drift in and out of the archive, making appearances sometimes years or decades apart; conversations and ideas evolve across the long durée of communal life. The tapes emphasize the radical diffuseness of the experience time, and the ways that conceptions of time differ as we shift scales from the individual, to the community, to the broadly historical. Indeed, there is a profoundly social experience of time that values duration, repetition and return, which is at odds with the accelerated pace of neoliberal capitalism and which, by consequence, may serve to mitigate some of its alienating effects.

3] The production of social relations.

Lefebvre notes how social relations, structured around class, race, gender, sexuality, and ability tend to reproduce themselves not as a result of inertia or passivity, but by a complex of material and discursive systems that maintain the outcomes of capitalist organization. This system is largely managed and sustained through discourse; as such it is important to take a critical stance toward the discursive practices in our everyday lives that shape our interactions with each other on a granular level. Indeed, there are many instances in which the social discourse inscribed on the tapes reproduces the hierarchies of dominant culture—for example, in the way that auditory space is unevenly distributed between men and women, in heteronormative attitudes toward sexuality and gender roles, etc.

However, one of the primary ways that these tapes critically interrogate and seek to reform social relations within the community is by reflecting on and refusing to resolve antagonism. The tapes contain numerous moments of debate and critique that centre on issues of race, class and gender—thinking, for example, about the ethics of performing poetry on people's morning commute to work where such performances are unsolicited; the role of privilege (male, white) in taking up physical and auditory space in public venues such as the train car or the classroom; the ethics of exhibiting one's work in a major gallery or signing with a mainstream publisher; the marginalization of certain figures because of their status as "minority" (read: ethnic) writers. Making these conflicts the content of artistic works extends the duration of their critique, shaping social relations in the moment of our present encounter with them as much as in the past. That is, from the vantage of the present, where history galvanizes around certain official narratives of how things came to be, the debate, critique and dissent in these recordings remind us that history is always contested and might have been otherwise.

Furthermore, some of the more performance-oriented recordings sought to use improvisatory tactics as a way of breaking out of inherited social roles and relations, forging new ways of being among each other that foregrounded embodied and non-verbal communication. For example, Kiyooka, Maxine Gadd, Rhoda Rosenfeld and Trudy Rubenfeld undertook a collaborative music practice that took place over the course of several years. In these routine jam sessions, they played instruments, improvised melodies, lyrics and sounds, and through it came to "experience some level of harmony" (par 1), as Gadd expresses in recent correspondence. In Michael de Courcy's 1998 film *Voice: Roy Kiyooka* (1998), Gadd explains: "If we talk, the words are so destructive sometimes ... The music's not an escape from what we do subjectively, alone. It's an escape from what we do with words together, collectively" (00:12:24.07).

That is, the group recognized how easily social relations could default to the hierarchical structures of patriarchy, classism, and white supremacy when language itself is constrained by those very same structures. Conscious effort is needed to expose and resist them, through creative strategies other than the linguistic or representative. In this manner, the tapes trace a self-possessed, self-critical fashioning of social relations through the staging of antagonism, while investigating other critical ways of being together that divert from the structures of social hierarchy and competition.

4] The reproduction of daily life.

In *Revolution at Point Zero: Housework, Reproduction, and Feminist Struggle* (2012), Silvia Federici defines reproductive labour as "the complex of activities and relations by which our life and labour are daily reconstituted" (5)—such as housework, cooking, and activities of emotional and physical care. Reproductive labour is the core of everyday life because it comprises the essential activities that allow that life to continue. Importantly, this labour is usually uncompensated and unevenly distributed along gendered lines. Because reproductive labour is unwaged, it has been overlooked in historical struggles that centre on the reform of wage labour and as such still constitutes an area of 'invisible' labour that is no less essential for the transformation of class relations and economic structure.

I would argue that there is a parallel reproductive labour that takes place outside the ambit of the nuclear family household *in the community,* which creates the conditions for the community to reproduce itself and undertake the work of cultural production. The reproductive labour of the community can be seen in activities such as the maintenance, cleaning and repair of communal spaces; the management of archival records and communal histories; the labour of conviviality including cooking, serving, hosting, and greeting friends and guests; care for community members when they are ill or in distress; and the labour of artistic and emotional support including reading, editing and providing feedback on friends' work.

These activities are all essential for a community to survive and thrive; they create the necessary conditions for the long duration of social time and the thickness of social networks. But this labour is so often overlooked in traditional accounts of arts and literary history precisely because it produces no tangible product—it only reproduces the community itself. Perhaps most importantly out of all these different forms of production, the tapes make reproductive labour audible because they document the minute and diverse activities of care that go into keeping the community afloat. And because the recordings so often straddle the line between community and domestic spaces, we can observe how the structures of reproductive labour operate in each—the places where the household's division of labour spills over into the space of the community, but also the moments where roles are more actively deliberated and contested. The tapes create the possibility for communities to recognize and valorize the labour that goes in to their making, and affirm the importance of these activities in the way that their collective histories are narrated.

5) The production of the subject.

Townsend-Gault's essay takes on a curious causality in its move from subject to community: when a subject articulates himself through artistic discourse he positions himself as an "exemplary act" (16) after whom other "inarticulate" subjects might follow. That is, while her account acknowledges the way that discourse itself is socially inflected and context-specific, her emphasis is on the way that the subject manoeuvres those discursive structures, pulling himself by his own bootstraps as it were.

However, what if the opposite is equally true: that collective self-fashioning creates the conditions by which subjects might articulate themselves more fully? That collectives not only define and invigorate the language that we use to express ourselves, but also play an important part in transforming the material conditions through which their members experience the world? By way of example, we can think of the important social, artistic, and political work of the Japanese Canadian redress movement, which recognized a collective experience rooted in colonial violence, racism, and displacement—but also resiliency, community activism and social justice. We can also think of the various Vancouver arts collectives that were marked by a social as well as aesthetic vangardism—for example, groups like Intermedia or bill bissett's blewointment press, which brought together formally experimental writing and visual art with anticapitalist, feminist and queer politics.

Kiyooka moved within the circles of these and many other collective formations, and there is no doubt that each one conditioned the ways that he articulated himself as a subject. There is a fluid, reciprocal relationship between subjects and communities: communities produce subjects through encounter and relation. Each encounter impresses upon the subject, and in the process shapes the way that they conceive of and express themselves. However, subjects also produce communities: each interaction between subjects acts as a kind of social *clinamen*—a minute swerve of particles that alters the course of history as these movements accrete, incrementally setting things on a different course. In this way, subjective self-articulation cannot be separated from communal self-conception: each pronounces the other in turn.

The tapes capture something of this complex social interplay between subject and community. Over and over they present us with moments of encounter that, in their unpredictability and novelty, expand the possibilities of how we might be together in the world—both the enunciative possibilities of discourse, and the material possibilities of how we live together and share space.

Ultimately, Kiyooka's audio archive presents us with a liminal object in many respects that requires new theoretical and methodological approaches to arts and literary history. On the one hand, the tapes create a minimal distance between the empirical facts of everyday life and their representation in art, in so doing providing the necessary critical distance by which we might consider their philosophical, political and ethical dimensions. As Lefebvre insists, this process is crucial in transforming the way we live, as all specialized areas of life—culture, politics, economics—have their basis in everyday life. On the other hand, the recordings foreground the relationships between individuals, and gesture toward the larger productions of community that transcend the production of objects: the spiritual production of space and time, and the reproduction and sustenance of the community itself. Kiyooka's tapes are a truly singular register of the collective forms of labour that subtend cultural production in a particular time and place; however, they also direct our attention to the ways that communities always have the power to transform the material conditions in which they exist.

Kiyooka's long poem "of seasonal pleasures and hindrances" opens with some lines of marginalia written "at the back of lot 1408" on the Westminster Highway in the fall and winter 1973–'74: "*I love you* is a vocal / variable to be interpreted / by the vibrations" (1997: 93, original emphasis). The poem is dedicated to "richard, linda, paul, lisa, fen yee, mariko, jenny, eric & ol' peat" (93). These lines encapsulate the community-based ethos of Kiyooka's sound recording project, what is at its most fundamental an ethical and political project rooted in sociality.

These vibrations produced by the voice—in speech, in conversation, in encounter—are the substance in which the variable articulations of a community are composed. They are the connective tissue between individuals, never complete in the moment of utterance but always anticipating the response and interpretation of another. The vibrations fill the spaces of our everyday lives, giving them a social texture—the roadways that we use to navigate our neighbourhoods and cities, the homes that we open up to our family and friends, and the public spaces where we move alongside one another, making and shaping each other in the process. Perhaps most importantly, vibration acts as a minimal swerve, a resolute opening of potential or possibility against the closures of seamless capital.

Acknowledgements

Writing is the product of many labours and kindnesses. I would like to thank Judith Copithorne, Maxine Gadd, Maria Hindmarch, Daphne Marlatt, Rhoda Rosenfeld, and Trudy Rubenfeld for sharing their time and invaluable insights during a series of interviews in the spring of 2017. Their words have attuned me to what a community can accomplish. I am grateful for the support the estate of Roy Kiyooka, particularly Fumiko Kiyooka, who consulted with me throughout the writing process and gave me permission to reproduce excerpts and photos of the audio recordings. Finally, my thanks are due to Ryan Fitzpatrick and Janey Dodd for their keen editorial eyes and ears during the early stages of writing this chapter, as well as Juliana Pivato for her work in assembling and editing this collection.

Works Cited

Aronsen, Lawrence. *City of Love and Revolution: Vancouver in the Sixties*. Vancouver: New Star Books, 2010.

Bernstein, Charles. "Introduction." *Close Listening: Poetry and the Performed Word*. Ed. Charles Bernstein. New York: Oxford University Press, 1998.

Bürger, Peter. *Theory of the Avant-Garde. Minneapolis: University of Minnesota Press, 1984.*

Debord, Guy. "Perspectives for Conscious Alterations in Everyday Life."
   The Everyday Life Reader. Ed. Ben Highmore. London and New York:
   Routledge, 2002: 237–249.

De Certeau, Michel. *The Practice of Everyday Life.* Berkeley, CA: University
   of California Press, 1984.

Federici, Silvia. *Revolution at Point Zero: Housework, Reproduction, and
   Feminist Struggle.* Williamsburg, NY: Autonomedia, 2012. Print.

Fong, Deanna. "Othertalk: Conversational Events in the Roy Kiyooka Digital
   Audio Archive." *Un/Archiving the Literary Event: CànLit across Media.*
   Ed. Jason Camlot and Katherine McLeod. Montreal: McGill-Queens
   University Press, 2019 (forthcoming).

Gadd, Maxine. "Re: Kiyooka audio recording & permission for conference."
   Received by Deanna Fong, 6 Dec. 2016.

Gilbert, Gerry. "Laughter: Five Conversations with Roy Kiyooka." *artscanada* 202/203 (winter 1975–76). Reproduced on *CCCA Canadian
   Art Database.* Web. 18 Jul. 2017.

Federici, Silvia. *Revolution at Point Zero: Housework, Reproduction, and
   Feminist Struggle.* Williamsburg, NY: Autonomedia, 2012. Print.

Kiyooka, Roy. "At the Cecil Hotel." *Roy Kiyooka Audio Archive.* Vancouver:
   Simon Fraser University Special Collections, 1970. Digitized audiotape
   (MP3).

----. "GG + RK Talking at the CBC." *Roy Kiyooka Audio Archive.* Vancouver:
   Simon Fraser University Special Collections, 1981. Digitized audiotape
   (MP3).

----. "In Conversation with Dave Howard." *Roy Kiyooka Audio Archive.*
   Vancouver: Simon Fraser University Special Collections, 1981. Digitized audiotape (MP3).

----. *Laughter* (Unpublished Manuscript). Vancouver: Simon Fraser University Special Collections, 1975.

----. "Roy + Alvin + Gerry" *Roy Kiyooka Audio Archive.* Vancouver: Simon
   Fraser University Special Collections, 1981. Digitized audiotape (MP3).

----. "No. 5 Highway." *Roy Kiyooka Audio Archive.* Vancouver: Simon
   Fraser University Special Collections, c.1972. Digitized audiotape (MP3).

----. *Pacific Windows: Collected Poems of Roy K. Kiyooka.* Ed. Roy Miki.
   Vancouver: Talonbooks, 1997.

----. "Trudi [sic] & I Talking." *Roy Kiyooka Audio Archive*. Vancouver: Simon Fraser University Special Collections, 1982. Digitized audiotape (MP3).

Lefebvre, Henri. *Everyday Life in the Modern World*. Trans. Sacha Rabinovitch. New York: Harper & Row, 1971.

Miki, Roy. "Unravelling Roy Kiyooka: A Re-assessment amidst Shifting Boundaries." *All Amazed for Roy Kiyooka*. Ed. John O'Brian, Naomi Sawada, Scott Watson. Vancouver: Arsenal Pulp Press, 2002.

Sheard, Sarah et al. "Transcript of Roy Kiyooka Conference, October 1–2, 1999." *All Amazed for Roy Kiyooka*. Ed. John O'Brian, Naomi Sawada, Scott Watson. Vancouver: Arsenal Pulp Press, 2002.

Townsend-Gault, Charlotte. "The Living of Modern Life—in Canada." *Roy Kiyooka* (Exhibition Catalogue). Ed. Cate Rimmer and Nancy Shaw. Vancouver: Artspeak Gallery and the Or Gallery, 1991.

Voice: Roy Kiyooka. Directed by Michael de Courcy, performances by Maxine Gadd, Roy Kiyooka, Rhoda Rosenfeld, and Trudy Rubenfeld. Michael de Courcy Films, 1998. Digitized film.

Serial Positionings:
Roy K. Kiyooka's "Conceptual Art Trips"

Felicity Tayler

A copy of Roy Kiyooka's *Transcanada Letters* (Talonbooks, 1975) sits in a beam of sunlight upon my desk. Canada Post delivered the book from Vancouver to Montreal after I ordered it from an online bookseller. My desire to own a copy of *Transcanada Letters* arose after a first visit "out West" to the Contemporary Literature Collection at Simon Fraser University, where Kiyooka's papers are housed. My trajectory, moving east to west, echoed the coast-to-coast narrative of Canadian nationhood. In this narrative, Vancouver currently plays the role of a thriving twenty-first century metropolis, which evolved from its earlier image as a "fantasy dream" at the edge of British Dominion and American Western expansion (Berelowitz, 3). Since the 1970s, when *Transcanada Letters* was published, Vancouver has increasingly adopted the identity of a Pacific Rim city. In this alternate narrative, the city plays the role of an essential node in global trade routes reaching out to Asia, just as its artists are tangled up in the complex cultural, political, and economic factors folded into the term "globalization."[39] The imaginary space mapped throughout the pages of *Transcanada Letters*, however, troubles the attempt to link the locality of its narrative, or the identity of its author, to a defined territory.

Roy Kenzie Kiyooka (born in Moose Jaw, Saskatchewan, 1926; died in Vancouver, 1994) is a nisei, or second-generation, Japanese Canadian artist and poet. His *Transcanada Letters* reproduces a series of approximately 250 items of correspondence addressed from Kiyooka to an array of family, friends, and colleagues between 1966 and 1974.

Individual photographs are inserted between the pages of text, notably, family portraits, while there is also a multi-page collection of 576 photographs from his travels that is arranged in a conceptual grid.[40] Within the pages of *Transcanada Letters*, a conceptual "aesthetics of information" pertains to both the inked impressions of linguistic signifiers and to the photographs printed in halftone patterns.[41]

The dates and return addresses included with each letter act as a collection of temporal and geographic coordinates, which track Kiyooka in his travels eastward and westward through multiple geographic locations across Canada, southward into the United States, and westward across the Pacific Ocean to Japan. The "transcanada" narrative begins with a description of his first visit to Japan, but this experience is conveyed as if the reader were eavesdropping because the text is filtered through an interim report on his activities first sent to the Canada Council for the Arts. His next geographic displacement is signalled by a letter without an addressee, perhaps a draft of a poem, sent from Montreal, Quebec. The final letters of the book are sent from a cabin at Qualicum Beach, British Columbia, where Kiyooka observes, "the circling the eddying" of birds between the different environmental conditions of the sea, the earth, and the sky.

As if to complement his own body's movement between complex cultural environments, the visual qualities of the text printed on the pages of *Transcanada Letters* reflect Kiyooka's attention to the arbitrary and conventional nature of the linguistic sign; notable in the unusual choices he made for word or line breaks in prose, it is also present in pages of concrete poetry, or in his mimesis of the formatting required for project budget and grant reports. A series of citations throughout *Transcanada Letters* attests to Kiyooka's eclectic reading habits in which multiple cultural references converge—extracts from biographies of Tom Thomson, citations of Marshall McLuhan's aphorisms, Herbert Marcuse's theories, Walt Whitman's and William Blake's poetry, are interspersed with reader responses to articles from *artscanada* and *Playboy* magazine, among many other sources. Kiyooka's colourful language, unusual syntax, and a deliberate disregard for capitalization and other rules of English grammar resonate with deeply personal (and strikingly ambivalent) views upon family matters, aesthetic theories, and shifting political positions. Tangled narrative threads chronicle the collaborative development of several projects with small publishers such as Toronto's Coach House Press, as well as with respected museum and gallery directors—but also reveal the nomadic conditions imposed by his employment in teaching positions scattered across the country.

Transcanada Letters has led some authors to reflect upon the multi-layered complexities of the Asian diaspora in relation to Canadian citizenship and national culture. Roy Miki has described *Transcanada Letters* as the "contrary geography" of a nisei reading the country from west to east and as a negation of the traditional Euro-Canadian narrative of settlement, east to west (Miki, 143). Responding to Benedict Anderson's notion of a nation as an "imagined community" constituted through linguistic standardization and the centralized production of printed matter, Smaro Kamboureli has looked to *Transcanada Letters* as an example of how Canadian literature might instead produce an "unimaginable community ... constituted in excess knowledge of itself, always transitioning" (*Trans.Can.Lit*, x). For Kamboureli, *Transcanada Letters* is an example of how to take a recognizable symbol of national unity—the TransCanada Highway—and divert its use value from social, cultural or trade policies enacted by those institutions that regulate identity in a national context.

This chapter argues that *Transcanada Letters* is a conceptual bookwork that reflexively moves between image and text. I explore how *Transcanada Letters* uses formal strategies to interrogate the book as an object, calling attention to how the book as a material form is imbued with ideological properties, not a neutral carrier of textual content. I also want to explore aspects of the book that are not-so-directly related to questions of Asian Canadian identity.

Throughout the period covered in *Transcanada Letters*, Kiyooka's exploration of his Japanese ancestry was doubly bound up with a critique of the consumer economy and the post-war liberal democracy that was the common form of government in Canada and the USA. Kiyooka's reworking of the TransCanada Highway as a symbol of nationhood draws upon visions of "the West" (and the Pacific Rim) as it simultaneously inhabited the countercultural imagination. Caravans of "tripping" mobile travellers (some of them war resisters) engaged with "utopian dreams" in their rejection of the Vietnam War, post-war consumer capitalism, and the technocratic organization of American society (Auther et al, xxx). Canada sometimes occupied an idealized position in this imaginary. Consider, for instance, Allen Ginsberg's comment in 1969 during a visit to Vancouver that "Trudeau is a 'hippie' … sort of a hippie, I hear" (Webster, n.p.).

This chapter situates the development of Kiyooka's practice of conceptual photography and, by extension, his conceptual bookwork, at the overlap between neo-avant-garde and countercultural scenes in Vancouver in the 1960s and 1970s—always keeping in mind that the multiplicity of coordinates mapped throughout *Transcanada Letters* complicates the idea of locality. Curator Grant Arnold has associated the development of conceptual photography in Vancouver with an "anarchic" social scene in which lifestyle politics countered the "culture of the commodity" (Arnold, 88). Kiyooka left the city in 1964, only to return permanently in 1973 after teaching in multiple locations including Montreal and Halifax; nonetheless, he stayed in touch with local scenes throughout this period through visits with his daughters, letters exchanged with friends and colleagues, and by reading copies of the countercultural newspaper, the *Georgia Straight*. This chapter also complements existing scholarship from literary studies by foregrounding the visual aspects of book design and by emphasizing that the printing of books is itself a photographic process. Following the Canadian centennial period, books had symbolic value in the consolidation of French and English reading publics, but *also* contributed to the formation of a countercultural readership attracted to open form poetics and intermedial artistic practices, including conceptual photography. In order to address these issues I will focus on a family portrait inserted by Kiyooka between two pages of letters, which allows me to reflect on his sensitivity to the intricate relationship between print culture, identity, and the nation-state. In contrast, the photographic series *Long Beach BC to Peggy's Cove Nova Scotia* (1971) opens up a discussion about his conceptual and countercultural affiliations, and I also address the poetics of "localism" in projective verse as it traverses the semantic registers of texts and images.

Intermedial Forms and Altered Consciousness

The front and back covers of *Transcanada Letters* show a multi-coloured illustrated map of the country, overlaid by black and white snapshots of the East and West coasts that are clasped in the left and right hands of the artist (Fig. I). The map's swirling amorphous shapes hold out the promise of an expansive psychedelic geography, as if one might "trip" through altered states of consciousness into another sense of place. Two snapshots confirm Kiyooka's presence on both edges of the continent at a specific time and location. A tiny figure perched on the craggy rocks directs our gaze towards the crashing waves and swirling tidal pools of the ocean. But the expansive visual field of the photographs is displayed alongside a grid indicating measurements of longitude and latitude. A scattering of notations anchors the meaning of the colours to the "rational" explanation provided by the legend of the geological map. "Cratonic Regions" designate rock formations across the continent, which have been enumerated (and therefore commodified) according to the soil quality and exploitable natural resources contained within Canada's geopolitical borders. But on this book cover Kiyooka has placed this grid between his hands, thereby turning the national territory into a material form that the artist can use to construct an imaginary space. This play between image and text introduces multiple semantic registers and indicates Kiyooka's awareness of how the technologies of book publishing use an invisible typographic grid to structure all visible marks (both text and images) on the printed pages.

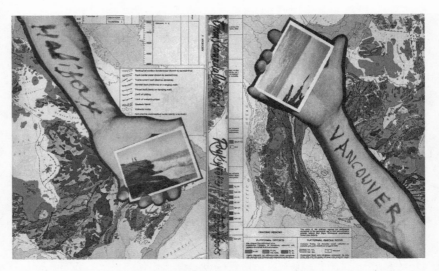

Wrap-around cover of Roy K. Kiyooka, *Transcanada Letters*. Talonbooks, 1975, 28 × 22 cm, closed; 28 × 46 cm, open. With permission of Kiyo Kiyooka. [Photo: author]

Kiyooka designated this, his "book-of-letters," as a companion to the exhibition catalogue produced the same year for the retrospective exhibition *Roy K. Kiyooka: 25 Years* (Kiyooka, *Transcanada Letters*, 358).[42] The exhibition, organized by the Vancouver Art Gallery, and its two accompanying publications marked his success as an established Canadian artist celebrated for his abstract painting. Kiyooka developed a distinctive hard-edge geometric style by the mid-1960s following his relocation from the Regina College of Art to teach at the Vancouver School of Art in 1959. His arrival in Vancouver had a significant impact upon younger painters in the city, as the hard-edge forms and tendency to work in series differed from the regional style of lyrical abstraction, which artists such as Jack Shadbolt (1909–1998) produced in response to the surrounding coastal landscape. Furthermore, Kiyooka's take on the New York School of abstract painting was less that of critic Clement Greenberg's formalism and closer to the ritual ideograms pursued by Barnett Newman.[43] On the one hand, as curator Diana Nemiroff notes, a sense of locality can be detected in the urban landmarks that influenced Kiyooka's compositional forms (such as the elliptical shape of the Granville Street Bridge); on the other, his style of abstraction transforms these signifiers of locality into a transcendent "spiritual confrontation that could take place anywhere" (Nemiroff, 225). This spiritual dimension, as it developed from Kiyooka's forays into painterly abstraction in the 1950s, was congruent with his experience of heightened perceptual states induced through hallucinogens such as peyote (Reid 279). His exploration of altered consciousness continued throughout the 1960s and 70s, with the use of LSD and marijuana (F. Kiyooka, *Reed*, 40:57). This detail is significant because it expands our understanding of his "local" reference points in Vancouver: Kiyooka frequented an early bohemian scene that gathered in venues such as the Cellar Club or the Sound Gallery for live performances of jazz, poetry, lightshows, and dance. In the second half of the 1960s this scene overlapped with a wider countercultural movement that valued nomadic patterns of travel. Thus, the locality of *Transcanada Letters* includes psychedelic tripping as well as multiple, concrete landmarks scattered across several urban and rural sites in North America, Japan, and Europe which he may, or may not, have physically visited.

Kiyooka's engagement with poetry and conceptual photography is sometimes linked to his abandonment of painting in 1969, as if the two modes were incompatible.[44] However, his exploration of printed text and photographic images paralleled his painting practice from the early 1960s onwards, as Kiyooka engaged with intermedial "happenings," recorded sound, and collaged material found in mass media sources. One of his first projects upon arrival in Vancouver was to organize an event with three of his students.[45] Images clipped from old magazines were then projected and combined with a polyphonic arrangement of prerecorded music to produce a multi-sensory environment. The presence of Charles Olson, Robert Creeley, Allen Ginsberg, and others at the 1963 Vancouver Poetry Conference has been cited as an important influence on Kiyooka's adoption of open form poetics; also important was his experience of the annual Festival of Contemporary Art, which brought figures of the American neo-avant-garde to the city, such as John Cage, Merce Cunningham, Robert Rauschenberg, Gerd Stern, Stan Brakhage, and Bruce Connor. In 1964 and 1965, the Festival provided a platform for these neo-avant-garde practices to converge with the media theory of Marshall McLuhan, who proposed that the technological environment was an extension of the body's sensorium.[46]

Susan Sontag has used the phrase "erotics of art" to describe strategies of the neo-avant-garde which echoed the countercultural desire to reconfigure the body's sensorium through aesthetic experience.[47] In the late 1960s, Vancouver's Intermedia Society was a site where McLuhan's notion of the sensorium could interface with the countercultural idea of altered consciousness. For many of Kiyooka's friends and colleagues in Vancouver, with whom he remained in touch during his absence, the radical potential of eros was a powerful means to politicize McLuhan's insight that shifts in communications technologies would affect human spatial awareness, moving away from the linearity of the printed word towards a multisensory, acoustic, collage-like environment (Fairnbarn, 81–91). In a letter to his wife Monica, reproduced in *Transcanada Letters*, Kiyooka favourably describes one of their babysitters: "She tells me about her acid trips. She is a friend of the children and very very gentle. I wld [sic] say she was one of the tribe Marcuse talks about in the *Georgia Straight* vol. 3/no. 51 (March 28/ April 3rd'69 issue)" (Kiyooka, *Transcanada* Letters, 43–44). This reference to theorist Herbert Marcuse and his connection to Vancouver through Kiyooka's citation is worth noting. When Marcuse lectured at Simon Fraser University in 1969, he argued that eros, the Freudian psychological drive for life, was the impulse behind a polymorphous eroticization of the body in relation to the surrounding environment —both the natural and media environment (Fairnbarn, 82).

Using McLuhan's vocabulary, it could be said that *Transcanada Letters* acts as a "probe" (Cavell, "McLuhan in Space," 93, 146). The book deliberately uses the "old media" of the printed page to produce a counter-environment to the communications media universe, which Scott Watson has argued was then being adopted as a "national value" in Canada (Watson, n.p.). McLuhan predicted that film, television, and radio would lead to the end of national cultures and the revival of collective identification through a post-national "tribal" affiliation formerly associated with oral cultures. He also believed that, due to their attention to form and material processes, artists were in a unique position to reveal this shift to a post-national space. They could produce "counter-environments" as new media technologies replaced older forms that nonetheless remained as residual traces of an older culture.

In 1975, the year that *Transcanada Letters* was published, the book form had symbolic value in the building of a national culture. Foreign media had historically dominated Canadian markets, but the debates over Canadian sovereignty in the 1960s and 1970s, as well as heightened opposition to US intervention in Vietnam, foregrounded the ideological role of this imported media; for many commentators, "American" images of the world were inculcating "Canadian" consumers (Cavell, "World Famous," 85–92). Within *Transcanada Letters,* Kiyooka draws a parallel between the discourse of Canadian cultural nationalism in the period following the First World War and that of the 1970s when he rereads Tom Thomson's serialized approach to painting as "conceptual art trips" akin to his own serial writing and photographic practice (Kiyooka, *Transcanada Letters,* 161).

Kiyooka's *Transcanada Letters* can be positioned in relation to the many Canadian and international Conceptual Art bookworks where photography and the codex form converge. Exhibitions such as Anne Moeglin-Delcroix's *Esthétique du livre d'artistes, 1960–1980,* or Matthew S. Witkovsky's *Light Years: Conceptual Art and the Photograph, 1964–1977,* and scholarly studies such as essays included in *The Photobook: From Talbot to Ruscha and Beyond,* have contributed to an understanding of the conceptual bookwork as a genre that combines photographic technologies and the form of the book in a reflexive exploration of the material and metaphorical consequences of reproduction. The ways in which the genre lends itself to the documentation of ephemeral acts or to circulation through unconventional distribution channels has also been foregrounded in exhibitions such as *Global Conceptualism: Points of Origin, 1950s-1980s* and *Traffic: Conceptual Art in Canada, 1965–1980,* as well as scholarly studies including Johanna Drucker's *A Century of Artists' Books* and Liz Kotz's *Words to be Looked At: Language in 1960s Art.* Furthermore, Moeglin-Delcroix, Drucker, and Kotz all recognize that conceptual bookworks and poetic genres such as concrete poetry and projective verse share a common preoccupation with language and image as material signifiers, just as the distribution networks and readerships for these publications overlap.

Within this discursive framing, the genre of conceptual book-works is sometimes described as a "cheaply produced paperback" following the example of Edward Ruscha's travel narrative, *Twenty-Six Gasoline Stations* (1965).[48] As in Ruscha's travel narratives, the sequencing of the pages in *Transcanada Letters* acts as an ordering system that arranges banal snapshots according to a grid. Theorist Sianne Ngai has observed that in the work of Ruscha, this sequential arrangement produces a minimal affective response in a reader, which reflects the suppression of emotion within the information and communication systems driving post-industrial economies (Ngai, 777–817). Kiyooka's approach differs from Ruscha's analytic conceptualism in that his images are *not* generic or banal; instead they convey what Michael Ondaatje appreciated as an affective excess of "commonplace moods" when he read the book (Ondaatje, n.p.). Reconsidering *Transcanada Letters* as a conceptual bookwork rather than a literary work allows for a discussion of excess as an aesthetic strategy that is in keeping with the appearance of low-quality production values, or the misleading "cheap paperback" appearance of this book. The quarto format (22 × 28 cm) of *Transcanada Letters* resembles the exhibition catalogue, which Talonbooks simultaneously printed to accompany *Roy K. Kiyooka: 25 Years*. Despite *Transcanada Letters'* resemblance to an exhibition catalogue in size, its soft-cover perfect binding, relatively inconsistent print quality, poor contrast between lights and darks in the images, and bleeding ink between pages means that the book appears to have more in common with paperback genres than with high-quality art books. While Talonbooks took on the exhibition catalogue as a commercial print job, it was underwritten and distributed by the publisher, the Vancouver Art Gallery. In contrast, when Talonbooks acted as publisher for *Transcanada Letters*, Kiyooka's aesthetic choice of a non-standard trim size was incompatible with a vision of the press as a viable contender in a subsidized literary publishing industry.

Talonbooks, the publisher of *Transcanada Letters*, began as a poetry imprint, but also supplemented their funds as the printer for exhibition catalogues and other materials that reflected the interests of overlapping countercultural and avant-garde social milieus in Vancouver. The press was part of a network of physical and imaginary meeting places that included spaces such as the Vancouver Art Gallery, the Intermedia Society, and the New Era Social Club, bars such as the Cecil Hotel, the pages of *Tish* magazine, and the *Georgia Straight* newspaper.[49] *Transcanada Letters* marks a moment of transition for the press, when it consolidated resources in order to become a financially viable business. In this sense, Kiyooka's bookwork was a commodity produced for the literary market and subsidized "with the assistance of the Canada Council," as it states in the colophon. However, Karl Seigler (who joined Talonbooks as business manager in 1974, with the mandate to make the press commercially viable) remembers that *Transcanada Letters* was the last extravagant project that the press undertook: "the project was so expensive that no other publisher wanted to touch it" (Seigler, n.p.). By the standards of the publishing industry, the counter-cultural attitude assumed by Kiyooka's conceptual bookwork was one of excess.[50]

Literary scholars who have engaged with *Transcanada Letters* tend to focus on the textual content of the book, at best treating the pictorial elements as mere illustration, secondary to the text. The 2005 reprint of *Transcanada Letters* has actually done away with the striking cover illustration and the full-bleed images of the title and end pages.[51] Intrusive margins have been added around the eighteen-page photographic series, which was originally printed so that the gridded images exceeded the edge of the pages. These cost-saving omissions have consequences for readers' experience of the work in ways that run counter to Kiyooka's earlier aesthetic decisions. Visually, the pages of textual content may at first seem to outnumber the images included in *Transcanada Letters;* however, on a closer reading, the images (over 576) outnumber the pages of text. Furthermore, these images are not subordinate to the letters' contents. Instead, photographic images operate in a complementary relationship to text—what Roland Barthes has described as "relay" as found in cartoons, comic strips and film (Barthes, 41). The linguistic message of the text works in parallel to the iconic message conveyed by images, advancing the action, as Barthes explains, "by setting out, in the sequence of messages, meanings that are not to be found in the image itself" (41).

As *Transcanada Letters* followed fourteen other printed works, it could be said that Kiyooka's aesthetics of emotional and material excess are informed by a long-term engagement with the material processes of publishing. His previous forays are linked both to poetry and to the circulation of images and text in the visual arts press.[52] A first book of poetry, *Kyoto Airs* (Designed by Takao Tanabe for Periwinkle Press, 1964) received a favourable review in *Tish 25* (June 1964) (Hogg, 2). Kiyooka's "Vancouver Poems" appeared in George Bowering's magazine, *Imago* II (1965), the same year he produced a series of collages to illustrate Bowering's *The Man in Yellow Boots/El Hombre de las Botas Amarillas* (1965). His literary conversations were not restricted to the *Tish* magazine circle. For instance, Kiyooka also produced a dreamily psychedelic series of Xerographic illustrations to accompany Dorothy Livesay's poems in *The Unquiet Bed* (Ryerson Press, 1967). Livesay's book, and Kiyooka's first self-illustrated book of poems, *Nevertheless These Eyes* (Coach House Press, 1967), both share mirror-like reflective dust jackets and textures derived from repeated acts of photo-copying. *StoneDGloves* (Coach House Press, 1970) marks Kiyooka's turn towards the conceptual bookwork combining image and text. Kiyooka's photocollages catalogue the gloves discarded by anonymous workers at the site of Expo '70 in Osaka, Japan.[53] Scott Toguri McFarland has argued that the photocollages, and the poems which overlay the images, are an "ideogrammatic assemblage" that not only anchor the meaning of the gloves as a sign of labour conditions in a global information economy, but also act as a memory-trace of the vapourized bodies of victims of the atomic bomb (Fig. 2) (McFarland, 119). *The Eye of the Landscape,* Kiyooka's contribution to the *BC Almanac(H)C-B* (National Film Board of Canada, 1970), includes serial images showing sunlight traversing the pages of a monograph on the life of the post-Impressionist Dutch painter, Vincent van Gogh. Kiyooka has inserted his own images between the pages of the book. This photographic series printed on newsprint paper continued his conceptual investigation into authorship, identity, the photographic process, and mass reproduction techniques. The serial poem *letters purporting to be abt Tom Thomson* (1972), published in *artscanada* magazine, again pursues a reflection upon authorship and

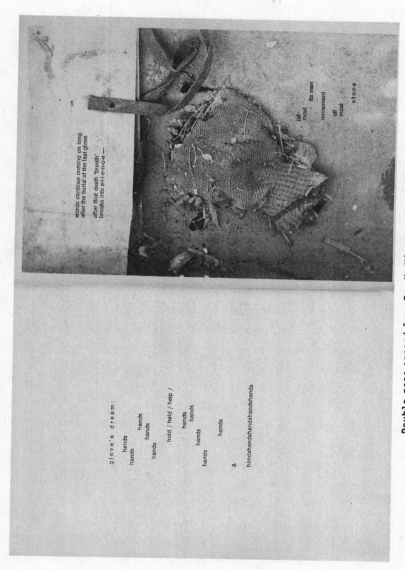

Double-page spread from Roy K. Kiyooka, *StoneDGloves* (Toronto: Coach House Press, 1970, n.p., 23 × 34 cm, open). With permission of Kiyo Kiyooka. [Photo: author]

identity as constructed through images and text circulated in mass cultural forms—this time, inhabiting the pages of a magazine with a mandate to promote national culture.[54]

In the commercial offset photolithographic printing process, image and text are fixed to the printing plate by exposing a film negative derived from photographs taken of pasted-up layouts of elements arranged on a grid. This common mode of reproduction means, as Kotz has observed, that both open form poetics and conceptual photography share an indexical mode (Kotz, 5). Within *Transcanada Letters*, the book form, its textual content, and the photographs work as equalized systems of signification, which gather together images and text as discrete units of relational information. Sheryl Conkelton has similarly described Kiyooka's aesthetic choices as a "personalized formalism" that uses narrative as a grid or ordering system placed over intimate content (Conkelton, 109). When this cataloguing of emotional space is read through conceptual aesthetics of information, it becomes evident that *Transcanada Letters* plays with the connotative meaning of the photographic "subject."

As Conkelton has also suggested, Kiyooka's *Transcanada Letters* bears comparison with conceptual bookworks produced by his contemporary, Michael Snow. For instance, the bookwork *Michael Snow/A Survey* (1970) was produced as the exhibition catalogue for the artist's solo show at the Art Gallery of Ontario. Regardless of the book's "subject" (which would be Snow himself), the catalogue engages with the limits of representation as determined by the specific qualities of photography and its processes. Alongside the textual accounts of the artist's career, several pages of the catalogue assume the form of a souvenir album, tracing the artist's family lineage back to the 1800s in a series of graphic layout grids. *Transcanada Letters* shares some features with *Michael Snow/A Survey*, including Kiyooka's exploration of the graphic layout of the book as a sequenced narrative structure and his presentation of his family lineage in relation to his status as a "Canadian artist." But there is an important distinction to be made as well. Snow uses the bookwork to show how photography and photo-mechanical reproduction technologies produce flattened representations of entities in the "real" world. In contrast, Kiyooka's photographs engage with the "performativity of documentation" discussed by Phillip Auslander (Auslander, 5). His photographs stage identity in an analogous mode to speech acts, which require a reader's reception to complete the event.

Transmissions Across Multifaceted Affective Spaces

Kiyooka includes a series of family portraits in *Transcanada Letters*, the second of which is a snapshot depicting six children posing in a field (Fig. 3). They appear to stand on top of crusty snow. Behind them, leafless trees mark the property line. I imagine the children shivering as they jam their hands into their pockets. The unmistakable icon of a Toronto Maple Leafs hockey club sweater peaks out from the waistband of one of the boy's unseasonably short pants. At first, the relationship of these children to each other, or to Roy Kiyooka, is ambiguous for me, as the image is simply captioned: "Opal, Alberta: Early '40s / *left to right:* George, Roy, Harry, Joyce, Frank and Irene." This image is inserted between two letters dated to Kiyooka's 1971 arrival in Calgary to teach for a semester at the Provincial Institute of Technology and Art. Kiyooka spent most of his childhood in the city, but it was also a site of racially motivated hostilities amplified by national policy enacted in the Second World War (Miki, "Inter-Face," 43). The Kiyooka family was fingerprinted and identified as "enemy aliens" under the War Measures Act, just as the city became a flashpoint for violence. Kiyooka's schooling was interrupted three weeks into grade ten when his family made the difficult decision to relocate to a single room cabin in Opal, Alberta, taking up the brutal work of farming life alongside other displaced Japanese Canadian families (Miki, "Coruscations," 304). In the photograph, Joyce, Frank, and Irene (three younger siblings) grin for the camera, but to my eye, George, Roy and Harry face the camera with expressions of defiance, confusion, and unease. Rather than using a first person pronoun in the caption, Kiyooka has chosen to identify "Roy" in the third person. This suggests an emotional distancing from the photograph, as it fixes the figures portrayed in that time and place.

"Opal, Alberta: Early '40s," in Roy K. Kiyooka, *Transcanada Letters* (Vancouver: Talonbooks, 1975, n.p.).
Note the bleeding of ink between pages. With permission of Kiyo Kiyooka. [Photo: author]

Kiyooka's identity formation, as it is shared with us throughout the pages of *Transcanada Letters*, moves between historical episodes and Kiyooka's later experiences. These temporal dislocations call attention to the contradiction arising between a racial category that was legally designated as the nation's "other," and Kiyooka's later conflicted desire to contribute images to the symbolic order that defined a national culture. Following the war, Kiyooka returned to Calgary from Opal to study under Illingworth Kerr (1905–1989) and Jock Macdonald (1897–1960) at the same institution in which he would later teach. There he was introduced to the tradition of the Group of Seven painters, and it was then that he articulated his desire to become a Canadian artist: "I remember saying to one of my friends at the time that one of my ambitions was to become a great Canadian painter, that was in my third year of art school" (R. Kiyooka, *Reed*, 10:22). Macdonald was a follower of the Group of Seven landscape painters but was also deeply engaged with techniques of Surrealism as a means of unhinging the unconscious from repressive social forces (Spikett, *Reed*, 19:30). While studying alongside veterans who had been trained to kill people who "looked " like him, Kiyooka reflected upon his own wartime experience of conflict between an ethnic ancestry originating "elsewhere" and "Canadian" cultural norms reinforced through government policy, print, and broadcast media.

As *Transcanada Letters* solicits the reader's engagement with Kiyooka's affective relationship to the nation-state and its symbolic order, the bookwork communicates a contradictory state of multiple associative belongings. Literary critic Glen Lowry has observed that Kiyooka's photographs and letters work together to create a kind of bond with the reader that is experienced as a "liminal space of mutual being" (Lowry, 376). This diffusion of authorship can be understood as a mode of political address with reference to queer theorist José Esteban Muñoz's term "disidentification," which he proposes is an identity formation that occurs as "the enacting of self at precisely the point where the discourses of essentialism and constructivism short-circuit" (Muñoz, 6). According to Muñoz, a moment of conflict supposedly takes place at the threshold between private life and images circulating in the public sphere, just as *Transcanada Letters* transposes the "private" register of letters and family photographs into the "public" pages of the book. For instance, the portrait Kiyooka includes of himself and his siblings transmits two contradicting, yet mutually occurring, affective spaces. The older boys' unease conveys the alienation of children with unstable citizenship status who labour for a subsistence living on their family's farm. But I am simultaneously bemused by the happiness of the three younger siblings huddled around the Maple Leafs sweater.

"Locus" is Media

Transcanada Letters corresponds to a mode of conceptual art in which tension is created between the affective experience of an individual and the discursive production of a subject positioned on a grid. Art historian Eve Meltzer has argued that this approach indicates an "antihumanist turn" taken through structuralism during the late 1960s and early 1970s. Meltzer explains that the anticipation of a world managed through information systems meant that the idea of a humanist subject imbued with individual agency and a central substance or "essence" was overlaid by a structuralist understanding of language as a system of imposed grids that discursively produce subjectivity (Meltzer, 8–25). Meltzer's rereading of Conceptual Art in affective terms can be compared to recent discussions of "Romantic Conceptualism" as a variant on the dry, analytic side to the movement.[55] This variant of conceptualism contrasts the rational process implied by the repetition of serial forms with the messy subject of bodies, emotions, and sensuality. In this sense, it has affinities with countercultural refusals of a public sphere dominated by either corporate or state control of mass media because it works to recover repressed modes of perception and affective sensibility (Heiser, n.p.).

Pages 2 and 3 of the 18-page photoseries, *Long Beach BC to Peggy's Cove Nova Scotia* [1971], in Roy K. Kiyooka, *Transcanada Letters* [Vancouver: Talonbooks, 1975, n.p., 28 × 46 cm]. With permission of Kiyo Kiyooka. [Photo: author]

Although the structuralist grid is present throughout *Transcanada Letters*, it is most visually striking in *Long Beach BC to Peggy's Cove Nova Scotia* (1971), a photographic series that unfolds as a travel narrative across eighteen pages that mimic the serial repetition of frames on a contact sheet (Fig. 4).[56] Pictorial qualities such as horizon lines and point-of-view shift as frequently as modes of transport. Kiyooka's photographs show a group of travellers moving from van to canoe to horse and buggy. Alongside views of wilderness vistas and communications towers, seen through dirty windows or framed in rearview mirrors (Fig. 5), Kiyooka shows us images of himself amidst a busload of longhaired and mustachioed friends. In many images the lighting is atmospheric, imbuing industrial landscapes, domestic scenes, and candid portraits with an ethereal quality. At times the high contrast of these images produces romantic chiaroscuro effects, or overexposes the features of friends who I imagine goofing around as they refuse to pose for the camera. An extended shutter speed creates a disorienting lack of focus in nighttime scenes, evoking a van bumping along, following the curve of a row of streetlights.

The cross-country photo-series catalogues his move to take up a teaching position at the Nova Scotia College of Art. At the time, the College was a complement to the Conceptual Art movement as it developed in New York City, benefitting from the use these artists made of printed matter to transcend distances. Visiting artists included Lawrence Wiener, Joseph Kosuth, Dan Graham, and Vito Acconci, each of whom published contemporaneous bookworks to Kiyooka's *Transcanada Letters*. This environment prompted Kiyooka's discovery that the quintessential painter of Canadian landscape imagery, Tom Thomson, was a conceptual artist.

He was also inspired to organize the *Halifax/Vancouver Exchange*, an event that took place as artists travelled between the cities. Eleven artists from Vancouver visited Halifax between 6 and 11 March 1972 as half of a two-part event.[57] A group portrait featured in *Transcanada Letters* shows this group huddling together outside the clapboard storefront of the Palm Lunch restaurant while being pelted by wet falling snow (Fig. 6). The caption tells us that this jovial bunch has just

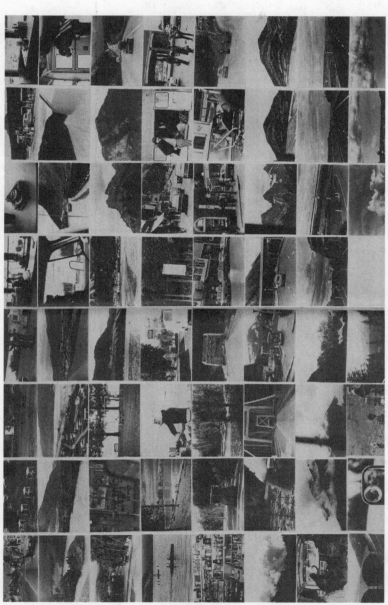

Detail from the photoseries, *Long Beach BC to Peggy's Cove Nova Scotia* [1971], in Roy K. Kiyooka, *Transcanada Letters* [Vancouver: Talonbooks, 1975]. With permission of Kiyo Kiyooka. [Photo: author]

eaten a "Big Meal" at the Chinese Canadian restaurant, which acts as a signifier of Asian Canadian community on the East Coast.[58] Art historian Virginia Solomon has discussed *Exchange* as a performative mapping of an alternate space, that of "Canadada," where the private realm of desire shapes a new experience of public life (153). As several West Coast participants extended their trip to visit with artists they knew in New York, it is also important to recognize how the events Kiyooka initiated from Halifax positioned his affective relationship to Vancouver within a multi-locational conceptual geography.[59]

Long Beach BC to Peggy's Cove Nova Scotia uses an eclectic grouping of photographic styles to index the experience of Kiyooka's body as it responded to the locations he travelled through. The camera acts as an extension of his body, recording his sensorial experience of the world and coordinating this emotional space with specific times and environmental conditions. In this way, the coordinating function of conceptual photography maps out a "landscape" in an analogous mode to the principles of projective verse, which inform Kiyooka's letters and poetic texts. Arnold has noted that the contrast between the mobility captured in the images and the gridded layout is reminiscent of Charles Olson's poetics of "localism" (Arnold, 98). Likewise, Lowry notes a resemblance between the textual content of *Transcanada Letters* and the first volume of Olson's *Maximus Poems* (1953), which is also composed as a series of letters addressed to the citizens of an imaginary city. "Localism" is the principle in projective verse of writing from one's "locus" in response to the immediate surrounding. Olson used "proprioceptive," a physiological term, to describe a process of composition working through responses arising within the body as it moves through space.[60] A kind of mapping is therefore performed on the page by using the typewriter to transcribe the poet's breath patterns when speaking the verse out loud. The reader moves across the semantic field of the page, navigating through a multifaceted syntax, multiple voices and polysemous cultural codes experienced through both text and images.

Halifax/ Vancouver: Exchange

front row, left to right: Bruce Parsons, Don Druick, Glenn Lewis, Carole Itter, Gerry Gilbert, Toby MacLennan, Zoe Druick, Alistair MacLennan

back row, left to right: Peter Zimmer, David Martin, Ellison Robertson, Doug Waterman, Michael Morris, Ian Murray, Gathie Falk, Charlotte Townsend, Anita Martin, Dave Rimmer, Mr. Peanut, Cheryl Druick, Mary, the Boss, Two Waitresses, Roy Kiyooka

Halifax, Spring '72
After a Big Meal at the Palm Lunch

"Halifax /Vancouver Exchange," in Roy K. Kiyooka, *Transcanada Letters* (Vancouver: Talonbooks, 1975, n.p., 28 x 22 cm). With permission of Kiyo Kiyooka. (Photo: author)

This correspondence between conceptual photography and projective verse illuminates Kiyooka's complex relationship to Canada, and to a sense of place existing somewhere beyond a print-based national imaginary bounded by the geopolitical entity. In keeping with projective verse, Kiyooka writes *Transcanada Letters* from his "locus." However, in a letter from Kyoto to Montreal, he reveals that his locus is coordinated in relation to multiple national territories, multiple urban sites, and to communications media, specifically, television:

'here' as over 'there' or almost 'anywhere' theres television-
you get the so-call'd 'real world' comin' at u via tecni-
color'd visors: Locus is 2 eyes in affront of a teley screen
'anywhere' ... (Kiyooka, *Transcanada Letters*, 55–56).

Works Cited

Arnold, Grant, and Karen Henry, editors. "Reference/Cross Reference: Conceptual Art on the West Coasteference/Cross Reference: Conceptual Art on the West Coast." *Traffic: Conceptual Art in Canada, 1965–1980,* Vancouver Art Gallery, 2011.

Arnold, Grant, and Karen Henry. *Traffic: Conceptual Art in Canada, 1965–1980.* Vancouver Art Gallery, 2012.

Auslander, Philip. "The Performativity of Performance Documentation." PAJ, vol. 84, 2006, p. 5.

Auther, Elissa, and Adam Lerner, editors. *West of Center Art and the Counterculture Experiment in America, 1965–1977.* University of Minnesota Press, 2011.

Barthes, Roland. "Rhetoric of the Image." *Image, Music, Text,* translated by Stephen Heath. Hill and Wang, 1977.

Berelowitz, Lance. *Dream City: Vancouver and the Global Imagination.* Douglas & McIntyre, 2010.

Bowering, George. "The Man in the Yellow Boots/El Hombre De Las Botas Amarillas." *El Corno Emplumado,* 16 Oct. 1965.

Byrd, Antawan I., et al. *Art Cities of the Future: 21st Century Avant-Gardes.* Phaidon Press Limited, 2013.

Cavell, Richard. *McLuhan in Space: A Cultural Geography.* University of Toronto Press, 2002.

----. "World Famous Across Canada, Or Transnational Localities." *Trans. Can. Lit: Resituating the Study of Canadian Literature,* by Smaro Kamboureli and Roy Miki, Wilfrid Laurier University Press, 2007.

Ching, Barbara, and Jennifer A. Wagner-Lawlor. *The Scandal of Susan Sontag.* Columbia University Press, 2009.

Conkelton, Sheryl. "Roy Kiyooka: '... The Sad and Glad Tidings of the Floating World ...'" *All Amazed For Roy Kiyooka,* edited by John O'Brian et al., Arsenal Pulp Press, 2002, pp. 101–116.

Di Bello, Patrizia, et al. *The Photobook: From Talbot to Ruscha and Beyond.* I.B. Tauris & Company, Limited, 2012.

Drucker, Johanna. *The Century of Artists' Books.* Granary Books, 2004.

Fairnbarn, Catherine Rebecca. "A Short Trip on Spaceship Earth: Intermedia Society, 1967–1972." University of British Columbia, 1991.

Foster, Hal, et al. *Art Since 1900: Modernism, Antimodernism, Postmodernism*. Vol. 2, Thames & Hudson, 2011.

Goodwin, Helen, et al, curator. "The Medium Is the Message." Morris and Helen Belkin Art Gallery Archives, Belkin Art Gallery Fonds, 13.4–5.12. Accessed 14 Oct. 2014, http://vancouverartinthesixties.com/archive/19.

Heiser Jörg. *Romantic Conceptualism*. Kerber, 2007.

----. "Moscow, Romantic, Conceptualism and After." *e-Flux* 29, Nov. 2011, www.e-flux.com/journal/moscow-romantic-conceptualism-and-after.

Hogg, Bob. "Bob Hogg." *Tish*, vol. 25, June 1964, p. 2.

Kamboureli, Smaro, editor. "Dear Chris, Richmond, B.C., 1974." *Transcanada Letters*, by Roy Kiyooka, Talonbooks, 1975.

Kiyooka, Fumiko, director. *Reed: The Life and Work of Roy Kiyooka*. 2010.

Kiyooka, Roy. "Roy Kiyooka Fonds." *Contemporary Literature Collection*, Simon Fraser University, Vancouver.

----. *Transcanada Letters*. Edited by Smaro Kamboureli, NeWest Press, 2005.

Kotz, Liz. *Words to Be Looked at: Language in 1960s Art*. MIT Press, 2010.

Lewis, Glenn. "National News." FILE, Apr. 1972, pp. 6–7.

Lowry, Glenn. "Afterword." *Transcanada Letters,* edited by Smaro Kamboureli. NeWest Press, 2005.

Marcuse, Herbert. *An Essay on Liberation*. Beacon Pr., 1969.

Mariani, Philomena, et al. *Global Conceptualism: Points of Origin, 1950s-1980s*. Queens Museum of Art, 1999.

McFarland, Scott Toguri. "Un-Ravelling *StoneDGloves* and the Haunt of Hibakusha." *All Amazed for Roy Kiyooka*, edited by John O'Brian et al., Arsenal Pulp Press, 2002.

Meltzer, Eve. *Systems We Have Loved: Conceptual Art, Affect, and the Anti-Humanist Turn*. Chicago University Press, 2013.

Miki, Roy, and Smaro Kamboureli, editors. "Preface." *Trans.Can.Lit: Resituating the Study of Canadian Literature*, Wilfred Laurier University Press, 2007.

----. "Coruscations, Plangencies and the Sybillant: After Words to Roy Kiyooka's *Pacific Windows*." *Pacific Windows*, edited by Roy Miki. Talonbooks, 1997, pp. 315–316.

----. "Inter-Face: Roy Kiyooka's Writing, A Commentary/Interview." *Roy Kiyooka*, edited by William Wood, Artspeak Gallery, Or Gallery, 1991.

----. editor. "Tom Thomson as/in Roy Kiyooka." *The Artist and The Moose: A Fable of Forget*, by Roy Kiyooka, Line Books, Burnaby B.C., 2009.

Moeglin-Delcroix, Anne. *Esthétique Du Livre D'artiste: 1960/1980: Une Introduction à L'art Contemporain*. 2nd ed., Mot Et Le Reste, 2012.

Muñoz, José Esteban. *Disidentifications: Queers of Colour and the Performance of Politics*. University of Minnesota Press, 1999.

Nemiroff, Diana. "Geometric Abstraction After 1950." *The Visual Arts in Canada: The Twentieth Century*, edited by Brian Foss et al., Oxford University Press, 2010.

Ngai, Sianne. "Merely Interesting." *Critical Inquiry*, vol. 34, 2008, pp. 777–817.

O'Brian, John. "White Paint, Hoarfrost, and the Cold Shoulder of Neglect." *Roy Kiyooka*, Artspeak, Or Gallery, 1991, pp. 19–25.

Ondaatje, Michael. "Letter from Michael Ondaatje, 19 May 1976." Received by Roy Kiyooka and Daphne Marlatt, Roy Kiyooka Fonds, MsC 32.6.8 Kiyooka Correspondence, Ondaatje. *Contemporary Literature Collection*, Simon Fraser University, 19 May 1976, Vancouver.

Reid, Dennis. *A Concise History of Canadian Painting*. Oxford University Press, 1988.

Roelstraete, Dieter. "Urban Renewal: Ghost Traps, Collage, Condos and Squats." *Intertidal: Vancouver Art & Artists*, edited by Scott Watson, Antwerp & Vancouver: Museum Van Hedendaagse Kunst Antwerpen and the Morris and Helen Belkin Art Gallery, The University of British Columbia, 2005, pp. 30–49.

Scherf, Kathleen. "A Legacy of Canadian Cultural Tradition and the Small Press: The Case of Talonbooks." *Studies in Canadian Literature*, vol. 25, no. 1, 2000, pp. 131–149.

Solomon, Virginia. "Conceptualism and Canadada at the Halifax/Vancouver Exchange." *The Last Art College: Nova Scotia College of Art and Design, 1968–1978*, edited by Gary Neill Kennedy, Art Gallery of Nova Scotia, 2012.

Taylor, Felicity, and Carole Itter. "Telephone Interview." 10 July 2014.

"Vancouver." *Art Cities of the Future: 21st Century Avant-Gardes*, by Antawan I. Byrd et al., Phaidon Press Limited, 2013, pp. 297–319.

Wah, Fred. "Introduction." *Net Work Selected Writing*, by Daphne Marlatt, Talonbooks, 1980, pp. 15–19.

Watson, Scott, and Dieter Roelstraete. *Intertidal: Vancouver Art & Artists*. Morris and Helen Belkin Art Gallery, 2005.

Webster, Jack. "Ginsberg and Webster." *Georgia Straight*, 4 Apr. 1969, pp. 9–12.

Witkovsky, Matthew S., and Mark Godfrey. *Light Years: Conceptual Art and the Photograph, 1964–1977*. Art Institute of Chicago, 2012.

Acknowledgements

My thanks go to the reviewers for their comments, which helped to shape this text alongside the editorial direction of Dr. Johanne Sloan and the attentive eye of karen elaine spencer. The conversations I had with Dr. Roy Miki, Daphne Marlatt, Carole Itter, and Henry Tsang were crucial to understanding Roy Kiyooka's presence in life. Erick Swanick, Head of Special Collections, and Keith Gilbert, Special Collections Assistant, helped me to pull traces of this presence from the Roy Kiyooka Fonds in the Contemporary Literature Collection, W.A.C. Bennett Library, Simon Fraser University.

The Pivot of Athwartedness: Roy Kiyooka's "Pacific Windows"

Veronica J. Austen

Published as a full issue of *The Capilano Review* in August 1990, Roy Kiyooka's "Pacific Windows" exists on the periphery of Kiyooka's canon. Despite the various ways in which this text could be considered the culmination of what Kiyooka deems his "photo/ glyphic epic" ("Notes" 94), "Pacific Windows," unlike his other photoglyphic texts *StoneDGloves* and *Wheels*, has achieved scant critical attention.[61] Perhaps the relative neglect of this text is a testament to the power of a collected works in framing scholarly discourse. Understandably, at 96 pages, the length of "Pacific Windows" in its photoglyphic form was prohibitive for its inclusion in the collected works, so unlike *StoneDGloves* and *Wheels*, which appear with their photographs, "Pacific Windows" appears as text without images in *Pacific Windows: Collected Poems of Roy K. Kiyooka*.[62] Its role in Kiyooka's photoglyphic epic is, thus, obscured.

With an excerpt of "Pacific Windows" forming the opening epigraph of *Mothertalk: Life Stories of Mary Kiyoshi Kiyooka* and thereby providing a poignant introductory portrait of Kiyooka's mother, the poetic text of "Pacific Windows" does have its own power and provenance. Nevertheless, as Kiyooka's published poem-essay "Notes Toward a Book of Photoglyphs" attests, "Pacific Windows" is largely a narrative about the expressive potential of the visual; hence, if Kiyooka's collected works is the key means through which contemporary readers come to know his oeuvre, the inclusion of an imageless "Pacific Windows" could easily cause the importance of this text to be undervalued.

In its photoglyphic form, "Pacific Windows" splits each page in half, one photograph appearing right-side-up on the top of the page and another, most often the same photograph, appearing upside-down on the bottom of the page. A band of text, white sans-serif font on black background, separates the two images; one line of text is encountered right-side-up and one upside-down. The reading process is such that one follows the continuous poetic line until the book's conclusion, at which time, one may rotate the book upside-down and continue reading, the end of the book now becoming its start, the same poetic narrative beginning anew. The narrative focus is itself also bifurcated, its attention split between a portrayal of a visit from the speaker's mother and a portrait of the speaker's city, Vancouver and all its various foibles and particularities. Framing these foci is the narrative's overarching depiction of a man's engagement with photography and its "bitter-sweet, past-tense, poignance" (Kiyooka, Insert n. pag.).

The textual narrative of "Pacific Windows" begins with the speaker looking at "All the photographs of windows and doors, all the lintels, ledges, / unspoke captions" that "no longer belonged to him" (n. pag.).[63] It continues to describe the speaker and his mother examining "all the old photos" (n. pag.), including "the casually taken / photos sandwiched between Pearl Harbour [sic] and Hiroshima that had a special / poignancy for both of them" (n. pag.). By the conclusion of the narrative, the speaker is not just a character within the narrative "Pacific Windows"; he too is somehow a reader of this text of which he is a product. The speaker is "gladful that the last snap / he had taken of [his father] got included in Pacific Windows" and "as each darkening / page reassumed its silences the book fell out of his hands" (n.pag.).

Since "Pacific Windows" depicts the speaker's relationship with photographs and the textual self that they both reveal and create, I argue that this work is central to an understanding of Kiyooka's theorization of the "inter-face," a concept introduced by Kiyooka in a 1975 interview with Chris Varley for the *Roy K. Kiyooka: 25 years* exhibition catalogue and elucidated in a later article/interview by Roy Miki that is now foundational to Kiyooka scholarship, "Inter-face: Roy Kiyooka's Writing, A Commentary/Interview." As I will discuss, the "inter-face" in Kiyooka's thinking is both a characterization of his approach to verbal/visual relations and an expression of his theory of cultural athwartedness. Furthermore, as a manifestation of Kiyooka's ideas regarding "inter-face," "Pacific Windows," specifically in its photo-glyphic form, signifies Kiyooka's achievement of an articulation of self not immediately available to him through either visual or verbal expression alone. As Kiyooka describes in "Notes Toward a Book of Photoglyphs," "Pacific Windows" involved him in a process of "looking for impeccable / photo-glyphic moments, those gestural/nuances to / launch me into the mundane domain of the willing 'i'" (82). This search for 'i' that "Pacific Windows" represents is both a negotiation of voice—the expressive potentials of word *and* of image—and, by extension, a navigation of cultural inheritances and positionings.

Much has been made of Kiyooka's trajectory as an artist and his agile movement between visual and verbal forms. Committed more to astonishment than to any one art form,[64] Kiyooka followed his creative impulses, leaving behind a successful career in painting for various other expressive media, most significantly writing and photography. While Kiyooka's departure from painting was also informed by his dismissal of the values of the "fucken art game" (Kiyooka qtd. in O'Brian and Watson 7) and its commodification of creativity, his evolution as an artist towards writing also reflects a pursuit of a fulfilling form of self-expression.

Kiyooka's much quoted response to Roy Miki's question "Why, then did you need to write?" was simply, "I wanted to claim some kind of articulation for myself" (Miki, "Inter-face" 64). As characterized by Miki, Kiyooka, who was predominantly an abstract expressionist painter, "remained wary" ("Afterword" 305) of representing the complexity of his personal experience visually, particularly that of the exclusionary politics of World War II. Miki states, "As a painter, Kiyooka gained national and international recognition for his brilliant paintings, but as he discovered this medium did not allow him the space to explore the more personal dimensions of his family history" ("English" 5–6). As Kiyooka explains, art forms like "'writing and photography and later music'" could allow him "'to plumb [his] unplummed [*sic*] self'

(RK Papers)" (qtd. in Miki, "Afterword" 317) and satisfy an "urgency in Roy for testimony and witnessing" (O'Brian and Watson 9). Given language's well-documented and -discussed role in power relations, it is no wonder that Kiyooka would equate his "survival" with "a quest for language as the modality of power" (Miki, "Inter-face" 67). "[C]ontrol over orders of discourse" may be "a powerful mechanism for [the dominant to] sustain[] power" (Fairclough 74), but to claim the right to language is to create a space for oneself amidst these discourses.

Kiyooka's assertion that writing for him equals a pursuit of articulation, coupled with his announcement that "Painting gave [him] a face, writing a voice" (Kiyooka, "Intersections" n. pag.) may suggest that he dichotomizes visual and linguistic systems of communication, giving more power and agency to writing. And yet, for Kiyooka, writing as an art form is rarely divorced from the visual. Kiyooka's "writing" — suggested by Miki to have "bec[o]me the most effective mode of articulating the personal, familial, and communal conditions of being Japanese Canadian" ("Inter-face" 57–58) — is not, in fact, exclusively linguistic. When defining "inter-face," which, as I have said, is part Kiyooka's conceptualization of visual/verbal relations and part, as I will soon elaborate upon, his description of cultural athwartedness, Kiyooka importantly does not stop with just identifying the binary between painting (face) and writing (voice). The sentence continues: "but its [sic] not a matter of choosing" (Kiyooka, "Intersection" n. pag.). As Kiyooka asserts in *Pacific Rim Letters*, the visual and the verbal arts "have always been twinned in [his] life. They, along with all [his] other curiosities, stem from the same pan-Pacific sources, etc." (203). For Kiyooka, "what has to be understood is how the two inform each other" (Miki, "Inter-face" 73).

It may be easy to interpret his move to writing as a commentary on the insufficiency of visual expression, but, to Kiyooka, neither the visual nor the verbal is really satisfactory on its own. What the visual offers, and requires, is "its own language," one that is "not transferable, in its uniqueness, its exactitude. [...]. It has its own experiential dimension, that you simply grab, and walk away with—mute" (Kiyooka, "With Roy Kiyooka" 29). In other words, the visual "can't be accessed through language, not really" (Kiyooka, "Inter-face" 64). The visual is beyond verbal expression because, to Kiyooka, it is about the experience; verbal expression, on the other hand, requires one to "situate oneself somewhere outside of the experience" (Kiyooka, "With" 18). Both the visual and the verbal communicate, but, as Kiyooka concludes, "[t]he one activity complements the other and both together give [him] a context for articulation more than either discipline per se (Kiyooka, "With" 18).

His gravitation towards linguistic expression, after all, did not provide a complete or easy cure for Kiyooka's struggle to communicate. Despite his claim that writing gave him voice, his star-crossed love of language is a key theme throughout much of his writing. As Joanne Saul has noted, Kiyooka "uses the word 'tongue' in almost every collection, particularly in compound words like 'tongue-tied,' 'tongue-twisted,' 'cleft-tongue,' 'flying-tongue,' and 'mother-tongue'" (89). Kiyooka's repeated focus on the tongue signals a compromised agency over voice, his own body figured as the betrayer. As much as Kiyooka's cultural conditions have "*left [him]* with a tied tongue" (Kiyooka, "We Asian" 116, emphasis added), the metaphors he uses— namely, "tongue-twisted" ("Kyoto Airs" 12), "tied tongue" ("We Asian" 116)/ "tongue-tied" ("Pear Tree" 208; "Wheels" 171), and "cleft tongue" ("We Asian" 117) reveal a struggle against internalizing the blame for this difficulty in speech. To be tongue-twisted is to be confronted with difficult language that tests and perhaps conquers the mouth's agility. To have a tied or cleft tongue, however, is not to confront a difficult external opponent, but rather to possess bodily difference that renders speech difficult. In either case, the focus of Kiyooka's choice of metaphors is on his own lack, the insufficiency of his body to complete the task at hand.

Beyond conveying self-doubt, Kiyooka understandably also expresses doubt in English as a vehicle for his self-expression and self-representation. Confronting a system of communication that would not accommodate his relationship with his mother who spoke predominantly in Japanese, Kiyooka approached English as a language "rampant with fissures" (Kamboureli 339). English too is that which named him "enemy alien" during WWII, making "that, dumbfound, yellow kid" (["October's Piebald"] 23) unfindable.[65] As Tara Lee asserts, English renders Kiyooka "vulnerable" precisely because of his "belief that it was his own" (144), a belief destroyed by Canada's WWII treatment of Japanese Canadians. In English, Kiyooka can be "nothing but [his] disparate / nomenclature" ("Notes" 87). To use the language that has rendered one "nothing" is to navigate quicksand, performing a treacherous balancing act between English's proffered opportunities and oppressions.

As various others have assessed, unable to comfortably claim a language, Kiyooka creates one, what he deems "inglish" (Miki, "Afterword" 304). With non-conventional punctuation, phonetic spelling, and word play, Kiyooka's aesthetic is testament to Kamau Brathwaite's argument, albeit from a different cultural context, that experimentation with language is a key means to upend racist and colonialist ideologies. As Brathwaite asserts, it is in the "misuse of [European languages] that [one] perhaps most effectively rebel[s]" (31). Building upon Roy Miki's observation that "It is here, in this transitional space ["between the necessities driving the artist and the necessities driving the writer" (Miki, "Inter-face" 57)], that the imagination of Kiyooka resides" (Miki, "Inter-face" 57), I argue that Kiyooka's "misuse" of language is about more than textual experimentation.

The 'inglish' Kiyooka creates is not, in fact, merely a textual language; it is one that makes use of the communicative potential of the visual. As Jay MillAr cleverly describes, "As a writer [Kiyooka] would art-iculate" (66). Kiyooka's 'inglish' is part text, part visual arts, the communicative insufficiencies of each expunged or made meaningful in their coming together.[66] As a photoglyphic narrative manifesting his theory of the "inter-face," "Pacific Windows" depicts Kiyooka's cultural athwartedness in such a way that neither the verbal nor the visual could have accomplished alone. Kiyooka may have intended "inter-face" to describe his fluid movement between visual and verbal art forms, but importantly, "inter-face" becomes also an expression of his navigation of cultural inheritance and hyphenated identity. Kiyooka describes his experience of English—the language of his daily life and art, but a language his mother did not use—as its own kind of "inter-face." He explains, "If you grow up in that kind of 'inter-face,' it's very poignant, because not to have been able to write in Japanese is to never have been able to have demonstrated to my mother that ... well—" (in Miki, "Inter-face" 70). The incompleteness of this thought, Kiyooka's drift into silence, reflects the crack at the root of his experience of cultural identity. To not experience an ease of belonging amidst his Japanese heritage, and yet to be excluded from his birth nation—Canada—because of it, is to be caught on multiple outsides.

This experience of life in the interstices has been described by oth-ers using multiple metaphors: Homi Bhabha's third space, Gloria Anzaldua's borderland, Mary Louise Pratt's contact zone, Dionne Brand's Door of No Return, and Fred Wah's hyphen or swinging door. For Kiyooka, the metaphor of choice is athwartedness. Describing his own experience of being finger-printed and named "enemy alien" by Canadian authorities during the Second World War, Kiyooka asserts that "being beholden to the white culture, its institutions, [he has] nonetheless grown up athwarted" ("Inter-face" 71). His much quoted definition of athwartedness reads, "You are of it, and you are not, and you know that very clearly" ("Inter-face" 71). Kiyooka's choice of "athwarted" as his descriptor resonates with multiple meanings. De-notatively, "athwart" can refer to that which traverses or stretches across two spaces ("Athwart, adv. and prep.")—for example, 'the storm moved athwart the shores of the lake.' As such, "athwart" figures the experience of hyphenated identities in terms of a journey between mul-tiple sites/selves. At the same time, "athwart" denotatively signifies opposition ("Athwart, adv. and prep.")—for example, 'his experience ran athwart the ideal.' This denotation thereby figures the experience of athwartedness in terms of contestation. Furthermore, beyond the denotative meaning, "athwarted" also resonates with the meaning of its segmented part, "thwarted"; to be "thwarted" is to be opposed and defeated ("thwart, v."). Kiyooka's choice of term in both its denotative and connotative possibilities, thus, captures a movement between po-sitionalities, a movement ripe with conflict and risk.

Although many of Kiyooka's texts can be seen as explorations of this experience of athwartedness, "Pacific Windows" is vital to his development of this concept, its visual and verbal components combining to perform what I assert is the pivot of athwartedness. Miki, drawing upon Wah's conceptualization of the hyphen, similarly classifies athwartedness in terms of the action of pivoting. Kiyooka's athwartedness, in Miki's words, is a "pivot between insiderness and outsiderness" ("Inter-face" 72). This conception of athwartedness as a pivot between identities recalls Wah's use of the swinging door as a symbol for movement between and through multiple cultural identities.[67] Describing the door separating the kitchen from the café of his family's Chinese restaurant, Wah writes: "open up with a good swift toe to the wooden slab that swings between the Occident and the Orient to break the hush of the whole café before first light the rolling gait with which I ride this silence that is a hyphen and the hyphen is the door" (*Diamond Grill* 16). It is this action of the pivot, and its subsequent complexities and discomforts, that I contend "Pacific Windows" makes manifest.

The textual narrative of "Pacific Windows" depicts a speaker — seemingly Kiyooka's autobiographical 'I' — negotiating various pivot points. This speaker has one foot in the past via the photographs that he is viewing and one foot in his current "polis" — Vancouver. As well, through his relationship with his mother, this speaker is shown to be pivoting between his connection to one side of the Pacific — Japan — and the other — Canada. As described in "Pacific Windows," the mother is the pivot point around which others rotate. Although she has come to Kiyooka in Vancouver for a visit, she is the one around whom the family rotates: "all / through the summer her grandchildren and great grandchildren *came and / went*" (n. pag., emphasis added). As figured by Kiyooka, these visits are both to a respected and caring family matriarch (who "knit[s] thick woolen slippers" (n. pag.) for them) and to the Japan she represents.

In Kiyooka's broader oeuvre, his mother — Mary Kiyoshi Kiyooka, Kochi-born daughter to a samurai and first-generation Canadian — is consistently constructed as a link to Japan. For example, in "We Asian North Americanos," Kiyooka asserts that "She and she alone reminds [him] of [his] Japanese self" (116). Beyond representing Japan, however, she too is made to symbolize for Kiyooka a less contentious blending of cultural identities than that which he experiences. In "Pacific Windows," she is the one who can speak of "all the / family ties they had on both sides of the pacific" (n. pag.); she is "the last link to the sad and glad tidings / of the floating world" (n. pag.). Although Mary's real experience was likely much more complex, for the Kiyooka narrating "Pacific Windows," Mary does not experience the unsettlement of hyphenated identity. Her occupation of space is portrayed as certain and steady. While Mary is depicted as "plac[ing] a tiny foot *firmly* on the livingroom / floor" (n. pag., emphasis added), Kiyooka, in the latter part of this text is left to wander, literally or via memory, through the "Peripatetic images [of Vancouver that] haunt his waking hours" (n. pag.).

Unlike the characterization of his own athwartedness, Kiyooka asserts that "all that had befallen [his mother] in a country too vast to imagine let alone put a / name to" has "composted an indigenous panpacific midden" (n. pag.). In this imagery, Kiyooka's mother is not valued solely for her embodiment of the family's Japanese heritage; she is, in fact, valued for her decomposition of separate identities into one. The vagueness of the wording means that the country that is "too vast to imagine let alone put a / name to" (n. pag.) can be either Japan or Canada, or in fact, be some combination of the two. Both sides of the Pacific are figured as coming together in Kiyooka's mother to form a pan-Pacific midden — a wished-for, if not realized, fertilized ground out of which a family can grow. (But importantly, it is not the mother herself who forms the pan-Pacific midden; it is "all that had befallen her" (n. pag.) that does so, suggesting an acknowledgement that this envisioned blending of identities has involved some form of assault and trauma.)

In these constructions of the mother, she, and her experience, is the ground, but one that is dangerously ephemeral. She is the "last link" (n. pag.); she is in the midst of "dwindling years" (n. pag.); her "gestures" are "faultless but frail" (n. pag.). In Kiyooka's characterization, she may represent the hope for a unified identity, but the space that she occupies is not available to future generations. She cannot bear their weight: her lap has grown too small to support "even the smallest grandchild" (n. pag.). She may be cast as the midden that could fertilize the generations, but the generations cannot root themselves to that centre — literally, her lap — and the stability/fulfilment of identity that it promises. Instead Kiyooka and the future generations, coming and going, circle around her, facing the constant threat of losing the security of even that gravitational pull.

Beyond the textual narrative's depiction of this navigation of identity/ies, it is the visual qualities of "Pacific Windows" that most fully enact the unsettled circling of those athwarted. Although the images are not clearly readable in terms of place—in other words, the photographs are not recognizable as picturing specifically Japan or Canada —the fact that each page contains two images and lines of text—one set right-side-up; one set upside-down—casts the page to be the "pacific windows" of this text's title. In its visual form, the page connects two narrative spaces, much as the Pacific Ocean itself connects Japan and Kiyooka's Vancouver. Furthermore, the visual form of the text, with the page holding both an upright and an upside-down narrative, involves the reader in multiple pivot points. Not only can each individual page be rotated, but at the conclusion of the narrative, one can rotate the book and begin the same poetic narrative again, each poetic line now paired with a different photograph. The pivoting of this reading process functions to perform a relationship between the spaces of the page, and thus between the cultural spaces that render Kiyooka athwarted.

Kiyooka's vision for "Pacific Windows" may be that "each page / its mirrored-image a / whole thing" ("Notes" 93), but importantly, the two parts of each page are, in fact, not mirrors of each other. If they were, not only would the lines of the images stretch into each other, but also the same poetic line would appear for both halves of the page, one instance rendered largely illegible, appearing upside-down and backwards, as if seen through Alice's looking-glass. Instead of being reflections of each other, the two halves of the page come together dependent upon the 180 degree rotation of the image. As such, the visual aesthetic of this text foregrounds not the wholeness of a page, but rather its fragmentation. The two narrative spaces may occupy the same page, but they do not compost together to become the pan-pacific midden that the mother is constructed to represent. Instead, as a representation of Kiyooka's negotiation of multiple cultural spaces, the pages of "Pacific Windows" perform a disconnect, a mismatch between the spaces that must be navigated.

Because the page includes one image and a 180 degree rotation of the same image (with a few notable exceptions that I will soon discuss), the vectors emanating from each photograph are necessarily blocked from each other, preventing the unification of the page. As conceptualized by Gunther Kress and Theo van Leeuwen, vectors are "depicted elements" within a visual plane "that form an oblique line" (57). In Kress and van Leeuwen's development of this concept, vectors "may be formed by bodies or limbs or tools" (57), in other words by any object (even an eyeline) that creates a linear connection between elements in an image. Although their focus, which casts vectors as creating an image's action, equates vectors particularly with diagonal lines, if one interprets vectors to be related to the Gestalt principle of continuity that assumes that one's eyes follow where a line leads, then vectors, no matter their direction, become a key marker of how objects in an image are related to one another. Consider, for instance, the vectors created by the flower petals on the opening page of "Pacific Windows" (see Figure 1). Where the vertical lines reach up and down towards each other, they do not match. Where the diagonal lines do at times suggest they could meet each other, their meeting requires a harsh change of course. In other words, a vector heading towards the right in one image meets up with a vector heading towards the left in the other image, or vice versa, this change in directionality signifying the agility required to traverse both spaces together.

The rotation of the image also means that the vectors stretching towards the opposite half of the page are completely severed; for example, the parking meter that appears in many of the images offers a vertical vector, but the rotation of the image means that top-to-bottom, the parking meter appears on opposite sides of the page.[68] Nevertheless, more often than not, the vectors reaching through the centre of the page are just slightly askew. For instance, in the page featuring a woman —Kiyooka's mother perhaps?—standing at a water's shoreline, the lines created by the woman's legs reach for each other and yet just miss (see Figure 2). While the incomplete union of the photographs on each page is sometimes jarringly apparent, it is these small, almost imperceptible, mismatches between the two spaces that reveal fissures that are perhaps all the more disruptive. After all, Kiyooka's dilemma of cultural identity is not simply that he encountered exclusion. The harshness of Kiyooka's athwartedness was instead that he was both "of" Canada and its "white anglo saxon protestant" ideologies and yet "not" of it ("Inter-face" 71). The pivoting of each page of "Pacific Windows" visualizes this experience, the photographs showing themselves — and hence, the differing cultural spaces they embody — to be both "of" each other and yet not capable of being at one with each other.

Figure 1   Figure 2

Similarly, the pivot enacted at the conclusion of the narrative when one can turn the book upside-down and continue reading uncovers another disconnection. The book's format promotes a reading process that allows the narrative to loop and form a continuous circle, the initial end becoming a secondary beginning, the secondary end becoming a third beginning. The syntax of this narrative, however, both promotes the possibility of continuity and yet performs its disruption. The narrative loops as follows, the period at the end of "eyelids" serving as the book's pivot point bringing together end with new beginning:

the first rain in weeks came through the open window and laved
    his eyelids.
Like the rain-spattered pages of a Romance novel left behind on
    a holiday
beach: All the photographs of windows and doors, all the lintels,
    ledges,
unspoke captions, no longer belonged to him. (n.pag.)

The fact that there is a period between the ending "eyelids" and the
beginning "Like the rain-spattered pages" suggests a full stop dividing
end from beginning. And yet, the "Like" clause, in fact, floats syntacti-
cally; if it weren't for the punctuation and capitalization, this clause can
conceivably connect either to what precedes it or to what proceeds from
it. The "first rain in weeks" can "lave[] his eyelids" "like the rain-spattered pages" or "[l]ike the rain-spattered pages of a Romance novel left
behind on a holiday / beach" "[a]ll the photographs" may "no longer
belong[] to him" (n. pag.). The syntactic floating of the "Like" clause
is made all the more apparent by the unconventional use of the colon
at its conclusion. The more common punctuation mark between
"beach" and "All the photographs" would be a comma.

    With the unconventional use of a colon and subsequent unconven-
tional capitalization of "All," the "Like" clause is barely more syntac-
tically connected to what comes after it than to what preceded it. As
such, this "Like" clause becomes a syntactic bridge between the end
and beginning that suggests a pathway between the two but that also
constructs this space-between as a possible "no-man's land" (Wah 73)
of compromised movement. In that I am envisioning this "Like" clause
to be a manifestation of the space-between cultural identities, I am
casting this clause to be an embodiment of Fred Wah's theorization of
the hyphen. As with the hyphen, the "Like" clause functions as a
marker that both "binds and divides" (Wah 72). The "Like" clause may
be a pathway between two narrative spaces, but to travel onto and off
of this bridge is to confront barriers. In this way, Kiyooka's syntax
becomes a performance of his athwartedness, a condition of being
wherein he inhabits two spaces that interconnect and are not entirely
divorced from one another, and yet that are not fluidly unified either.

In addition to this disrupted narrative loop and to the fissures performed by the interrupted vectors between the two halves of any one page, additional formal features of this work perform Kiyooka's athwartedness and its implications. Although every page of "Pacific Windows" seems uniform in format, in fact, not every page features two of the same image; three anomalies in page layout occur. For example, one page contains an upright photograph of an urban environment—a building—on the top of the pages, while a photograph of a natural setting—a forest with corn-like stalks in the foreground—appears at the bottom. Furthermore, although the pattern of the rest of "Pacific Windows" would dictate the image of the natural environment be positioned upside-down, it is not readably placed as such.

While this particular anomaly may possess less interpretable significance than the other two anomalies that I am about to discuss, the existence of these anomalies at all speaks to the dilemma of athwartedness and the complex negotiation of (un)belonging that it entails. Each anomalous page is "of" some greater whole—namely, the larger book-length poetic narrative—and seems to follow its pattern. Nevertheless, even though the differences are obscured, they remain present, disrupting the unity of the whole. These anomalous pages, thus, become an expression of the belonging-but-not-quite of Kiyooka's existence.

One of the other anomalous pages features a triptych of portraits (See Figure 3). The upright and the inverted halves of the page include the same three parts, but these parts appear in differing orders. Left to right, the top triptych features:

- a close up of a man's face[69] with eyes, nose, mouth, and chin apparent, the top of the frame rendering his forehead incomplete;
- a slightly less close-up image of the same man's right eye, nose, and mouth, the mouth and nose slightly cropped;
- and again the same man, this time his left eye apparent but nose and mouth remain outside the frame and even the glasses covering his eye are cut-off before the nose-bridge.

Figure 3

What this initial ordering of the triptych offers is the appearance of
two relatively complete faces; the centre and right frames do not quite
cohere, but all the parts that go into a normalized face—two eyes, one
nose, and one mouth appear. This top triptych, thus, continues the
focus in "Pacific Windows" on doubling: two photographs and two
lines have appeared on each page; the narrative has had two foci—
Kiyooka's mother's visit and the city of Vancouver; Mary Kiyooka has
linked two sides of the Pacific; and Kiyooka himself combines two

identities—Canadian and "enemy alien." This triptych, in its ordering of parts, offers two renderings of the same man. The inverted triptych, however, changes the order of its parts, with the most complete portrait now appearing in the centre, severing the other two frames from each other. What had been two versions of the same man, one albeit slightly disjointed, is now one portrait that has destroyed the other. As such, the pivot of this page reveals a visual narrative wherein an attempt to privilege one identity—to bring it into the centre—is to render impossible the other.

The earlier introduced Figure 2—the image of an older woman standing on the shore and looking out at the water—also offers an anomaly to this text's use of the same photograph for the top and bottom of the page. While both the upright and inverted image features the same content, the inverted image appears markedly out of focus. This pivot towards lost clarity functions in the context of the narrative's broader representation of the speaker's relationship with photographs and the memories that they manifest. In that photography represents "not a memory, an imagination, a reconstruction, [...], but reality in a past state: at once the past and the real" (Barthes 82), this pivot towards blurriness performs the ephemerality of that past moment. This "reality in a past state" cannot stay in focus, the continuity of its presence is in doubt. This photograph gone blurry reveals photography's false promise of permanent preservation of the past.

This movement between images thus serves to illustrate the textual narrative's construction of the speaker's ambivalent, and somewhat troubled, relationship with photographs and the past they depict. The textual narrative begins with the lament that "All the photographs [...] / [...] no longer belonged to him" (n. pag.). As he peruses these photographs, he is confronted with his disconnection from "each passing / face" (n. pag.). Each face has "its own thatch, its half-shuttered windows and closely-guarded door" (n. pag.). These descriptions cast photographs as possible thresholds—windows, a door—that connect viewer to subject, and yet the promise of this passageway is spoiled—the windows are half-shuttered; the door guarded. And yet, later in the narrative, the speaker conveys more confidence in the power of photography to resurrect the past: "While he was printing the / photos he found himself leafing through, he habitually revisited the site of their / initial disclosure" (n. pag.).

Photographs in this depiction have the capacity to transport the viewer to the place and time they represent. While the arc of the textual narrative suggests a growing confidence in photographs as elegiac re-constructions of the past and while the pivot of Figure 2 suggests the opposite, a doubt in the ability of photographs to render a moment immortal, the looping aesthetic of "Pacific Windows" keeps these at-titudes in perpetual flux. The textual and visual narratives do not land and remain upon a validation of photography or conversely a nihilistic disbelief in its affective potential; instead these contradictory attitudes vacillate as the narrative proceeds, not to an end, but to a pivot back to a beginning. As much as the pivot towards blurriness in Figure 2 suggests the possible loss of that past moment, the page can pivot again and clarity be regained; the past can come back into focus.

The ambivalence in this speaker's attitude towards photographs expresses in part the speaker's contentious relationship with the past that results from the athwartedness of his experience. The ideal expe-rience of time as conveyed in "Pacific Windows" is one of continuity. The epigraph, a passage by Henry Corbin, expresses as much: "Every-thing that the indifferent call the past comes forth only in direct pro-portion to our love, itself the source of the future" (qtd. in "Pacific Windows" n. pag.). In this phrasing, not just "our love," but "the past" that is formed out of "our love" for it, is the "source of the future." Similarly, in the narrative itself, when the mother eulogizes "those she knew who had recently passed away" (n. pag.), she announces "how each of them passed their presciences onto / those who were alive and kicking" (n. pag.). In this vision, the past perceives the future and thereby impacts the present; all time frames remain in contact.

This desired continuity, however, is revealed in "Pacific Windows" to be unachievable because of the trauma of the Kiyookas' exclusion during WWII. Kiyooka writes,

. . . . In the end it was the casually taken
photos sandwiched between Pearl Harbour and Hiroshima that
   had a special
poignancy for both of them, though they agreed that even these
   couldn't
foretell what the post-war years had in store for them" (n. pag.).

This phrasing identifies a biographical pivot point, the Second World
War, a time that rendered Kiyooka into two incommensurable identities, Canadian and enemy alien. As described here, in the family's visual
narrative, this period of photographs is a hyphen, a distinguishable
marker between moments, one that bridges the time before and the
time after the war, but that also represents the disruption caused by
that wartime period. While "Pacific Windows" constructs time ide-
ally as continuous, the past revealing the future, the war is described
here as having disturbed this continuum. In retrospect, Kiyooka and
his mother can see that the photographs and the past that they document could not predict just how changed their lives would be amidst
of the legacy of WWII's exclusion and racism. One time is discontinuous with the next.

    This reference to, but absence of, these photographs ultimately also
conveys a reluctance, if not inability, to represent this time during WWII
that led to Kiyooka's feelings of athwartedness. The textual narrative
describes the perusal of these particular images and their poignance, but
these images are not readably present in the visual narrative of "Pacific
Windows." The textual narrative does not describe these images so readers cannot know if any images chosen for "Pacific Windows" are indeed
the ones with "special poignancy" (n. pag.). Their absence, or at least
their lack of clear identifiers, may in part speak to a continued difficulty in articulating that experience of exclusion or, in fact, represent
a preservation of privacy. In "Notes toward a Book of Photoglyphs,"
Kiyooka identifies the dilemma of using autobiographical images: "'our'
/ once-published" photographs are "no longer 'personal'" (79). "Pacific
Windows" is a narrative about the perusal of personal photographs;
"Pacific Windows" is also a narrative that engages its audience in the

viewing of what Kiyooka names "Autobiographical Images" (Berger 92). Nevertheless, the narrative form of "Pacific Windows" exposes barriers to intimate revelation. Kiyooka may have found a visual/verbal medium that allows for a modicum of articulation, but even in this medium much goes unrevealed. In the end, Kiyooka's athwartedness is both in the speaking/showing that the aesthetic form of "Pacific Windows" prompts, and in the silences that remain.

These silences and barriers to revelation are performed by the verbal/visual relationships set up by the page layout. With a textual line running beneath each upright or inverted image, the textual narrative is positioned as caption to the photographs. In this way, the page is arranged such that the text may anchor the meaning of the image or the image illustrate the meaning of the text. John Berger explains the traditional function of captions:

> In the relation between a photograph and words, the photograph begs for an interpretation, and the words usually supply it. The photograph, irrefutable as evidence but weak in meaning, is given a meaning by words. And the words, which by themselves remain at a level of generalisation, are given specific authenticity by the irrefutability of the photograph. Together the two then become very powerful; an open question appears to have been fully answered. (Berger and Mohr 92)

Kiyooka, however, upturns this expectation. The words, for the most part, bear no recognizable connection to the image they accompany. They do not contextualize the photograph; they instead make overt both the lacunae of information the reader confronts when viewing these photographs and the lack of photographic evidence to "authenticate" the textual narrative. The photographs may suggest that an "authenticity" exists, but the details of the pictured events go unspoken, and hence, readers are given a window into a life, but are positioned to remain distant observers, players in a game of 'you think you see me, but no, you don't.'

For example, one of the most important and memorable statements of the text—"they both knew she was the last link to the sad and glad tidings / of the floating world" (n. pag.)—carries across two pages and is accompanied in the upright reading with multiply exposed images that layer a foreground of people walking along a street with smaller glimpses of people at leisure in a park-like setting. While the palimpsestic nature of these images may aesthetically relate to the theme of "floating," the content of the images does not illustrate the textual narrative. As well, the identities of neither the people nor their location are readable; Kiyooka's possible connection to any of the people or locations goes unstated. When "Pacific Windows" is flipped upside-down to be read back to front, this significant part of the textual narrative then appears with two images of rockscapes, the first a collection of boulders and the second a pair of glasses sitting on a gravelly ground. Again, the specific context of these images remains illegible, and their connection to the textual narrative is a non-sequitur.

In juxtaposing words and images so as to suggest, yet deny, a relationship between them, Kiyooka positions his readers at a site of disjuncture. The composition of this text denies static meaning for both the images and the textual lines. Since one photograph is framed by two possible "captions" and since each "caption" frames two different images, the visual/verbal relations are shifting and unsettled. Even though the captions and photographs cannot be said to directly name nor illustrate each other, the significance of each line and photograph shifts as it is placed in a different relationship. In this way, "Pacific Windows" manifests Kiyooka's vision of it as a "kaleidoscopic narrative" (Insert n. pag.). If one turns the kaleidoscope's end, a somewhat slow and tentative pulling apart begins, until all of a sudden, glass particles climax, shift, and fall into a new pattern to start anew the next coming apart and recovery.

Much as the various pivots of "Pacific Windows" revealed fissures —vectors that reach for, but miss, each other; syntax that promises, but disrupts, cohesiveness; a page layout that sets up, but breaks, a pattern—this mismatch between word and image expresses further Kiyooka's condition of athwartedness. Both the visual and the verbal narratives strive towards an articulation and both achieve this goal, but incompleteness and silence remain. Through its photoglyphic form, "Pacific Windows" performs an experience of self wherein one's parts, in all their fluid complexity, do not always cohere into a whole. As the text pivots and its fractures become overt, Kiyooka elucidates a navigation of multiple, and at times colliding, identities.

Acknowledgements

I acknowledge the support of a University of Waterloo/SSHRC Seed Grant in the production of this work. Furthermore, I would like to thank Laura Bayer for research assistance and Dr. Guy Beauregard for reviewing this paper and providing important feedback.

Works Cited

Anzaldúa, Gloria. *Borderlands/La Frontera: The New Mestiza*. 1987. 2nd ed. San Francisco: Aunt Lute, 1999. Print.

"Athwart, adv. and prep." *OED Online*. Oxford University Press, June 2017. Web. 1 July 2017.

Barthes, Roland. *Camera Lucida: Reflections on Photography*. 1980. Trans. Richard Howard. New York: Hill and Wang, 1981. Print.

Berger, John. "Appearances." *Another Way of Telling: A Possible Theory of Photography*. By John Berger and Jean Mohr. New York: Pantheon, 1982. 81–129. Print.

Bhabha, Homi. *Location of Culture*. New York: Routledge, 1994. Print.

Brand, Dionne. *A Map to the Door of No Return: Notes to Belonging*. 2001. Toronto: Vintage, 2002. Print.

Brathwaite, Edward. *Folk Culture of the Slaves in Jamaica*. London: New Beacon, 1970. Print.

Conkelton, Sheryl. "Roy Kiyooka '... the sad and glad tidings of the floating world...'" *All Amazed for Roy Kiyooka*. Ed. John O'Brian, Naomi Sawada, Scott Watson. Vancouver: Arsenal, 2002. 101–15. Print.

Fairclough, Norman. *Language and Power*. London: Longman, 1989. Print.

Gilbert, Gerry. "Laughter: Five Conversations with Roy Kiyooka." *arts-canada* 32.4 (1975–76): 11–21. Print.

Kamboureli, Smaro. "Afterword: For What it's Worth." *Pacific Rim Letters.* Ed. Smaro Kamboureli. Edmonton: NeWest, 2005. 330–49. Print.

Kiyooka, Roy. Insert. "Pacific Windows." *The Capilano Review* 2.3 (1990): n. pag. Print.

----. "Intersections." Interview by Chris Varley. *Roy K. Kiyooka: 25 Years.* Vancouver: Vancouver Art Gallery, 1975. n. pag. Print.

----. "Kyoto Airs." *Pacific Windows: Collected Poems of Roy K. Kiyooka.* Ed. Roy Miki. Burnaby: Talon, 1997. 7–24. Print.

----. *Mothertalk: Life Stories of Mary Kiyoshi Kiyooka.* Ed. Daphne Marlatt. Edmonton: NeWest, 1997. Print.

----. "Notes toward a Book of Photoglyphs." *The Capilano Review* 2.2 (1990): 76–94. Print.

----. ["October's Piebald Skies & Other Lacunae."] Untitled excerpt. "A Celebration of Roy Kiyooka." *Brick* 48 (1994): 13–23, Print.

----. "October's Piebald Skies & Other Lacunae." *Pacific Windows: Collected Poems of Roy K. Kiyooka.* Ed. Roy Miki. Burnaby: Talon, 1997. 277–90. Print.

----. "Pacific Windows." *The Capilano Review* 2.3 (1990): n. pag. Print.

----. *Pacific Rim Letters.* Ed. Smaro Kamboureli. Edmonton: NeWest, 2005. Print.

----. "Pear Tree Pomes." *Pacific Windows: Collected Poems of Roy K. Kiyooka.* Ed. Roy Miki. Burnaby: Talon, 1997. 195–222. Print.

----. "With Roy Kiyooka." Interview. *White Pelican* 1.1 (1971):18–35. Print.

----. "We Asian North Americanos: An Unhistorical 'Take' on Growing up Yellow in a White World." *West Coast Line* 24.3 (1990): 116–18. Print.

----. "Wheels: A Trip thru Honshu's Backcountry." *Pacific Windows: Collected Poems of Roy K. Kiyooka.* Ed. Roy Miki. Burnaby: Talon, 1997. 135–78. Print.

Kress, Gunther, and Theo van Leeuwen. *Reading Images: The Grammar of Visual Design.* London: Routledge, 1996. Print.

Lee, Tara. "Representing the Body in Roy Kiyooka's *Kyoto Airs.*" *Dandelion* 29.1 (2003): 142–61. Print.

McFarlane, Scott Toguri. "'Kiyooka' and the Desert of Living in General."
    Dandelion 29.1 (2003): 14–31. Print.

Miki, Roy. "Afterword: Coruscations, Plangencies, and the Syllibant: After
    Words to Roy Kiyooka's *Pacific Windows*." *Pacific Windows: Collected
    Poems of Roy K. Kiyooka.* Ed. Roy Miki. Burnaby: Talon, 1997.
    301–20. Print.

----. "English with an 'i': Imagining Japan in the Poetry of Roy K. Kiyooka."
    The Canadian Literary Society of Japan 21(2013): 3–13. Print.

----. "Inter-Face: Roy Kiyooka's Writing A Commentary/Interview." *Broken
    Entries: Race Subjectivity Writing.* Toronto: Mercury, 1998. 54–76. Print.

MillAr, Jay. "Portraits of Kiyooka." *Dandelion* 29.1 (2003): 65–68. Print.

O'Brian, John, and Scott Watson. Introduction. *All Amazed for Roy Kiyooka.*
    Ed. John O'Brian, Naomi Sawada, Scott Watson. Vancouver: Arsenal,
    2002. 5–10. Print.

Pratt, Mary Louis. *Imperial Eyes: Travel Writing and Transculturation.*
    London: Routledge, 1992. Print.

Rae, Ian. *From Cohen to Carson: The Poet's Novel in Canada.* Montreal:
    McGill-Queens UP, 2008. Print.

Saul, Joanne. *Writing the Roaming Subject: The Biotext in Canadian
    Literature.* Toronto: U of Toronto P, 2006. Print.

"Thwart, v." *OED Online.* Oxford University Press, June 2017. Web. 1 July
    2017.

Wah, Fred. *Diamond Grill.* Edmonton: NeWest, 1996. Print.

----. "Half-Bred Poetics." *Faking It: Poetics and Hybridity: Critical Writing
    1984–1999.* The Writer as Critic. 7. Edmonton: NeWest, 2000. 71–96.
    Print.

Diddling the Archive:
The Crooked Speech of Roy Kiyooka's
The Artist and the Moose

Max Karpinski

In the "Afterword" to Roy Kiyooka's *The Artist and the Moose: A Fable of Forget* (2009), Roy Miki quotes Kiyooka's introductory remarks from a reading of the manuscript held at the Kootenay School of Writing (KSW) in 1990: "Every two years I would take it out and go through the thing in its entirety and literally rewrite it. I don't know what I was trying to do … There was this interminable sort of fumbling, you could say" (qtd. in "Afterword" 137). Although *The Artist and the Moose* was published posthumously, fifteen years after Kiyooka's unexpected death in 1994, it had been in production since the late 1960s. Kiyooka's comments at the KSW begin to articulate the text's singularity as well as what might be called its potential to trouble or unsettle the field of Canadian literature. This paper takes Kiyooka's self-deprecating description of the history of the text's production seriously; I argue that, in the context of the text's critique of the institutionalization of Canadian literature, *The Artist and the Moose* occupies a unique position as a document continuously recomposed and reconfigured alongside and in response to the crystallization of the twinned discourses of centralist nationalism and cultural nationalism. Indeed, Miki explicitly links the text to the "period of heightened nationalism" inaugurated by the Canadian centennial, as well as to Northrop Frye's "Conclusion" and the "nationalist literary project" of the *Literary History of Canada* ("Belief" 45). Considering Miki's assertion that Frye invents a "'pastoral myth' that functions as the origin of Canadian literature" ("Belief" 31), I read *The Artist and the Moose* as constituting both a pointed rebuttal to the myopia of Canadian literary nationalism as well as offering an alternative genealogy of literary production in Canada, one that emerges precisely from its refusal to traffic in the dominant Canadian literary paradigms.

This reading positions Kiyooka's text as engaged in a double movement: simultaneously retrospective and *critical* in regards to the contemporary distribution of the sensible, and yet also invested in a future-oriented and *affirmative* politics that imagines otherwise. I follow a number of contemporary critical theorists and scholars who have turned their attention to the ways in which a particular set of reading practices have constellated around the term "critique," in such a way as to delimit the work of the literary critic.[70] Fred Moten, for example, describes the contemporary "reduction of intellectual life — to reduce study into critique, and then at the same time, a really, really horrific, brutal reduction of critique to debunking" (*Undercommons* 120). Similarly, Bruno Latour repeatedly returns to the word "debunk" in his challenge to what might be understood, more broadly, as the hermeneutics of suspicion that underlies some models of critique. "The critic," for Latour, "is not the one who debunks, but the one who assembles" ("Why" 246). In this move, which posits "drawing together" over "tearing down," he asks us to consider "What would critique do if it could be associated with *more*, not with *less*, with *multiplication*, not *subtraction*" ("Why" 248, emphasis in original). Shared between these two articulations of the limits of critique is a sense that negation cannot be enough. Rather, critique must be understood as simultaneously a refusal of the established order of the visible and the sayable, as well as a suggestion of an alternative ordering. This would be to think the act of negation or refusal as also generative; or, as Moten and Stefano Harney put it, embrace "abolition [not] as the elimination of anything but abolition as the founding of a new society" (42).[71]

In this quick sketch, I am repositioning "critique" as removed from the work of debunking and as invested, instead, in an avowedly political action that might be understood, following Jacques Rancière, as a "*re*distribution of the sensible" (*Politics* 43). Rancière develops the notion of the "distribution of the sensible" as a way to describe the systematic parceling out of the possibilities for participation in a common or shared sphere of relations. If "Politics revolves around what is seen and what can be said about it, around who has the ability to see and the talent to speak, around the properties of spaces and the possibilities of time" (*Politics* 13), then the distribution of the sensible manages those abilities, talents, and spaces, and hence dictates, for some, the "exclusion from participation in what is common to the community" (*Politics* 42–43). Rancière develops this model, one premised on a fundamental equality of all human subjects, as a way to describe the self-organizing mobilizations of those heretofore excluded from participation in the political sphere. In other words, politics happens when those who have been denied the ability to speak assert their fundamental equality as speaking beings through the act of speaking. These newly articulate subjects make their utterance undeniable, and deploy it to forcefully intervene in the common sphere of discourse. These interventions function as redistributions, as moments that re-articulate or re-negotiate the previously accepted systems and structures that preclude properly democratic participation in the political sphere.

Rancière is clear on the possibilities for artistic or aesthetic practices to engage in redistributive, political acts. In terms that map onto Rancière's description of politics, Franco Berardi offers the poetic as "the semiotic concatenation that exceeds the sphere of exchange and the codified correspondence of the signifier and signified" (149); in other words, poetry is a semiotic assemblage that exceeds the limits exercised upon language by regulatory grammars. Berardi's understanding of the poetic charges it with an inherent redistributive capacity. Poetry, in this model, refutes the possibility of any transparency to speech, as embodied by "the codified correspondence of the signifier and signified." In the context of Rancière's politics, this model of the poetic can be understood as a space from which to begin to think the emergence of the model of critique that I have gestured to above. Beyond negating, refusing, or rebutting, Berardi's poetic appears as an inherently excessive utterance, one that might also be turned towards the imagining of alternative ways of being and relating.

This idea of the poetic utterance as somehow existing alongside a transparent regulatory speech that demarcates the horizon of the sayable or the "field of the possible" (Berardi 16) finds an analogue in what Latour theorizes as the "crooked speech" of politics. In *An Inquiry into Modes of Existence* (2013), Latour attempts to locate the "interpretive key[s]" (48) that delineate the tactics of communication specific to individual disciplines. He locates the fundamental contradiction of the democratic political system in a crisis of representation: "people are obstinately critiquing political representation for something that it can never procure: they are asking it to 'express faithfully'—and thus mimetically—the 'political opinions' of billions of beings" (334). In the sphere of the political, representation (speaking-for) can never be transparent. Latour's version of this claim is that "political reasoning *never goes straight*"; representations are never "straightforward, flat, clean" (333, emphasis in original). Rather than positing the inherently crooked speech of politicking as a failure or crisis to be rectified, crooked speech emerges in this model as precisely that which must be maintained and cultivated. Crooked speech becomes the means towards articulating a future collective that takes into account those beings (human and non-human) who had previously been excluded from the count: "What will he have to do to situate *appropriately crooked speaking* once again at the centre of our civility as the only means to collect the collective, and above all to universalize it?" (355, emphasis in original).

"Appropriately crooked speaking": isn't this a beautiful description of the poetic? If crooked speech names the fundamental operation of political representation and utterance, then we might look to the inherently crooked speech of poetry and experimental writing as a site through which we can begin to negotiate the boundaries of the new, more equitable and just, collective. Rancière, too, invites a connection between the act of writing and the constitution of a particular group in common: "Writing always traces much more than the signs it aligns; it also traces a particular relation of bodies to their souls and to other bodies, and of the community to its soul. It is a specific distribution of the sensible, a specific structuring of a common world" (*Mute* 94). This passage returns to Berardi in its insistence upon writing's excessiveness, which can be understood as both a characteristic semantic expansiveness and the text's circulation and effect beyond the realm of pure discursivity. Rancière, however, is explicit in suggesting that this excess can be understood as the foundation or ground of a "common world." This line of argument posits the poetic as more than a disruptive or negative force, turned against the linguistic and material structures it seeks to undermine; the poetic becomes, instead, productive and propulsive, a site of creativity and an enactment of Daniel Heath Justice's injunction to "imagine otherwise" (qtd. in McKegney 318). Put differently, we can conceive of the poetic, in terms that map onto what I have described as the double pose of the alternative model of critique, as simultaneously recalcitrant and aspirational.

If crooked recalcitrance operates as a critique of contemporary social relations, I want to offer the aspirational quality of the poetic as a desire for the articulation of a "common world," a term that appears in both Rancière's and Latour's writing. Indeed, in *Politics of Nature* (2004), Latour imagines how it might be possible to "convoke the collective" (57), that is, how to begin "to compose a common world" (8) that takes into consideration the existence, needs, and demands of non-human beings or "propositions" (83) that continually assert their presence. Pairing Rancière and Latour, we might arrive at the image of the poet as the *crooked*, that is, not-straight, speaker of politics, constantly engaged in articulating a redistributive utterance that *encircles* the common world. The common world, as I want to offer it, is thus never settled and constantly under renegotiation. Rancière understands any articulation of a common world as positing a renegotiation of inclusion and exclusion from participation in the shared sphere of politics: "The assertion of a common world thus happens through a paradoxical mise-en-scène that brings the community and the noncommunity together" (*Disagreement* 55). This is a constantly open and incomplete process; for Rancière, "A 'common' world ... is always a polemical distribution of modes of being and 'occupations' in a space of possibilities" (*Politics* 42). Any articulation of a common world, then, involves the imposition of order; but in naming each instance "polemical," Rancière also foregrounds the disputatious nature and the partial quality of each and every iteration of a common world.

Crooked poetic speech, then, represents a constant desire to rene-gotiate the limits of the common world and to extend and expand the boundaries of the collective. But, and this is of the utmost importance, this model of political and crooked speaking foregrounds, always and from the very beginning, the polemical, disputatious, and partial as-pect of any common world, as well as the *differences that remain* be-tween any and all constituents. That is, these invocations of a common world must not be understood, following Lauren Berlant, as "the de-sire for a smooth plane of likeness" (395). Berlant's corrective resonates with Moten's description of the Mississippi Freedom School curriculum from 1964. As Moten tells it, those involved were asked to consider a series of questions:

> What do we not have that we need, what do we want or want to get? But the other question, which is, I think, prior to the first in some absolutely irreducible way, is what do we have that we want to keep? ... What that second, but prior, question presupposes is (a) that they've got something that they want to keep, and (b) that not only do those people who were fucking them over not have everything, but that part of what we want to do is to organize ourselves around the principle that we don't want everything they have. (121)

Moten's history here challenges Rancière's notion of what might be construed as an amicable coming together of "the community and the noncommunity," and opens the possibility of a common world predi-cated on a refusal of participation alongside the perpetrators of his-torical violence and exclusion. The "undercommons" emerges, for Moten and Harney, as a deployment of the commons concept that attempts to surface the constant, already-present resistances that constitute ways of being with others. Similarly, Berlant outlines the commons concept in a way that resonates with how I want to position the work of crooked speech: "[as] a way to view what's broken in sociality, the difficulty of convening a world conjointly, although it is inconvenient and hard, and to offer incitements to imagining a livable provisional life" (395).

Berlant's construction returns us to the double pose of critique with which I opened this paper. Crooked speech both points to "what's broken in sociality" while also "imagining a livable provisional life," a different or redistributed model of relationality. Indeed, Kiyooka's *The Artist and the Moose* suggests that these two aspects of crooked speaking are inherently and necessarily *linked*. That is, Kiyooka's text performs a critique of what's broken as a necessary first step, prior to supplementing critique's negations with positive livable and provisional constructions. Inasmuch as the text can be reduced to a narrative plot, *The Artist and the Moose* follows a nameless protagonist who has been "fingered" by "the Royal Commission on 'The Status of a Genuine Multi-Cultural Aesthetic for Canadians in the 21st Century' ... to write a White Paper" (16). Originally from a small town in Saskatchewan named Forget,[72] the protagonist travels to the "National Archives" in Ottawa, where he pores over "The Canadian History Texts" (17) in the hopes of fulfilling his mandate. His quest transforms into an obsession with the suspicious death of Tom Thomson, figured in the text as Tom Aplomb. The protagonist's desire to unravel the mysterious circumstances of Aplomb's death is linked to a question about the canonization of Canadian artists and the fabrication of a uniquely Canadian aesthetics. As Smaro Kamboureli reads it, the text's shift into detective story is less about Aplomb's death than it is about answering "both how and why Aplomb/Thomson emerged as a cultural hero" (23).

Both the search for the sordid truth beneath the official narrative of Aplomb's death and the quest to articulate a "Genuine Multi-Cultural Aesthetic for the 21st Century" fail, of course. And yet, in my reading, it is precisely in this failure that the recalcitrance of crooked speech becomes intertwined with aspiration; it is in the protagonist's failure that resistance and refusal circumvent sheer negation and emerge as productive. To better understand this shift, we might recall Latour's revaluing of critique as "*multiplication*, not *subtraction*," mentioned above. Recalcitrance operates at multiple levels in *The Artist and the Moose*: it describes the text's insubordination, its refusal to uncritically inherit narratives about the Canadian nation-state and

Canadian culture contained within the official (and always capitalized) "Canadian History Texts"; but it also names a formal resistance, one that presents itself as an interpretive irreducibility. Miki represents this second recalcitrance as the text's paradoxical invitation to "interpretation at the same time that it undermines the closure of settled meanings" ("Afterword" 164). We might also link it to Kiyooka's understanding that "a text is never completed, but finally 'abandoned'" (Miki, "Afterword: Coruscations" 302). In other words, and as a sort of microcosmic model of the common world's ceaseless improvisation and experiment, the text is never closed and never finished.

The text's refusal of the official narratives of nation becomes immediately available from the moment the protagonist begins his archival investigations. Along with Ol' Moose/Ol' Twig-eater (a magical moose that performs as the protagonist's mentor during his quest), Kiyooka rejects "the Tundra Blues" (13) as a mode of relating to the Canadian landscape. Instead, he attends to the ways in which land and landscape were instrumentalized in the fabrication of the Canadian nation-state, and particularly to the ways "the Official Documents" construct "a hostile Tundra, with every footnote diminishing both 'Moose' and 'Native'" (24). Deep within the archives, Kiyooka's protagonist quickly understands that the dominant Canadian trope of a hostile and awe-inspiring natural world underwrites both the material dispossession and violence enacted on Indigenous peoples as well as the degradation and reshaping of the land. Taking a cue from the nursery rhyme referenced in the text's first line, I read the protagonist as engaging in what I term an archival "diddling" that opens the National Archives to the play and presence of voices otherwise excluded or "diminished." The protagonist's dalliance in the Archives infuses the Official Documents with an oppositional excess, one that simultaneously undermines the dominant tropes or paradigms and offers an alternative opening onto the composition of a common world.

In this paper so far, I have endeavoured to position crooked poetic speech as the simultaneous cultivation of a critical attention to our contemporary distribution of the sensible and a future-oriented politics that imagines otherwise. While I seek to pull this double pose from

The Artist and the Moose, Miki has described Kiyooka's earlier texts as operating in a similar manner in that they "open a productive janus-like space: linked to the 'past' as a minority writer who underwent the era of cultural nationalism, but pointing to a 'future' that may be witness to radical cultural transformations" ("Unravelling" 79). Indeed, as Miki's statement suggests, the critical stance that runs through Kiyooka's texts might be tied to his experience as a "minority writer," and as a *Nisei* in predominantly white western Canada. Kiyooka was born in 1926 in Moose Jaw, Saskatchewan to first-generation Japanese immigrants. He has referred to himself as "a white anglo-saxon protestant with a cleft tongue" (qtd. in Miki, "Inter-Face" 49) while also describing a sense of "growing up athwarted ... You are of it, and you are not, and you know that very clearly" ("Inter-Face" 51).[73] At the same time as they index an undercurrent of violence or exclusion, both of these descriptions position Kiyooka simultaneously within and askance of the dominant culture. If Berardi, above, attributes an inherent redistributive capacity to poetic utterance, Miki recognizes a similar aspect within the speech of the "minority writer": "the lexicon of RK's inglish ... emits a sonic resonance exceeding the bounds of a pale face English" ("Afterword: Coruscations" 315).

Kiyooka's "cleft tongue" and his "inglish" offer two notions of a crooked speech that simultaneously works through the dominant, colonial language while also, by necessity, torqueing or tweaking it from within. A connection might be drawn between these models of troubled and/or troubling speech and what Kamboureli describes as the "saboteur"[74] aspect of the protagonist from *The Artist and the Moose* (26). Responding to Kiyooka's invocation of the "cleft tongue," Miki reads it in terms that resonate with my articulation of crooked speaking: "[the cleft tongue] suggests a kind of perversity within the form ... perverse not in an immoral sense but as a disruptive force" ("Inter-Face" 49). This clandestine and resistant movement through the symbols and structures of the dominant culture is referenced directly in *The Artist and the Moose*. Early in the text, the reader is presented with a "Night Letter," ostensibly sent from Ol' Moose to his "Protégé" (13), the protagonist. "There's a WASP at the bottom of every Frontier

Simile," Ol' Moose warns: "If you don't flush'em out they'll surely knee-cap you. Otherwise, appropriate their awesome guile" (14).[75] Ol' Moose is the first to turn the protagonist on to the ways in which the dominant cultural representations of so-called nature reflect a colonial relationship to dispossessed lands. While cautioning his Protégé to remain vigilant, he also suggests a kind of appropriation from below as an appropriate response to the state's discursive violence or myopia. In other words, it is precisely the "cleft" in the tongue that allows Kiyooka to speak aslant through the Official Documents of the National Archives.

While the "cleft tongue" emerges as a powerful symbol that encapsulates Kiyooka's constant movement on the periphery or limit point of Canadian literary and artistic production, another bodily image recurs throughout Kiyooka's writing: the hand, and particularly the phantom hand. In *The Artist and the Moose*, the arrival of a package containing Tom Aplomb's pipe marks a turning point in the protagonist's search. The package is sent anonymously by "A Collector of Troop of 7 Memorabilia," who assures the protagonist that "nobody, as far as I know, has had their hands on it except one Tom Aplomb and yours truly who, for obvious reasons, has been most careful not to touch it" (26). This strange paradoxical construction shuttles between the different semantic inflections of having one's "hands on" something. That is, it uncouples corporeality (to touch) from possession (to have), or alternatively, belonging. Discussing *StoneDGloves*, a series of poems presented alongside a photographic catalogue of the discarded workers' gloves that Kiyooka stumbled upon at the Expo 70 site in Osaka, Japan,[76] Scott Toguri McFarlane mentions "the force of Kiyooka's ambivalent relationship to Japan and also to hands" (136). McFarlane locates this ambivalence in Kiyooka's teenage experience as a "(farm) hand" in Opal, Alberta, where his family relocated after his father and brother were both dismissed from their jobs in Calgary in the wake of the bombing of Pearl Harbor (137); he also notes that Kiyooka's "hand … was fingerprinted in 1941 by the RCMP and labelled 'enemy alien' on his mandatory identification card" (137). McFarlane's associations suggest that, from very early in his life, Kiyooka would have been acutely aware of the ways his body was read as *not* belonging in the "Canadian" spaces through which he moved.

McFarlane's reminders articulate the very real political stakes of both Kiyooka's linguistic practice and the work of *The Artist and the Moose*, a work that I have named, somewhat irreverently, archival diddling. I understand the two bodily images traced above as central to Kiyooka's writing: if the "cleft tongue" is that which marks the speech of the minority writer, offering at once a restricted or limited inclusion in literary circles as well as the means to critique them, then the "phantom hand" points to those external systems that delimit the movement of the racialized body. In other words, if the cleft tongue torques the poet's utterance, the phantom hand operates beyond his ken. In his own recollections of Opal, Kiyooka describes his sense of "a punitive fist [that] kept clenching and unclenching behind my back but each time [he] turned to catch it flexing it would disappear into the unlit corners of our small log house" (qtd. in Miki, "Inter-Face" 44). This image paints the individual racialized subject as always under threat; or, perhaps even further, the "punitive fist" floating unseen in the corners of the home suggests the impossibility of an outside, a space free from the violent incursions of the state. It is here that the "cleft tongue" attains its full force. Always the skewed speech of a "white anglo-saxon protestant," it is precisely *not* a "way out" or an opening onto a beyond. Rather, in its saboteur aspect and its operation from within the structures and paradigms of the dominant culture, the cleft tongue exercised in *The Artist and the Moose* might offer a useful model for imagining a compromised or "livable provisional life" in the contemporary moment (Berlant 395).

The Artist and the Moose opens with a question, voiced by one of the protagonist's archival assistants: "'Did you hear about the Moose that flew over the moon?'" (11). Already at work in "the archives of Tom Aplomb," the protagonist is initially wary: "He instinctively took the question to be just another diversionary tactic but having arrived at the probe's limits where even the inconsequential could matter, he answered in the negative" (11). The assistant explains that "according to an old Iroquois I met in a bar in Hull, Mother Goose got it all wrong when she was telling that story about the cat and the fiddle" (11). Her error originates in her "short-sighted[ness]," that is, her myopia; she is said to mistake "a bull-moose's testicles" for "a bagful of milk" (11). The assistant concludes the tale by suggesting that the protagonist "summon[] up that fabulous critter. After all, Tom Aplomb did include him more than once in his paintings, and depicts him as an indomitable earthling" (11). The first page of Kiyooka's novel thus presents Ol' Moose as the mistaken cow from the Mother Goose nursery rhyme "Hey Diddle Diddle."[77] The Moose himself represents the first instance of the playful torqueing of an inherited or prior text, a tactic that is also available in Kiyooka's tendency to pun on the names of historical figures.

Ol' Moose originates, therefore, in a nonsense rhyme, in an "inconsequential" or "diversionary tactic" that imparts the stuffy archive with a sliver of levity. Indeed, I want to suggest that the nursery rhyme referenced on the first page hangs over the text, infusing *The Artist and the Moose* with what might be understood as a formal embodiment of the inconsequentiality and diversion of the phrase "Hey, diddle, diddle." It is in this formal engagement that I locate the text's enactment of an "archival diddling." First, the protagonist diddles the archive in the sense of "to do for, undo, [or] ruin" ("diddle"), in that he undermines the tropes and narratives he inherits in the National Archives. Second, in his "exemplary failure" (107), this archival diddling becomes available as well as a "diddling away," a waste of time or a "trifle" that refuses the *telos* embodied by the archive ("diddle"). It is in this shuttling between negation and trifling that I read the fusing of recalcitrance and aspiration. That "origin of Canadian literature," the pastoral mythology of Northrop Frye—who appears in the text as "Friar Northtrope," an "adversary" of Ol' Moose's (85)—is diddled doubly; it is trifled with, as Kiyooka's cheeky choice in renaming Frye suggests, and it is undone or perhaps unsettled, revealed as a screen that installs and upholds a centralist, white supremacy.

This second sense of "diddling" relates to the tradition of skeptical critique that I have described as invested in unmasking sunken ideological content. His very first "afternoon" on the job (18), the protagonist begins to feel apprehensive about the relationship between his project and the nation-state. That is, from the outset, he registers an unease or anxiety about the "Texts" that the "Nation's Archives" offer as a means to articulate "a Genuine Multi-Cultural Aesthetic for Canadians in the 21st Century" (16). Immediately upon "swear[ing] his allegiance to the Crown" (17), he receives "[p]age after page of Anglo-Canadian History" which "proposed a parenthetical alignment with Indo-European man and his clandestine appropriation of all the Aboriginal Land that had virtually remained unsullied til 1492" (18). The protagonist names this alignment "a Textual Paradigm that threatened his alacritous quest" (18). In other words, upon his first foray into the state-mandated textual materials for the construction of a "Genuine Multi-Cultural Aesthetic," it becomes abundantly clear that the White Paper he has been tasked with writing is considered valuable less for any recognition and celebration of difference than it is for its consolidation of state power and its reiteration of those narratives of nationhood and belonging from which it is asked to inherit. To return to the image of the cleft tongue, the protagonist very quickly understands that there is no outside possible for his Mandate, no available exit from the Archive onto a "genuinely" equitable articulation of relations.

To recognize the White Paper in its capacity as a kind of propaganda is to acknowledge the ways in which the nation-state is always concerned with reiterating its shape, or, to recall the language invoked above, always concerned with reinstalling a particular distribution of the sensible. Rancière's term is instructive here in that it registers the exercise of power in the distribution of visible bodies, or, in material space. Before he travels to Ottawa, the protagonist receives "a wall-sized map of O Canada ... from Statistics Canada" (27); his impulse is to measure what appears to him as "an immense, *crenellated* land mass" (27, emphasis added). This adjective reappears in Ottawa, as the protagonist imagines the Rideau Canal as "a medieval moat completed with crenellated stone towers" (40). The first half of the OED definition offered for "crenellate" is "To furnish with battlements, to embattle" ("crenellate"). The "crenellated land mass" offers a concise image of the nation-state as both a site of contestation—a space that requires defending—but also, and importantly, a *constructed* site. In the context of the archive, this construction can be understood to occur on the discursive level, in the "[p]age after page of Anglo-Canadian History" that shapes a particular, polemical narrative of Canadian belonging and inheritance.

In its implication of both contestation and construction, the "crenellated land mass" and the "crenellated … towers" of the nation's capital infuse the artistic and discursive modes of production that appear throughout Kiyooka's novel with the threat of violence. A similar move is embodied in the renaming of the Group of Seven as the "Troop of Seven" (55). Presented as less of a collective and more of a regiment, this punning shift militarizes the Troop's aesthetics, and suggests that artistic representation, or cultural production more broadly, can be understood as related to the forceful means by which the nation-state asserts its shape and boundaries. Here, again, we can return to Rancière's description of the relation between aesthetics and politics; whereas, for Rancière, the political names the appearance and apprehension of a dissenting voice from within a particular distribution of the sensible, both Kiyooka and his protagonist are attuned to the ways in which aesthetic representations have contributed to the formation of the contemporary, "police" distribution of the sensible. The canonization of Thomson/Aplomb and the Group/Troop of Seven forms the ground of a particular strand of "Canadian" aesthetics, predicated on the "colonial vernacular" (36) of pristine, "wide open spaces naked of mist and fog" (35) and divested of Indigenous presence. This aesthetic operates through the colonial fiction of *terra nullius*, described by Miki as "the colonial assumption that the land—which was, in effect, stolen from Indigenous groups who inhabited it—was unoccupied or 'empty' and therefore destined or 'in waiting' to be colonized and transformed into a national possession" ("Afterword" 153). Aesthetic representation recapitulates settler-invader violence; the Troop of Seven is drafted to serve the nation-state's violent land grabs.

If the *"crenellated* land mass" illustrates the intertwining of discursive construction and military contestation that *The Artist and the Moose* both unmasks and critiques, it might also offer a means to write aslant from within the National Archives. The second half of the OED definition for "crenellate" offers this sliver of light: "to furnish with embrasures or *loopholes*" ("crenellate," emphasis added). The "loophole" names both a particular type of battlement or defensive fortification, as well as a means of escape or an outlet. In these twinned and inverted significations, the "loophole" thus emerges as a prime site of crooked speech. The protagonist of *The Artist and the Moose* first identifies the ways in which a canonical "Canadian" aesthetics, aligned with Thomson and the Group of Seven, has been deployed to corroborate or defend the nation-state's violence and exclusions. Furthermore, he recognizes that the state-sanctioned Mandate for a new, "Multi-Cultural," and future-oriented aesthetic serves the continued fortification of the nation-state. Although the protagonist flounders in this knowledge, Kiyooka's text itself, I would argue, performs the work of crooked speech, or the movement from the "loophole" that serves the nation-state to the "loophole" that operates to reorganize the distribution of the sensible.

One way to begin to think the text's reorganizational tactics is through its play with the term "Hero," a play that serves to undermine Tom Thomson/Aplomb's canonical role as "the 'Blameless Hero' at the heart of the Eastern Historian's mytho/poetic enterprise" (28). Ruminating on Aplomb's lionization, the protagonist of the text quotes an uncited passage in his "*Notebook*": "*In* [The Cratylus] *Socrates maintains that 'heroes' are so-called because they are born of love, 'eros' being contained in heroes*" (30).[78] Another unattributed quotation, appearing later, offers its own interpretation of Aplomb's popularity, beginning in a consideration of his aesthetics but swerving into what might be read as a pointed statement about the comfortable fact of his whiteness:

> (Tom) isn't popular for what aesthetic qualities he showed, but because his work is close enough to representation to get by with the average man.... . Then, in Canada, we like our heroes made to order, and in our own image. They mustn't be too good and, above all, not too different. (35)[79]

Reading these two passages together, I want to suggest that *The Artist and the Moose* imagines the possibility of calling forth remarkably different cultural heroes. These heroes emerge, nonetheless, as objects of "love" or "eros."[80] It is this tactic that embodies the simultaneous recalcitrance and aspiration that I name poetic crooked speech. In refusing to recapitulate the white, male, heroic individualism of Tom Aplomb, Kiyooka's text reroutes or diverts the national "eros" into two primary figures: Ol' Moose and the Nameless Algonquin.

If nothing else, Ol' Moose is a decidedly strange presence in the text. As mentioned, he is called into existence through a diddled version of the nursery rhyme "Hey Diddle Diddle." He is a non-human character—a literal moose—and yet he also seems to be a living archive of suffering that fuses disparate experiences, or an entity that offers commonality through the differential experience of various forms of violence: "Since 1492, Ol' Moose had contracted, without his consent, syphilis, trench mouth, gangrene, small pox, AIDS and cancer plus a whole array of noxious pimples. All these plus endless codicils, institutions, and surveillance systems" (68). Miki reads Ol' Moose as "both a victim of colonialism and an embodiment of the lands appropriated through invasion" ("Afterword" 155). Ol' Moose, then, might be understood as a materially manifest reminder of the violence that "Anglo-Canadian history" routinely conceals. And yet, while such a reading makes sense in the context of the protagonist's struggle with his Mandate and his critical perspective on the blind spots of the Texts in the National Archive, much of Ol' Moose's double recalcitrant and aspirational power lies precisely in the expansiveness and irreducibility of his character. That is, I would argue that Ol' Moose is *not* to be read as a symbol; rather, we are asked to engage his character across multiple frames of reference and to hold this complexity together.[81] This is also Jane Bennett's perspective on the appearance of non-human characters in fictional narratives. Reading Kafka's "The Cares of a Family Man," which features an animate spool of thread named Odradek, Bennett suggests that the importance of Odradek is that he appears as "ontologically multiple" (8). Odradek and Ol' Moose pose a problem or difficulty for human characters and for the reader. Against the canonization of Thomson/Aplomb as a hero "in our own image," Ol' Moose asks the reader to welcome, with love, a hero of radical strangeness, an entity available as both an individual non-human and a transhistorical embodiment of suffering and dispossession.

Ol' Moose and the Nameless Algonquin appear as alternative heroic figures, opposed to the narratives of Canadian belonging traditionally proffered by those "historians [who] were mostly old men with shiny domes" (36). They represent a formalized response to the protagonist's realization that "'History' also belonged to all men women and children, together with other sentient critters who could be said to possess an acute ear and an infallible nose for prosody" (36). Whereas Ol' Moose actively influences the protagonist's quest, the Nameless Algonquin emerges from his archival excavations. The Nameless Algonquin refers to the body exhumed by the real-life figure of Judge Little (renamed Judge Small in *The Artist and the Moose*). Little, trying to prove that Thomson was murdered and that his body had never been moved from Algonquin Park, dug up the initial gravesite to find "a casket with skeletal remains, and a skull with a hole in its side" (Miki, "Afterword" 159). Forensic analysis, however, demonstrated that *"the skull ... belonged to a Nameless Indian, a whole head shorter than the legendary Tom Aplomb"* (Kiyooka, *Artist* 71, emphasis in original). For Miki, this corporeal switch offers an exemplary moment of Kiyooka's tendency to multiply interpretative possibilities: "Has the white settler/artist ... in death, replaced the Native[?] ... has Aplomb *become* Native[?] ... Or does the act of digging up the past expose the visibility of a Native presence that has been suppressed?" ("Belief" 45). Responding to Miki's multiple questions, I want to suggest that the Nameless Algonquin embodies a formal expansiveness or excess in that his presence both multiplies interpretations and troubles the settled, inherited narrative of Thomson/Aplomb's life and death in the wilderness of Canada.

The protagonist himself recognizes the ways in which the Nameless Algonquin simultaneously undermines and expands the possibilities of the inherited narratives; in his words, the Nameless Algonquin "splice[s] reams-of-silences into the great Laurentian Legend" (40).

Kiyooka's phrase, here, captures the operations of crooked speech and identifies the aesthetic dissent that distinguishes Rancière's notion of the political. The insertion of "silences" into inherited "Legend[s]" points to the voices silenced, diminished, or excluded from the "Official Documents." But this tactic extends beyond a demand for recognition; rather, the "reams-of-silences" demonstrate the necessity for a reorganization of the "Laurentian Legend" and a rethinking of narratives of belonging or community that form the ground of a collective identity. These "reams-of-silences" echo in one of the protagonist's final gestures in the text: the official rescindment of his obligation to the nation-state. The protagonist is "laid off" before he is able to write the White Paper. Completing the termination process, "he placed his name (in Cree) on the bottom line of the official Document that gave him back his freedom" (102). Kamboureli describes the signature as an *"hors-texte,"* one the narrator "inserts into the cultural, historical, and political archive of Canada" (26). The signature, and its announcement in a parenthetical aside, might be understood as an implicit question about the nation-state's restriction of the horizon of the sayable. It re-centres the languages overwritten by governmental and juridical discourse. It represents another diddling of the nation-state's directive, another "silence" (the protagonist's name is never mentioned, in English, Cree, or otherwise) that functions as both an impossible interpretive clot and a generative site undermining the state distribution of the sensible.

At the text's close, after the "exemplary failure" of his quest (107), the protagonist "escape[s] into his destiny," vanishing "through the [loop?] hole in the middle of the small round pond" in his backyard in Forget (106). All that remains of his life's labour is "a hastily penned circle with a question mark in the middle" (107). This question mark is legible as the text's final silence, a gasp of despair or renunciation. And yet, I am inclined to read it as one last gesture towards the double pose of crooked speaking. In this reading, the question mark is an imperative, perhaps even a direction onto the Aesthetic the protagonist has been seeking. It is both the recognition of the necessity of critique, a demand to ask questions of the narratives we inherit, and an aspirational goal. To recall Miki's construction, the question mark reminds us to refuse the "settled" narratives. This word, of course, signifies doubly: refuse the stable and the closed, and refuse those narratives that "recapitulate a colonial vernacular" (Kiyooka, *Artist* 36), that operate by exclusion and that underwrite dispossession. As it appears emblematized in Kiyooka's question mark, poetic, crooked speech approaches the complex and the different with openness and hospitality. Indeed, this pose is one that Kiyooka felt intuitively in the wake of the centennial and the crystallization of a Canadian cultural nationalism with its concomitant exclusions and obfuscations. Speaking with Sheila Watson in 1970, Kiyooka muses on the place of the "Canadian" in so-called Canadian cultural production: "Canadian, for me, is a complex possibility. It (at least) has to include the obstinate, the weird, the recalcitrant, the bizarre and the fanciful—at least, that much" ("With" 22).

At least, that much: Even as he imagines cracking open those settled narratives of Canadian cultural nationalism, Kiyooka leaves space for other, different dissenting voices to surge in. Each of those adjectives —obstinate, weird, recalcitrant, bizarre, fanciful—inflects *The Artist and the Moose*. In its double diddling, signalled from the opening sentence, the novel embodies that critical/aspirational pose that I recognize in the work of crooked speech. Closing his essay that pairs *The Artist and the Moose* with Frye's "Conclusion," Miki allows himself a moment of fancy:

> [I]t is instructive to imagine the subsequent history of Canadian literary studies had this work achieved the canonic status of Frye, so that 'our' beginnings had been more preoccupied with forms of difference in our actually existing conditions rather than with the demarcation of identity boundaries. (47)

Although, as Miki quips, "literary studies do not have access to a crystal ball" (47), perhaps it is nonetheless possible to pull to the surface (exhume?) a singular, innovative, and political text written in Canada that exceeds or cracks any remaining vestiges of a calcified Canadian literature. That much, at least, is this paper's gambit: to articulate an alternative genealogy of innovative and political contemporary literature written in Canada, a genealogy that undermines the settled, inherited paradigms—the "Northtropes" of Canadian "Friars" —and that might be traced, instead, to the astonishing work of a prairie-born writer of Japanese heritage.

Works Cited

Anker, Elizabeth S. and Rita Felski. "Introduction." *Critique and Postcritique*, edited by Elizabeth S. Anker and Rita Felski, Duke UP, 2017, pp. 1–30.

Arnheim, Rudolf. *Visual Thinking*. U of California P, 1969.

Bennett, Jane. *Vibrant Matter: A Political Ecology of Things.* Duke UP, 2010.

Berardi, Franco. *The Uprising: On Poetry and Finance*. Semiotexte, 2012.

Berlant, Lauren. "The Commons: Infrastructures for Troubling Times." *Environment and Planning D: Society and Space*, vol. 34, no. 3, 2016, pp. 393–419.

Brown, Craig, Ed. *The Illustrated History of Canada*. 25th Anniversary Ed. McGill-Queen's UP, 2012.

Castiglia, Christopher. "Hope for Critique?" *Critique and Postcritique*, edited by Elizabeth S. Anker and Rita Felski, Duke UP, 2017, pp. 211–229.

"crenellate | crenelate, v." *OED Online*. Oxford UP, June 2017. Web. 11 July 2017.

"diddle, v.3." *OED Online*. Oxford UP, June 2017. Web. 11 July 2017.

Findlay, Len. "Always Indigenize!: The Radical Humanities in the Postcolonial Canadian University." *Unhomely States: Theorizing English-Canadian Postcolonialism*, edited byCynthia Sugars, Broadview, 2004, pp. 367–382.

Harney, Stefano and Fred Moten. *The Undercommons: Fugitive Planning & Black Study*. Minor Compositions, 2013.

Kamboureli, Smaro. "Introduction." *Critical Collaborations: Indigeneity, Diaspora, and Ecology in Canadian Literary Studies*, edited by Smaro Kamboureli and Christl Verduyn, Wilfrid Laurier UP, 2014, pp. 1–27.

Kiyooka, Roy K. *The Artist and the Moose: A Fable of Forget*. Edited by Roy Miki, LINEbooks, 2009.

Kiyooka, Roy. "With Roy Kiyooka." *White Pelican*, vol. 1, no. 1, 1971, pp. 18–35.

Latour, Bruno. *An Inquiry Into Modes of Existence: An Anthropology of the Moderns*. Translated by Catherine Porter, Harvard UP, 2013.

----. *Politics of Nature: How to Bring the Sciences into Democracy*. Translated by Catherine Porter, Harvard UP, 2004.

----. "Why Has Critique Run out of Steam? From Matters of Fact to Matters of Concern." *Critical Inquiry*, vol. 30, no. 2, 2004, pp. 225–248.

Love, Heather. "The Temptations: Donna Haraway, Feminist Objectivity, and the Problem of Critique." *Critique and Postcritique*, edited by Elizabeth S. Anker and Rita Felski, Duke UP, 2017, pp. 50–72.

Marlatt, Daphne et al. "A Celebration of Roy Kiyooka." *Brick, a literary journal*, vol. 48, 1994, pp. 13–34.

McFarlane, Scott Toguri. "Un-Ravelling *StoneDGloves* and the Haunt of the Hibakusha." *All Amazed for Roy Kiyooka*, edited by John O'Brian, Naomi Sawada, and Scott Watson, Arsenal Pulp Press/Morris and Helen Belkin Art Gallery/Collapse, 2002, pp. 117–147.

McKegney, Sam. "Indigenous Environmental Ethics and the Limits of Cultural Evolutionary Thinking." *Found in Alberta: Environmental Themes for the Anthropocene*, edited by Robert Boschman and Mario Trono, Wilfrid Laurier UP, 2014, pp. 305–327.

Miki, Roy. "Afterword: Coruscations, Plangencies, and the Syllibant: After Words to Roy Kiyooka's *Pacific Windows*." *Pacific Windows: Collected Poems of Roy K. Kiyooka*, edited by Roy Miki, Talonbooks, 1997, pp. 301–320.

----. "Afterword: Roy Kiyooka as/in Tom Thomson." *The Artist and the Moose: A Fable of Forget*, by Roy K. Kiyooka, LINEbooks, 2009, pp. 135–177.

----. "Belief as/in Methodology as/in Form: Doing Justice to CanLit Studies." *Critical Collaborations: Indigeneity, Diaspora, and Ecology in Canadian Literary Studies*, edited by Smaro Kamboureli and Christl Verduyn, Wilfrid Laurier UP, 2014, pp. 29–48.

----. "Inter-Face: Roy Kiyooka's Writing, A Commentary/Interview." *Roy Kiyooka*. Artspeak Gallery/Or Gallery, 1991, pp. 41–54.

----. "Unravelling Roy Kiyooka: A Re-assessment Amidst Shifting Boundaries." *All Amazed for Roy Kiyooka*, edited by John O'Brian, Naomi Sawada, and Scott Watson, Arsenal Pulp Press/Morris and Helen Belkin Art Gallery/Collapse, 2002, pp. 69–83.

Rancière, Jacques. *Disagreement: Politics and Philosophy*. Translated by Julie Rose, U of Minnesota P, 1999.

----. *Mute Speech: Literature, Critical Theory, and Politics*. Translated by James Swenson, Columbia UP, 2011.

----. *The Politics of Aesthetics: The Distribution of the Sensible*. Translated by Gabriel Rockhill, Continuum, 2004.

Thompson, John Herd with Allen Seager. *Canada 1922–1939: Decades of Discord*. McClelland and Stewart, 1985.

Wah, Fred. *Faking It: Poetics and Hybridity, Critical Writing 1984–1999*. NeWest Publishers, 2000.

The Imaginary of the Masculine "Northland": Asian-Canadian and Indigenous Kinships in Roy Kenzie Kiyooka's *The Artist and the Moose*

Tavleen Purewal

In Osaka, Japan, installing his sculpture "Abdu Ben Adam's Vinyl Dream" as part of the Canadian pavilion for Expo '70,[82] Roy Kenzie Kiyooka photographed the scattered gloves of workers at the world expositions' construction sites. These photographs circulated Canada as an exhibition entitled *StoneDGloves*, showcasing gloves tattered, fallen and forgotten, covered in dust and cement.[83] Now the exhibit is in print in what Roy Miki defines as a "poetry book doubling as a catalogue" (309), which experiments with the generic and thematic possibilities that arise out of poems positioned as captions for photos and as inscriptions atop photos. One of the images, for example, is overlaid with the text: "palimpsest/ palm poem." Palimpsest derives from the Ancient Greek "palimpsestos" and denotes "again scraped." To be scraped again suggests that the use-value changes and that the scraping cannot completely erase the previous text. Kiyooka evokes the idea of the palimpsest to gesture towards the layering of social realities within this representation of the glove, and to participate in a literary and critical tradition that has used the palimpsest to discuss the dynamics between erasure and repression, and the power relations of the visible and the barely visible.

Scott Toguri McFarlane examines the aesthetic possibilities of *StoneDGloves* through a geological context, like that of the palimpsest, wherein the gloves allude to visual and symbolic ghosts, archives, and archaeological excavations. He evokes these images through the historical framework of the hibakusha, "those affected by the bomb" during Hiroshima and Nagasaki, and the sociological context of the capitalist forces underwriting globalization with labour exploitation (124). McFarlane suggests that Kiyooka's photographic project "escalates" the "haunting effects" of the hibakusha, but I wonder how the project functions to concretize an abstract reality's forgottenness.

The publication's opening image of a worker's glove, a glove covered in dust and brittle in some areas due to the cement, is accompanied by the following text: "the way they fell/ the way they lay there/ the dust sifting down,/ hiding all the clues ..." The brief beautiful lines, beginning with iambs that descend into trochees, all end with a stress, an emphatic stamp to focus on and magnify what is otherwise softly occurring: a slow and light sedimentation of dust, a burial, which Stephen Morton observes in relation to the reader: "The reader is thus invited to participate in the retroactive articulation of the absent productive body, and to interrogate his/her own complicity in its erasure, or burial" (100).[84]

Whereas the "palimpsest/ palm poem" textualizes the interface of presence, absence, multiple significations, and contexts upon the surface, this caption-poem traces the process of the layers' coming together, a gradual sedimentation whose mode is defined by the poem's verbs. Sedimentation is a geological concept but figuratively envelopes the gloves to both concretize the glove from its place as forgotten rubble and emphasize its forgottenness—an ambivalence theorized in *Camera Lucida* by Roland Barthes' suggestion that each "photograph is a certificate of presence" but "it is without future" (87, 90). The gloves' relation to the photographer makes the definition of sedimentation capacious to include the metaphorical and literal significances of bonding and relation. The atemporal glove encounters the temporal photographer.

The relation between the photographer and the object of photography can be characterized with the same duality of repression and memorialization. One of the photo caption-poems, entitled "glove's dream," reads: "hands/ hands/ hands ... hold/held/help/ hands/ hands." A metonymy for the human body within labour conditions, the glove is also a literal glove, both significations which call out for a kinship by linking hands, putting one inside the other to feel life through touch. The glove dreams, then, for the process of sedimentation that buries it to also enact its metaphorical signification and reproduce a hand as representative of an emerging kinship, or even ownership. As the hand is the target domain for the sediment in this metaphor, there is still a literal bonding occurring between a hand and a glove. The metaphoric and literal align to signify kinship. This hand is the photographer, Roy Kiyooka, and the viewer and audience.

Kinship, then, is practiced within the rubble of stone and dirt, framing the emergence of solidarity and ethical relation between human and non-human, especially when one considers a grammatically reoriented kinship that goes beyond the biogenetic. Daniel Heath Justice articulates it succinctly: "kinship is best thought of as a verb rather than a noun, because kinship, in most indigenous contexts, is something that's done more than something that simply is" (150). Focusing on the doing allows one to conceptualize Kiyooka's project as a process.

One may also read Kiyooka as a process. His youth was marked by change and geographical fluidity: from Moose Jaw, Saskatchewan to inner-city Calgary, to Opal, Alberta. As Roy Miki intuits, "young RK was profoundly disturbed by this radical estrangement from place" (304). Both Smaro Kamboureli and Roy Miki have noted Kiyooka's "athwarted" relation to Canada, which could characterize his relation to the workers in Japan and to the Indigenous reality of this land.[85] To study Kiyooka raises a question about focus: how is the temporally specific lived experience of a Nisei photographer in Japan processed, without reducing the general experience of the Asian-Canadian identity in the colonial Canadian state? How can a critic analyze both the specific and the general without falling into the trap of inverse proportionality, whereby something present requires something absent, a concept I borrow from mathematics whereby one variable's increase results in the other's reduction. Moreover, there is a methodological risk of creating a noun, a presence, an essential object of study. Kiyooka notoriously resists the nouning of his identity. To study him as a verb, however, is not a critical approach I can manage yet. As such, I refocus on the emergence and function of kinship in *The Artist and the Moose: A Fable of Forget*, which is itself a shifting, transforming, and generative thematic that must be studied in its movement and creation, in its modality as a verb.

The Artist and the Moose: A Fable of Kinship and Poetics

Roy Kiyooka began writing *The Artist and the Moose* in the late 1960s and early 1970s, around the time when Anne Brodsky, the editor of *Artscanada*, solicited a submission from him. He sent in a serial poem, "letters purporting to be abt tom thomson" and, as Roy Miki remembers, handed out this poem during his reading of the novella in 1990 at the Kootenay School of Writing. Miki proposes that the "letters" accompany the novella and suggests that "the primary intent" of Kiyooka's work was "to reconstruct the poet's memories of the Group of Seven" (138). Consequently, in the posthumous publishing of *The Artist* in 2009, Miki appends the narrative prose work with the poem. It serves to reiterate the centrality of Tom Thomson, both as an early 20th century Canadian artist who influenced the Group of Seven and as a catalyst for the narrative.

The narrative of *The Artist and the Moose* follows a nameless protagonist from Forget, Saskatchewan (a real town in Saskatchewan named after a commissioner who contributed to the report on the Metis in 1884)[86] to Ottawa where he undertakes a project requested by the Royal Commission to write about "The Status of a Genuine Multi-Cultural Aesthetic for Canadians in the 21st century" (Kiyooka 16). His research for the mandate turns into an investigation of the mysterious disappearance of Tom Aplomb (Tom Thomson) which in turn explores the random yet predetermined, and tenuous yet inextricable connection between the protagonist and Tom Aplomb. Miki's autobiographical reading of this relationship suggests a literary kinship that needs to represent the colonial structuring of relation in Canada: "the figure of Tom Thomson may be filtered through [Kiyooka's] own subjectivity, but his subjectivity has been filtered through the 'vision of o canada true north strong and (barely) free' that Tom Thomson, as the 'true' Canadian artist, has been portrayed as embodying" (139). The protagonist is ensnared by Tom Aplomb as a mythic and national character and as one that he produces through his research, but he is guided away from this relationship by Ol' Moose, an Indigenous mythic figure whose representation exemplifies the vexed relation between Kiyooka and the Indigenous episteme in Canada.

The Artist and the Moose captures Kiyooka's fascination with geological imagery in material and metaphorical contexts in the way that it analyzes the palimpsestic relationship between labouring Asian-Canadian subjects and the erased and buried Indigenous presence. This Indigenous presence appears throughout the fable, a genre indicated by the novella's subtitle, manifesting as Ol' Moose and Pipe and other non-human and human characters such as the Algonquin man's skeleton. Ol' Moose is the protagonist's guide and a bodily representation of the colonization of Turtle Island as the "King of the Tundra" who "since 1492" undergoes violence (Kiyooka 13). Pipe is the smoking pipe of the painter Tom Aplomb (Thomson), and a representation of colonial artifacts and their function in producing a hegemonic national narrative. Ol' Moose demonstrates, moreover, that the geography blurs into the character to make it sociohistorically specific and locatable. Within a kind of chiastic structure, the Indigenous geography erupts the narrative through the ghostly and mythic Indigenous presence of Ol' Moose and the Algonquin man's skeleton. The eruptions represent an Indigenous epistemic intervention that puts under erasure the conditions for what I outlined above as the trap of inverse proportionality. Indigeneity is enduring and its presence resists decline even if Aplomb's presence saturates the text. By positioning Indigenous and Indigenous-representative characters in intimate kinships with the non-Indigenous characters, Kiyooka encodes kinship with the necessity of Indigenous presence within Indigenous epistemologies. Recurrent motifs of palimpsestic artifacts, people, surfaces, and geographies further unveil kinship as a process that occurs and is possible within the land.

Kiyooka's language is difficult. It is a difficulty that derives from the many semantic valences of his words that portray a dense mixture of polysemy and polyvalency. This technique is best exemplified in the multiple significations accrued in the names: Tom Aplomb is at once a reference to Tom Thomson and to the literal meaning of aplomb, a self-confidence or assurance that only a white character heralded for an 'authentic' artistic representation of Canada can inhabit; Vinnie Travail, for whom Aplomb is a "two-bit lover" (44), is given a grammatic valency for a name: travail as a noun signifies a laborious effort and as a verb denotes the engaging of labor, all of which play on the Old English homophone of travail as "time" and "work."

Kiyooka's words and phrases seem to be alive and continuously amassing meaning through the palimpsestic reality of meaning upon meaning, sediment upon sediment. Consequently, the language parallels the images in the text that are either dense concept-metaphors evoking the land, mountains, and natural elements, or literal images of sedimented and palimpsestic objects and surfaces like books, archives, paintings, and faces. Glen Lowry accords such a density of signification to the poetic voice, which he argues is translated into prose in Kiyooka's *TransCanada Letters*. A voice structured by poetic compression explodes the prose genre, and in the process, destabilizes the expressive Self/Author to signify either the author or the text.

Lowry marks the "I" of Kiyooka's letters as one that shifts, multiplies, and negotiates a "fragmentary nature of racialized subjectivity [and] also its problematic relationship to the community of communities it performs" (8). The protagonist thus can be read as an Asian-Canadian identity if we tie the slippages of Kiyooka's autobiographical and fictional "I" to include and temporarily inhabit the protagonist. The protagonist, furthermore, is nameless. The rare clues in the text attest to him being non-WASP (White-Anglo-Saxon-Protestant) and the one choice reference to the Rocky Mountains (104) suggests some association with Asian communities on the West Coast, like Kiyooka. The namelessness, moreover, represents a personhood framed by the logic of the *tabula rasa*, whereby the protagonist is open to the palimpsestic writings and rewritings of entities like the state, like Tom Aplomb, and Ol' Moose; but it also refuses categorical and deterministic meaning and identity. The protagonist disappears at the end of the narrative, inflecting his namelessness with a political and cultural refusal to being legible to the state.

It is the ending of the fable that began for me my work on the text. The last paragraph depicts the protagonist's "goodly wife" in Forget, Saskatchewan, left behind, looking at her husband's goodbye or possible suicide note: "a hastily penned circle with a question mark in the middle" (107). The note is a literal imagining of what Roland Barthes discussed figuratively about the photograph and its impact on the observer: "I am alone with it, in front of it. The circle is closed, there is no escape. I suffer, motionless. Cruel, sterile deficiency: I cannot transform my grief, I cannot let my gaze drift" (Barthes 90). The wife could inhabit Barthes' "I". As she stands in front of the note: is she grieving? Is she rendered motionless? Is her gaze fixated? Is her ambiguous, unspoken demeanor more enigmatic then what Barthes describes? Or, another concern, why is she left behind?

The protagonist, the narrator vaguely shares, "joined Ol' Moose in the Tundra" (106–107). Consequently, I trace the text's development of subjectivities, processes, and conclusions of the male characters' kinships, while noting that this development abandons its women characters or operates at the expense of these women characters. *The Artist* portrays a kinship experienced through literal and metaphorical processes of sedimentation, but does not account for the random and non-causal processes of sediments falling into place wherever that might happen. Instead, this sedimentation adheres to codes and channels of male-kin lines forming a kind of biogenetic kinship based on gender.

Ol' Moose and the Sedimentation of Kinships in and on Indigenous Land

A study of sedimentation, in the ways that it becomes a framework in the novella for characters to bond metaphorically and literally, allows one to change the focus from bodies to the relations between bodies and the signification of kinship that arises from physical intimacies and relations with Indigenous conceptions of land.[87] The metaphorical mode represents kinships between identity categories, the Indigenous, white, and Asian-Canadian, or non-specified racialized subjectivities, and the difficulties, fissures, and appropriations of these kinships. Meanwhile, the literal depicts the simultaneous physical bonding, doubling, and melding of bodies.

From the Latin *sedere*, to sit and to settle, sedimentation not only evokes geology—sediments settling at the bottom of a liquid—but also an unwitting association to settler politics and by extension, to settler-colonialism. Sedimentation thus etymologically gestures at the becoming of a settler identity: the sediment, like the diasporic subject and white settler, moves through seas and settles on a host land. I assert, however, that the unequal racialized realities of the diasporan and white settler result in very different movements and settlements. On the one hand, the etymology connotes a non-essential conception of sedimentation and so opens up the possibility of kinship outside the biogenetic and blood-quantum logics. On the other hand, discussed soon after, the originary violence of settlerhood that inhabits the term reveals the slipperiness of identity and of kinship. Glen Coulthard, in his powerful work *Red Skin White Masks*, advocates the necessity for settlers to educate themselves on the material and pedagogic role of land in Indigenous epistemology. He writes: "land as [a] system of reciprocal relations and obligations can teach us about living our lives in relation to one another and the natural world in non-dominating and non-exploitative terms" (13). Through this conceptualization, land's animated capacity teaches and produces relations, which in the context of *The Artist*, can foster encounters and kinships between racialized beings in Canada.

Shifting the focus from white settler-Indigenous and Indigenous-Indigenous kinships that Coulthard theorizes, Rita Wong in "Decolonizasian: Reading Asian and First Nations Relations in Literature" articulates a kinship between the titular communities—Indigenous and Asian Canadian—that foregrounds Indigenous epistemology and land as the organizing principle. Wong wonders what "happens if we position indigenous people's struggles instead of normalized whiteness as the reference point through which we come to articulate our subjectivities" (1). Whiteness then makes way for "First Nations values of interdependency and land stewardship" to highlight the intersections of "individual interactions and the level of larger socioeconomic frameworks" to not only inform subjecthood but kinship (15).

Her particular observations that "writers racialized as Asian cannot avoid making reference to the First Nations of this land" (3) illuminates Kiyooka's own self-conscious encounters with the present or absented Indigenous reality of this land. After attending an arts fest in Yellowknife, Kiyooka notes that many authors congregated "to read from our poetry/stories ... i wanta call it a gathering of a divers clan who only had their particular senses of a (Canadian) 'English' to make some sense out of their northland experiences. And, yes, we declaimed our poetry, some of it having to do with native Dene/Inuit Mythologies without a single actual native present."[88]

Kiyooka taps into the literary colonial phenomenology of the "northland" that absents the "native" from experience and authorship. His project in *The Artist*, thus, relives this exclusionary phenomenology through the demands of the "Mandate" (17). The protagonist inadvertently "stubbed his big toe on a paradigm that threatened to undermine his Mandate" (78). That paradigm that intervenes is Ol' Moose, a consistent character who foregrounds the relationship between the land and the Indigenous community. While Ol' Moose triangulates the relation between the protagonist and Aplomb, the land is the triangulating agent insofar as it is the condition by which kinships occur.

The triangulating is only possible if one considers land animate and pedagogical as Coulthard reminds us and as theorized in Jeannette Armstrong's essay "Land Speaking," which appears in *Speaking for the Generations: Native Writers on Writing*, edited by Simon J Ortiz. This collection of essays attempts to reposition Indigenous literary and cultural study in the specificity and intellectual milieu of Indigenous scholars and communities. Armstrong's essay furthers this project by grounding the study of Indigeneity and language in her ancestral land, the Okanagan, and by portraying herself as the transmitter or translator of theory that the land and her ancestors articulate. She transcribes what is "said in Okanagan": "the land constantly speaks. It is constantly communicating. Not to learn its language is to die" (176). The powerful declarative makes apparent that the land is a communicative subject that speaks whether or not a listening human agent is present. It becomes the duty of the inhabitant, of the person indigenous to the land, to listen and learn, without which they will linguistically and spiritually die.

Listening for the Okanagan is not exclusively about the aural apprehension of the listener: "Through my language I understand I am being spoken to, I'm not the one speaking" (Armstrong 181). When the land speaks, its communicative forces "move within as the colors, patterns, and movements of a beautiful, kind Okanagan landscape" (176). This 'movement' is the extra-linguistic force that characterizes "land language" (178). A non-verbal and multi-sensational relation develops within the human agent, and between the human and the land in a way that resembles Samuel Taylor Coleridge's articulation of the poetic process in the 1796 poem "Eolian Harp." The harp, like the poet's mind, is stimulated by an "intellectual breeze" that brings it into expression. The person indigenous to Okanagan, then, like Armstrong, is brought into expression through the "human words" that are used to translate land's language (Armstrong 176). To return to the idea that land's expressive patterns and movements occur within the human, Armstrong insinuates that land speaks itself. Precisely through articulating itself, land implicitly instills the listener with a sense of relation between the two. When the "beautiful, kind Okanagan landscape" speaks itself inside her, Armstrong recognizes that she relates to it.

Turning to *The Artist*, I note that Ol' Moose, the simultaneously mythic and contemporary animal, is a translator of the land language of the Tundra, but also takes on the qualities of the land. Ol' Moose appears in and out of the protagonist's narrative with his "avuncular profile" (42) to advise the protagonist against the dangers and oppressions of the "Mandate," not allowing him to be "another sacrificial victim to the Eastern Establishment's legerdemain" (13).

He also has his own narrative to live. The reader relearns the history of colonization from the perspective of this non-human entity. Ol' Moose is forced to confront post-1492 misrepresentations of itself through Canuck, Jesuit, and Whiteman discourses and decides to transform into "The Laughing Hulk of the Tundra" as a means of escape (13). The avuncular Moose transforms into "one part hill and one part tree" (13), a part of the landscape that undergoes historical, colonial, geographic, linguistic, and cultural violence. However, Ol' Moose exhibits the various entities of Turtle Island that are involved in strategies of Indigenous survival, and highlights the role of land, the Tundra specifically, in providing the space and epistemological tools to continue to survive: "he carried the vestigial remains of paradise in the tip of his antlers and thus was given to heap scorn on New World Puritans and their pretensions" (13).

Kiyooka crafts an image of an animated and animal-shaped landscape that moves toward a future that will confront his burden's "scorn" (13). The blurring of land with the non-human gives the narrative a grounding in and attention to the conventions of Indigenous mythology that give voice to the non-human and spiritual being. The blurring also articulates the complex reality of Indigenous survival that requires paradigm shifts in how we think about kinships between the human, non-human, and the environment in relation to resistance.

Resistance in *The Artist* is also articulated as an aggressive masculinized project. Though Ol' Moose never interacts with any human character other than the protagonist, he does visit the archives in Ottawa and has an uncomfortable encounter with Pipe, the artifact that belonged to Tom Aplomb. Pipe is pompous, entitled, bitter, and sardonic, and it intercepts the telepathic messages Ol' Moose sends to the protagonist (51). Ol' Moose and Pipe meet randomly, however, as Ol' Moose "stumbled over the pipe in his meanderings ... he picked [Pipe] up in his fore hoofs ... packed it full of lichen ... nearly blew his many-tiered antlers off. Whereas the distraught Pipe never again regained its former composure" (83). This passage undercuts Pipe's unsympathetic characteristics, humbles it, by violating its body. I cannot help but read the encounter as part of a rape joke, alongside its significations of Ol' Moose recontextualizing the colonial artifact as part of a smoke ritual, or rather rehabilitating it to its Indigenous context. Reappropriation, recontextualization, and rehabilitation are effective aspects of Indigenous resurgence, but its application in *The Artist*, and its implications of misogyny in action, a misogyny embedded in rape culture, undermines the symbolism of Ol' Moose's actions. This problematic masculinity is also what constitutes Ol' Moose's representation in the novel with regards to the Tundra.

Kiyooka depicts the Tundra landscape as both the abode and identity for Ol' Moose, which reproduces the conception of the North as masculine. In a letter to Phyllis Web in 1976, Kiyooka writes of his experience in Yellowknife: "[t]he Northland in those yrs was a very real place—it's where I underwent my initiation into manhood viz gruelling work and gambling" (Pacific Rim 17). The "Northland" here is a space of hostility with hard labour that allows a certain rugged and classed masculine ideal, "manhood," to emerge. Through work and gambling, one enters a manhood that is inextricable from the landscape and from the land's demands on the gendered body. In other words, the Tundra functions as a site in which a masculinity is developed and produced, communicating within the conventions of a masculine performance.

Introducing Forget, the narrator describes the geography as "the Tundra's tumulus silences," and later, as "sybillant-silences" (27). The first phrase signals the Tundra as a metaphoric and literal burial site of an Indigenous presence; "tumulus silences" depict the ice sheet as a silencing mound over the Indigenous graves—of bodies, of languages, of governance, etc. The second instance maps out the geography's linguistic scape wherein the protagonist's attuned ear hears the silent syllables of the Tundra to both make sense of and turn away from his project with the government. Consequently, the Tundra is capable of communication and land language, in Armstrong's terms, which, in conjunction with the gendered performance of Ol' Moose, teaches the protagonist an aggressive masculinity. This masculinity manifests itself in the sexual life of the protagonist: divided between impotent, sexually gratifying, and infertile spaces, all of which offer dissatisfying relationships with women. Furthermore, the labour required to work the land and the women parallels how Kiyooka imagines the North as laborious and "grueling." This imaginary sustains Malissa Phung's critique that the overlay of the labour narrative upon Indigenous lands valorizes settlers of colour who participate in the same colonial logics of working the land from terra nullius to a property they rightfully earned.[89]

"Settlers of colour" as a phrase recalls the etymology of sedimentation, and it is one of the abiding tensions in the text as the protagonist explores his racialized subjectivity of settlerhood if one continues to assume that Kiyooka is slipping in and out of the protagonist's "I." As a non-WASP and non-Indigenous, (Asian) person of colour, the protagonists' lived experience is shaped by the contours of the colonial state and of the absence of Indigeneity. Tracing the scholarship in diaspora studies that locates the advent of modernity in the slave-trade era and thus "erases Indigenous presence" (130), Bonita Lawrence and Enakshi Dua contemplate the positionality of such scholars and implicate them in the colonial project. They, amongst others, encourage decolonization studies to grapple with the complicity of people-of-colour on Turtle Island with settlerhood.[90]

A grappling must not limit itself to considerations of Indigeneity as part of the "pluralist framework," but it must acknowledge it as "foundational" for anti-racism work in Canada (137). The necessity for people-of-colour to engage with and foreground the Indigenous community and the land is clearly addressed in the text, as discussed, but the racialized settlerhood is an inflection of identity that the protagonist begins to understand through his experiencing of multiple kinships, especially with Ol' Moose. These kinships, additionally, emerge through the imagery of rock formation. The four male figures, Ol' Moose, the protagonist, Tom Aplomb, and the Algonquin man's skeleton, begin to mirror one another and to collapse into one other as sediments melding into and joining the masculinized Tundra.

The Inscription of Kinship as Male Friendship

The synopsis on the back of the book jacket, by Roy Miki, centres the concerns of the narrative around the mystery of Tom Thomson's death in Algonquin Park, which forms the basis for the kinship between Aplomb and the protagonist. With the appearance of the Algonquin man's skeleton, however, during a day of field research at "Tom Aplomb's hillside grave" (Kiyooka 79), the kinships are refocused, and the reader and the protagonist are forced to contemplate the significance of the relation between the Indigenous skeleton and Tom Aplomb. The protagonist names the former Nameless, and the latter Blameless (81), a mirroring of words and rhythms that signify the kinship between the nameless and blameless as compounded and unified, but with a difference.

The skeleton's appearance is one of the many Gothic tropes in the narrative. When the protagonist signs "the White Paper" in a quasi-Faustian moment of contract, he signs away his liberty "in an act of servitude" which will eventually lead to the failure of the project and to self-destruction. Alongside the deal with the devil, this mandate and the research it requires inflects the narrative with the Gothic themes of subterraneous revelations (all the episodes in the Archives), live burial (Pipe in the Archives), and what Eve Sedgwick identifies as doubling. According to Sedgwick, the gothic fear of the Other is one of doubling, wherein the self and the "outside life" become "counterparts rather than partners, the relationship between them one of parallels and correspondences rather than communication" (13). The Algonquin skeleton becomes a gothic Other insofar as it evokes "apparitions from the past" (Sedgwick 10), and doubles as Aplomb's body, which puts Aplomb's associations with authenticity and Canadian heroics in crisis.

Due to the mystery behind the death, the researchers dig up Tom Aplomb's grave and send the skull "and remnants to a forensic laboratory," after which they discover that the skull "belonged to a Nameless Indian, a whole head shorter than the legendary Tom Aplomb" (70–71). Taking the Algonquin skull to be literally insignificant and inconsequential — representative of how Indigenous lives and problems are easily sidestepped — the group of researchers do not pursue the questions for why this body, rather than Aplomb's, was unearthed.

The unearthing plagues the protagonist who finds Aplomb's veritable grave amongst the "marigolds," and contemplates the implications of the mistake while overlooking the great Algonquin lake:

> his mind superimposed a Nameless Algonquin's skull on top of a Blameless Hero's unrecoverable one. Noting the exactitude with which the hole in their respective temples overlapped and in effect became one, he came to the conclusion that both the earthed and unearthed skulls ... were nothing if not tailor-made to the Eastern Establishment's impeccable measurements (80).

Through superimposition, the protagonist imagines the skulls as a palimpsest. The passage calls attention to the work of sedimentation that occurs in the creation of a palimpsest, and that both the process and the product constitute the kinship between the characters. However, do the sediments fall upon one another naturally, resulting in a coincidence of "correspondence" (Sedgwick), sameness, as the identical holes signify a subterraneous and cross-geographical kinship? Or, does the unifying of skulls come about due to a different parallelism, whereby the superimposition of the protagonist enacts a similar dictate of causality or parallelism between the two skulls that the "Eastern Establishment" calculated and measured? The two skulls and bodies "became one" because they were made to become one. The state, or the structure of imposition that is a tool of the state, is the precondition for this kinship, but the Algonquin skeleton reveals a reality of kinship that the state cannot capture or control.

In one way of subversion, the narrative inversion of the Algonquin as "earthed," in contrast to the "unearthed" Aplomb, subverts scripts of buried spectrality; scripts of who is meant to be surfaced. In her introduction to *Critical Collaborations*, Smaro Kamboureli identifies the unearthing as pivotal, since

> '[n]o longer in the closet of colonial cover-up' (Miki, Afterword, 160), the Algonquin skull brings to light yet another plot repressed in the Colonial Texts the narrator has been poring over. The affiliation suggested here between Aplomb/Thomson and the unknown Algonquin man is of the kind that speaks of complicity, as well as of misbegotten and denied af/filiations" (26).

Accordingly, the skeleton's silence gestures at the predetermined failure of the national project that seeks identity through the monologic Mandate. This silence also emphasizes the gaps of kinship. Roy Miki, in "Doing Justice to CanLit Studes: Belief as/in Methodology as/in Form," asks the following questions about the two characters' kinship: "Had the white settler/artist Thomas Aplomb, in death, replaced the native, as the advocates of cultural nationalism would have it? ...

Or does the act of digging up the past expose the visibility of a native presence that had been suppressed?" (269). Here, as in Kamboureli's analysis, the kinship between Aplomb and the Algonquin recognizes and exposes the historicization of Indigenous absence, but Miki also gestures towards the white hegemony of representation. Tom Aplomb is an artist and his paintings of the Algonquin landscape generate an imaginary of Canada in which the Algonquin man's skeleton cannot participate except through being the object of representation: the surface upon which the imaginary is forced and imposed.

The forced unification of the skulls cannot reconcile the abiding dichotomy of the earthiness of the Algonquin and the unearthliness of Aplomb that prefigures the process of sedimentation as one of inverse proportionality: one is earthed and the other necessarily unearthed. "Given their similarities," the protagonist writes in his notebook, "the single most telling thing about each of them had to do with the fact that Tom Aplomb inscribed the unmitigated wilderness ... whereas the Algonquin adorned his own body with its calligraphic hues and thereby took the totem landscape with him" (81).

Aplomb's relation with the wilderness mimics the monologism of the "Official Documents" (24) that the protagonist must consult to write the White Paper. Writing in his notebooks early on, the protagonist creates an opposition between his work and the institutional work: "he noticed that the heaped-up Notebooks he was forever scribbling entries into had grown taller than the stack of Official Documents. Furthermore, the former kept encroaching on the latter and shoving them off his sturdy table." (24). His work must replace the official documents if it desires legibility, but his "own ruminations kept turning into palimpsests" (24) due to their dialoguing with what is already written (by official and personal history). The Official Documents, however, "keep reiterating the litany of a hostile Tundra, with every footnote diminishing both "Moose" and "Native" (24).

It is this erasure through representation and monologism that Aplomb practices by inscribing and imposing upon the wilderness. The wilderness thus takes its place alongside the "Moose" and the "Native," both acting as reducible concepts under the footnote. Within the textual margins, the wilderness and the Algonquin skeleton have a relation of reciprocity in which the Algonquin is "adorned" by the wilderness, which in turn undergoes a transformation as the Algonquin carries the inscription of the wilderness "with him" (81). The wilderness aesthetic writes itself upon the Algonquin, thus exemplifying, to build upon Armstrong's theorization, another kind of extra-linguistic communication that the land language teaches the Indigenous inhabitants. Further, the wilderness, like the land, is the triangulating agent that extends kinship to the Algonquin, but also ties him to Aplomb, thereby bringing two repelling poles together within its process of sedimentation to build with each other, upon each other in order to practice a life with strong, mutually beneficial bonds.

But, one cannot escape reading the description of the wilderness' inscription upon the Algonquin body as a trope that reinforces the colonial racist representations of Aboriginality. In addition to this, even within the erotic dynamics that emerge between the two, an interaction between a sexually dominant subject and a passive object, the text reiterates its thematic of kinship along male-kin lines. Perhaps both these problematics demonstrate the impossibility of a kinship of equal representation between the WASP and the Indigenous person. Even if the land and its sedimentary function prioritize Indigenous presence and the skull holes' sameness exaggerates the dichotomy of the earthed and unearthed bodies, the kinship between Aplomb and the Algonquin man defines the limits of what shape a relation with a white nationalistic entity can take. One could causally argue that land and a doubling and melding of characters thus will not produce generative and equitable kinships, since one will suppress the other deeper into the earth, but the relation between the protagonist and Ol' Moose provides an alternative example.

The protagonist and Ol' Moose come together at the end of the narrative in an act of willful solidarity and kinship with each other and the land, which emerges through a focus on listening that culminates in a climactic sedimentation. The text characterizes the act of listening as the act of touching. Thinking of his favourite radio program, the protagonist wonders about the faceless "gaggle-of-voices" and notes "[i]t was as if each voice had signalled something tangible about its owner's actual presence. That in fact their lips were close enough to kiss his fervent cheek" (36). The transmutation of voice to touch parallels the telepathic relationship of teacher-student between the protagonist and Ol' Moose that is materially manifested as a pimple. After his first appearance, Ol' Moose notifies the protagonist that "[i]t's time you thrashed the text," and he leaves "with his Protégé's pimple attached to his own avuncular profile" (42). This kinship along masculine and family codes ("avuncular") employs the pimple image to depict sedimentation's requirement of inverse proportionality: to relate, the pimple/ignorance must be excavated from the protagonist and sedimented onto Ol' Moose, one to the other, and not both.

The "avuncular" adjective for Ol' Moose at once connotes the patrimonial economies of inheritance that function to pass down teachings from Ol' Moose to the protagonist, and the potential homoerotics of kinship. In the Western canon, the most the Uncle figure transgresses sexually is by "relying on a pederastic/pedagogical model of male filiation."[91] The least, Eve Sedgwick notes, is as "a metonym for the whole range of older men who might form a relation to a younger man (as patron, friend, literal uncle, godfather, adoptive father ...) offering a degree of initiation into gay cultures and identities" (58). The intimate moment of transference, understood by the appearance of the pimple, alludes to a homoerotic culture of kin-doing. The final unification, furthermore, concretizes the codes of homoeroticism in an act of consummation. The Mandate quashed by Ottawa and forced to resign, the protagonist meets Ol' Moose in the Tundra: "Nobody but Aurora Borealis [witnessed the two], who pledged to dance a wild fandango ... when they got together and merged into a single transcendental being" (91). The kinship materializes as an immaterial fusion, as the two are abstracted into the realm of the transcendental, but grounded in the process of sedimentation carried out by the geographic materiality of the Tundra. Though a moment of emancipation, wherein the sedimentation of Ol' Moose's and the protagonist's bodies allows them to escape the current colonial structure of Canada, Kiyooka's text upholds the precondition of male-male bonds as requisite for growth and freedom. Further analyses of the homoerotic thread could interrogate the disappearance of the two as representative of the conceptual queering of futurity, in line with queer studies that theorize the queer as having no future, and as a subjectivity within no-future relations, such as the spinster aunt.[92]

The final consummation, furthermore, is framed as another inversely proportional relation, wherein one must shed its particular identity to join the other. The narrative continues after this consummation and retrospectively represents the protagonist's final act in Ottawa. After being "laid off," he needs to sign the Official document to take "back his freedom" (102). He signs in Cree, in contrast to the initial Faustian signing, thus gesturing toward an Indigenous and diasporic-settler kinship that promises emancipation for all, rather than for one group at the expense of another. With regards to the Mandate, the "Cree signature [also] inserts into the cultural, historical, and political archive of Canada what has been rendered as an hors-texte" (Kamboureli 26). Accordingly, the Cree signing inscribes an Indigenous epistemology into the legal and linguistic framework of colonial Canada, since it asserts a culture of knowledge based in the land, as Cree stands in for one of the land languages of the Laurentian shield. However, does not the Cree signing absent the protagonist's identity? Notably, as the protagonist meets Ol' Moose, he arrives emptied of a non-WASP identity, most significantly exemplified in his final note to his wife. "When his goodly wife came home ... she found a hastily penned circle with a question mark in the middle, pinned to his study door, and nothing, nothing more" (107).

The encircled question becomes the objective correlative for the protagonist's affect once his identity is lost, taken, or shed. All that remains, the note suggests, is the necessity for new questions to emerge, from which new identities may develop. What the circle denotes is the limited structures of identity and perhaps of kinship that are currently formulated by the state and colonial logics. To escape those and to fuse in solidarity with Ol' Moose, the text seems to suggest that one must efface the entirety of the Self as it stands within the current system. New systems outside the epistemology of the state are existent in the land, but again, the overarching system of patriarchy permeates both the current and the new.

It must be noted that the rich relationship between Ol'Moose and the protagonist, a kinship that occurs within the land and one that offers much to studies of homoerotic male kinships in the fable, develops at the expense of the women in the novel who function, conversely, as mild variants to the male experience of sexual impotency, frustration, and emotionally-lacking gratification of bodily desires.

Conclusion: Women, the Last Ones Standing; the Ones Left in the Dust

No, I am not discussing women here to intervene in the narrative of homoerotic kinship with a complaint about the neglect of women and of fulfilling heterosexual relationships in *The Artist*. Instead, I briefly outline here the difficulty of reading the reductive and limited representations of the women. The representation both indicates the novella's failure to address women in its system of generative and subversive kinships, and mimics the ideological reality of patriarchy. As mimesis, the text reveals the gap left by male-focused movements of resistance, and thus suggests that women are the answers, or at least, that they are the ones to ask the new questions required to construct a decolonial reality.

The text, however, creates a lot of suspicion around the protagonist's disappearance: is it suicide? Is it freedom? Both? If suicide, then the wife left standing is symbolic of the burden on women to continue, as they always have, with the resistance. If escape, then the wife has been left standing in the kitchen alone, legible only as a one-dimensional plot device, much like the other primary women characters: Rosie the Stripper, the clerk, and Vinnie Travail. The "Old Crone," who "was none other than a demented Vinnie Travail" (102), is an older, less attractive representation of a woman and her role is limited to parodying the Gothic trope of ventriloquism when she opens her mouth to sound the voice of Tom Aplomb at a gathering many years after the failure of the Mandate. The Gothic trope of ventriloquism functions to inject discomfort into the space of privilege and propriety, exposing these very spaces as improper and commercialized, but like the other women, the crone is used as a vehicle to expand on the complex and intellectually rich representations of the men.

The women in the narrative relate tangentially with each other through relations with the men, and do not participate—amongst themselves or with men—in any long-standing, satisfactory, or mutually benefitting relations.[93] There is "Rosie the stripper," a sex worker in Ottawa with whom the protagonist finds sexual gratification, but no emotional attachment. The sex working space is revealed to be as emotionally bankrupt as the other spaces of labour, like that of the Archival space and that of the domestic space. At home in Forget after having left Ottawa, when his wife asks about his evenings and weekends, he mentions "a dull night in Hull with one of the clerks" and the reliable "Rosie the stripper" (94), without conceding much detail. The wife teases him of her affairs and finally shares a more detailed account of her time with "Frankie the lanky kid" (95). "Chagrined," the protagonist remains quiet and contemplates the insular world one can inhabit, like the wife. The affective register of the home is palpably subdued. He does not share his thoughts with his wife, a coping mechanism of distancing and emotional opacity that colours his relations with the three women. They have direct, isolated lines of kinship exclusively through the protagonist, similar to the network of the women around Tom Aplomb, who emerge in the text through triangulated relations with Aplomb, to only provide their impressions of Tom, of the day of his death, and of his relations with Vinnie Travail (66–68).

The National Archive, further, embodies the ethos of the male-female relations in the text and stands in as a space of intellectual and sexual stasis for the male labourer. As a space for a phallogocentric insistence on the written, monologic word, the archives exemplify a heightened patriarchal colonial narrative of labour that, in part, undermines the masculinization of the Tundra by way of juxtaposing it as a competing source of knowledge. Writing about the marginalization of sex and sexuality as subjects of study in colonial North Indian archives, Charu Gupta depicts the correlation between the imperial governing body and the archives "where political and administrative history was the main focus and sexuality was rendered marginal" (13). The archives thus delineate, consolidate, and pursue nation-state narratives at the expense and suppression of desiring subjects.

However, Kiyooka's text goes further to suggest that the archival space itself, as an organizer of (phall)Logos (Irigaray), suppresses sex in rendering the protagonist impotent. The protagonist experiences some sexual desire and gratification with Rosie, but wonders about the clerk. "[I]n an unaccustomed moment of forthrightness," he asks "the combustible Clerk" to spend "a night in Hull" (82). The two move from bar to bar "bored out of their minds" and conclude that Hull was dull (83). Dull Hull seems to euphemize the sexually impotent state of their relation that is framed by the archival space. Further, when the archival work drives him to a failed suicide attempt (76), he immediately heads to an institutionally sexualized space, the strip club (77).

His life is marked by escapes, but the final escape into the Tundra has implications for the metaphorical mode of sedimentation that depicts the kinship between diasporic and Indigenous beings. Kamboureli asks: "Becoming as [the protagonist] does an elusive ghost himself, is his vanishing act one of mimicry or resistance, or both? Does he kill himself or is he spirited away by Ol' Moose?" (27). His doubling of disappearance does suggest mimicry—the protagonist mimics his Indigenous counterpart and leaves for the Tundra—but also exemplifies a resistance that arises out of limitations; if Indigeneity is rendered absent, then so is the diasporic settler, and therefore both can haunt the settler colonial state. However, the text also accounts for the irreconciliability of the theoretical conceptions of Diaspora and Indigeneity that conceptualize resistance diametrically.[94]

Nandita Sharma and Jared Sexton, both of whom address Dua and Lawrence's essay on decolonizing anti-racism, delineate the diasporic subject's disenchanted relation with the land and with territory that totalizes the subject as "nonnative" (Sharma 172), or as forced to indigenize (Sexton). Sharma, examining the development of the Indigenous subjectivity post-1492, observes that mobility became a problem for autochthonous self-realization—"movement and migration are posited as inherently colonizing" (171)—wherein "migrants come to stand as the ultimate nonnative" (172). Her essay refuses to contemplate reconciling the nonnative and native divide by considering Indigenous conceptions of land. Jared Sexton's "The Vel of Slavery," makes a similar refusal, but explicitly identifies the attempt at reconciling black resistance and Indigenous resistance as a project of indigenization and a violence to black subjectivity. Considering Dua and Lawrence's essay, Sexton concludes that "[i]f black-native solidarity is founded upon shared Indigenous worldviews, practices, and kinship structures, then the prerequisite for black people to move, politically and ethically ... is, in a word, re-indigenization" (588). Consequently, does the protagonist's Cree signing and kinship with Ol' Moose and the Tundra signal his indigenization? Is sedimentary kinship possible without the diasporic-settler merging into the Indigenous body?

Perhaps the protagonist's disappearance marks his landlessness, and, in tandem, the refusal of the land to indigenize him. In the end at Forget, the protagonist peeks through "the hole in the middle of the small round pond [and] could no longer see his own face" (106). He seeks his reflection in the pond for a moment of affirmation in the form of the Lacanian mirror stage's imaginary of wholeness. On the one hand, the lack of reflection exhibits the protagonist's inability to embody the unificatory project of the Canadian identity. On the other hand, the land becomes opaque to the protagonist's desire for recognition and kinship, which Sexton would characterize as the manifestation of Indigenous refusal for diasporic solidarity: "From indigenous perspectives, [black resistance is a] baseless politics [that] can only ever be a liability ... landless black people in diaspora cannot mount genuine resistance to the settler colonial state and society" (Sexton 589). Though specific to the Black diasporic experience, the distrust of the "landless" evokes Kiyooka's own "athwarted" relation to the nation and the land.

The image of the Rockies and the Tundra near the end of *The Artist*, however, prevents the naturalization of Indigeneity as spectral and vanished, and interrupts the reproduction of a non-WASP mimicry of the vanishing Indian trope. Before the protagonist's final note, Ol' Moose conveys his "last words to his Protégé" (104): "Before pharmaceuticals, the Rockies were bare rock ... now that we know there isn't a panacea for our hubris, it's once again bare rock/ incipient Void: O the Unmitigated Tundra" (104). Gesturing again at the complicity of everyone within the system, the text demystifies what "*our* hubris" (emphasis added, 104) concealed. The Rockies and the Tundra, however, are and were unconcealable, "[u]nmitigated," and irrepressible, which represents the resoluteness of Indigeneity. The absented and spectral kinship that exists between the protagonist and Ol' Moose, thus, continues unmitigated in its own right through its mediation and sedimentation by the land, even if as a diasporic being, the protagonist has a vexed relation with land.

The disappearance, thus, continues to articulate and practice kinship as long as the Rockies stand, humbling humankind; but where does the woman position herself? Can she also act within the parameters of the verbal mode of kinship, moving in and out of the land, paralleling the process of sedimentation? Or, is she the fallen, forgotten glove, interned in the sediment that collects at the base of the mountains? The "goodly wife," is the stonified and stunned observer, fixated by the death-image of the question mark, and the fallen glove accumulating the remains of the animated land that excludes her. Perhaps she could also be, like the women in Tom Aplomb's circle who give voice to create a narrative of Aplomb's life and death but ultimately get lost in the failure of the project, the tiny sediments that try but fail to fuse with the masculinized Tundra. They fall and remain forgotten, both as *StoneDGloves* and stones and gloves. Unlike the monumentalized and specified geographic and historical moment of *StoneDGloves*, these women are abstracted, ahistorical, and therefore, easily sidestepped by the reader, the photographer, and the artist and the moose.

Works Cited

Armstrong, Jeannette. "Land Speaking." *Speaking for the Generations: Native Writers on Writing.* Ed. Simon J Ortiz. Tuscon: U of Arizona Press, 1998. 175–194.

Barthes, Roland. *Camera Lucida: Reflections on Photography.* Trans. Richard Howard. NewYork: Hill & Wang, 1982.

Butler, Judith. *Giving an Account of Oneself.* New York: Fordham UP, 2005.

Dua, Enakshi and Bonita Lawrence. "Decolonizing Antiracism." *Social Justice* 32.4 (2005): 120–143.

Charu Gupta "Writing Sex and Sexuality: Archives of Colonial North India." *Journal of Women's History* 23.4 (2011): 12–35.

Coleridge, Samual Taylor. "The Eolian Harp." *Norton Anthology of English Literature.* 8 (Vol 2). New York: Norton. 426–248.

Coulthard, Glen. *Red Skin White Masks: Rejecting the Colonial Politics of Recognition.* Minneapolis: U of Minnesota Press, 2014.

Edelman, Lee. "Queer Theory: Unstating Desire." *A Journal of Lesbian and Gay Studies.* 2 (1995): 343–346.

Ensor, Sarah. "Spinster Ecology: Rachel Carson, Sarah Orne Jewett, and Nonreproductive Futurity." *American Literature* 84.2 (2012): 409–435.

Glissant, Edouard. *Poetics of Relation.* Translated by Betsy Wing. Ann Arbor: U of Michigan Press, 2010.

Heath Justice, Daniel. "'Go Away Water!': Kinship Criticism and the Decolonization Imperative." *Reasoning Together: The Native Critics Collective.* Eds. Craig S. Womack, Daniel Heath Justice, and Christopher B. Teuton. Norman, OK: University of Oklahoma Press, 2008. 147–168.

Irigaray, Luce. *This Sex Which is Not One.* Trans. Catherine Porter & Carolyn Burke. Ithaca: Cornell UP, 1985.

Kamboureli, Smaro & Christl Verduyn (Eds). *Critical Collaborations: Indigeneity, Diaspora, and Ecology in Canadian Literary Studies.* Waterloo: Wilfred Laurier UP, 2014.

----. Kamboureli, Smaro. "Introduction." 1–28.

----. Lai, Larissa. "Epistemologies of Respect: A Poetics of Asian/Indigenous Relation." 99–126.

Kiyooka, Roy K. "Afterword." *Pacific Windows: Collected Poems of Roy K. Kiyooka*. Ed. Roy Miki. Vancouver: Talonbooks, 1997. 301–320.

----. *The Artist and the Moose: A Fable of Forget*. Ed. Roy Miki. Burnaby: LINEbooks, 2009.

----. *Pacific Rim Letters: Roy Kiyooka*. Edited & Afterword by Smaro Kamboureli. Edmonton: NeWest Press, 2005.

----. *StoneDGloves*. Toronto: Coach House Press, 1970.

Lowry, Glen. "Roy Kiyooka's *Transcanada Letters*: re: reading a poet's prose." *West Coast Line* 36.2 (2002): 16–34.

Maracle, Lee. "Oratory on Oratory." *Trans. Can. Lit: Resituating the Study of Canadian Literature*. Eds. by Smaro Kamboureli and Roy Miki. Waterloo: Wilfred Laurier UP, 2007.

McFarlane, Scott Toguri. "Un-Ravelling *StoneDGloves* and the Haunt of Hibakusha." *All Amazed for Roy Kiyooka*. Eds. John O'Brian, Naomi Sawada, & Scott Watson. Vancouver: Arsenal Pulp Press, 2002. 116–146.

McKittrick, Katherine. "Worn Out." *Southeastern Geographer* 57.1 (2017): 96–100.

Miki, Roy. "Afterword." *The Artist and the Moose: A Fable of Forget*. Roy K. Kiyooka. Burnaby: LINEbooks, 2009.

----. "Doing Justice to CanLit Studies: Belief as/in Methodology as/in Form." Essays by Roy Miki, *In Flux: Transnational Shifts in Asian Canadian Writing*. Ed. Smaro Kamboureli. Edmonton: NeWest Press, 2011.

----. "Inter-face: Roy Kiyooka's Writing, A Commentary/Interview." Roy Kiyooka. By Roy Kiyooka. Vancouver: Artspeak Gallery; Or Gallery, 1991. 41–54.

Morton, Stephen. "Multiculturalism and the Formation of a Diasporic Counterpublic in Roy K. Kiyooka's *StoneDGloves*." *Canadian Literature* 201 (Summer, 2009): 89–109.

Phung, Malissa. "Are People of Colour Settlers Too?" *Cultivating Canada: Reconciliation through the Lens of Cultural Diversity*. Eds. Ashok Mathur, Jonathan Dewar, and Mike DeGagné. Ottawa: Aboriginal Healing Foundation, 2011.

"Remembering Roy Kiyooka: 1926–1994." *Story Archive. The Bulletin: A Journal of Japanese Canadian Community, History, and Culture*. 7 Feb 2014. Web. 2 June 2017.

Sedgwick, Eve Kosofsky. "The Structure of Gothic Conventions." *The Coherence of Gothic Conventions*. New York & London: 1986. 9–36.

----. "Tales of the Avunculate: Queer Tutelage in *The Importance of Being Earnest*." *Tendencies*. Durham & London: Duke University Press, 1993.

Sexton, Jared. "The Vel of Slavery: Tracking the Figure of the Unsovereign." *Critical Sociology* (2014): 1–15.

Sharma, Nandita. "Strategic Anti-Essentialism: Decolonizing Decolonization." *Sylvia Wynter: On Being Human as Praxis*. Ed. Katherine McKittrick. Durham & London: Duke UP, 2015.

Titley, E. Brian. "Forget, Amédée-Emmanuel." *Dictionary of Canadian Biography*. Web. 17 June 2017.

Wong, Rita. "Decolonizasian: Reading Asian and First Nations Relations in Literature." *Canadian Literature* 199 (Winter 2008).

English with an "i":
Imagining Japan in the Poetry of Roy K. Kiyooka [95]

Roy Miki

Japan beckons. where will my forked tongue lead me?
(*Pacific Rim Letters* 198)

Two days before one of several trips to Japan in the 1980s, Kiyooka wrote a letter to himself in which he comments on his ties to his ancestral country. He admits that "apart from whatever i learned from my parents and their asst. friends in Calgary before and after the war, almost all of what i came to know about Japan came thru translations of one sort and another, and so it is that my Japan is, among other things, an altogether habitable place in my mind: my callit duplicitous, ofttimes errant, mind. I take it that mind is itself grounded in language/s." (*Pacific Rim Letters*, 265) During his lifetime, Kiyooka developed a complex relationship to Japan, exploring as deeply as he could how he might close the distances, or if not close at least diminish the distances between his parents' homeland Japan and the Japan he came to imagine through the lens of his minority positioning in what was for him, at least in his formative years, an Anglo-dominant nation.

What is telling in Kiyooka's note is the importance he assigns to "language/s" that grounds the mind that imagines Japan from the distance of a Canadian cultural space that is so dominated by the power of the English language—against which Kiyooka's mother tongue, Japanese, would lose its hold in his mind in his efforts to hold his own in what was for him very much a WASP (white Anglo-Saxon protestant) country, particularly in the postwar years when he matured as an artist. In a revealing statement found in his papers, housed in Special Collections, Simon Fraser University, Kiyooka acknowledges that his brand of English—which he often referred to as inglish—is peculiar because it embodies the traces of Japanese, or more specifically Kochi-ben:

> beginning with 'kyoto airs' in '64 i've tried to shape the fragmented images of nippon i've carried with me my whole life long. odd to say that i learned to speak nihongo well enough as a child and spoke it into adolescence: but, given the circumstances, i never learned to read and write it. alas and alack. nonetheless, i do believe that my kind of inglish bears the syntactical traces of my parents' kochi-ben. (*Pacific Windows*, 320)

Kiyooka experienced a tension between a childhood immersed in spoken Japanese and the English of an Anglocentric society that he lived in, and this created in him a sense of doubleness: on the one hand, he felt tied to Japan through his issei parents and, on the other, he felt tied to Canada through birth and the need to accommodate the social and cultural conditions of his life. Once, when asked to reflect on his formation as an artist and writer, Kiyooka replied that he had "grown up athwarted." Like so many words in Kiyooka's inglish, this one asks to be mouthed ("athwarted") and simultaneously articulates a refined understanding of Kiyooka's social and cultural positioning, in his case a minority positioning based on being racialized as "Japanese" or "Asian" in a predominantly white Canada. Being "athwarted," in his explanation, means "You are of it, and you are not, and you know that very clearly." In other words, Kiyooka saw himself as both inside of Canadian culture and outside of it, and this in-between state, which he calls an "athwarted" one, meant that he would experience a doubled existence, straddling the boundaries between his "Canadian" birthright and his "Japanese" ancestry. Kiyooka goes on to say that he traced his consciousness of being athwarted back to the "1950s in the years following the war." It was a time when "the taint of racism was still left" (Miki, *Broken Entries*, 71) from the wartime period, when Canadians of Japanese ancestry were categorized by the Canadian state as "of the Japanese race," and thereby stripped of their citizenship rights, interned, and dispossessed.

Kiyooka was born on January 18, 1926, in Moose Jaw, Saskatchewan, but spent his childhood in the rough and tumble immigrant
Calgary neighbourhood called Victoria Park. In the words of his brother
Harry Kiyooka, also an artist, their neighbourhood combined "bigotry
/ gangs / street fights / families on the dole / hoboes / hand-me-downs—
the everyday reality of the 30s" (2). Interestingly, 1926 was the first
year of Showa ("Enlightened Peace"), a date that also coincided with
the death of his samurai-related grandfather. For his issei mother Kiyoshi Kiyooka, this conjoining of dates had auspicious importance,
because it meant that her son Roy Kenji—and this point is made in
Kiyooka's book *Mothertalk: Life Stories of Mary Kiyoshi Kiyooka*
(1997)—was born in a moment of transition from the old to the new
in Japanese history.[96] It was during this era of the Canadian nation-
state when Anglocentric values were powerful in Kiyooka's childhood
in Calgary— "Rule Britannia! Britannia rule the waves" —and these
values placed a high price on competency in English, the King's English.
For a kid of Japanese and/or Asian background at the time, English
took on a huge presence, Kiyooka's phrasing, as a "modality of power"
(*Broken Entries*, 67). When asked about his experience of acquiring
English in his childhood, he recalled: "Oh yeah, to me it had to do
with surviving—*survival*. At some level I needed to be able to come
to an articulateness by which I could stand in this world of literate
people, and hold my own. I had that as an actual drive" ("Roy Kiyooka,
An Interview," *Inalienable Rice*, 59).

Fast forward to 1942, and the racism directed towards Japanese
Canadians would result in their mass uprooting from the BC coast.
Although living far away from the coast, in Calgary, the Kiyooka family was also categorized as "enemy alien." His father lost his job, and
Kiyooka, then in grade 9, was removed from school, thus terminating
his formal education. Forced to relocate, the Kiyooka family moved to
a small Ukrainian farming town, Opal, Alberta. When Kiyooka regained
some freedom of movement it was already 1946. By then a young man,
he turned his attention to his dream of becoming an artist. He enrolled
in Calgary's Institute of Technology and Art (now the Alberta College
of Art and Design), graduating in 1949. By the mid-50s he had so

immersed himself in the world of art and artists, excelling in his art practice to such a degree that he was awarded a prestigious scholarship to study art at the San Miguele de Allende school in Mexico.

In the years ahead, as Kiyooka got progressively more involved in the contemporary art world, he was always a force in the circles he moved in—in Regina in the late 1950s, in Vancouver, in the early 1960s, and in Montreal, where he was when he received the Expo70 commission. But through all of this experience, he always remained a singular figure, "of" the most progressive art forms of his generation, and yet "not of" the mainstream cultural world because of his marginalization as a minority artist of Japanese ancestry. As a painter, Kiyooka gained national and international recognition for his brilliant paintings, but as he discovered this medium did not allow him the space to explore the more personal dimensions of his family history. These dimensions included their mistreatment when categorized as "enemy alien," and their familial and cultural ties to Japan, more specifically to the Shikoku region where his parents were born and raised, his mother Mary Kiyoshi in Tosa and his father Harry Shigekiyo in Umagi-mura. For Kiyooka, this difficult relationship to Japan was made tangible in the plight of his sister Mariko who was trapped in Japan during the war and who continued to live there after the war, estranged from the rest of her family.

* * *

This short account of Kiyooka's relationship to Japan and to the Japanese language can hardly do justice to the complexities of his personal and family history. As a way of providing an overview of this history, and to suggest some directions for further research, I have chosen to focus on three poetic works that were drafted and/or based in Japan, written on three different occasions: *Kyoto Airs*, *Wheels*, and *Gotenyama*.[97] By dwelling on a key moment in each of these works, I will propose a pattern in Kiyooka's imagined Japan, a pattern in which we see him move from a sense of estrangement, through a painful but creative encounter with his Japanese Canadian past, to an acceptance, even a strong affirmation, of Japan—and the Japanese language of his past—as a poetic resource for his work. In this process we move from the early 1960s to the mid-1980s.

Kyoto Airs

It was during the summer of 1963 that Kiyooka made his first trip to Japan as an adult.[98] He travelled to Kyoto, where he finally connected with his sister Mariko. He also began work on his first book of poems, *Kyoto Airs*, published a year later by Periwinkle Press, a press run by fellow Japanese Canadian artist Tak Tanabe. The poems are carefully composed, each word in their short lines placed meticulously, the lines moving down the page, as Kiyooka explores the social and cultural elements of Mariko's world. His attention is intense as he takes in these elements, almost as if he were surveying the landscape as a first time explorer. What comes into his perceptual field—a haniwa horse, a sword, the road to Yase, the stone garden of Ryoanji, a children's shrine—is framed through the eyes of a stranger to Japan but one who carries an imagined Japan within him. So he informs his reader: "I am a Canadian painter / come home to pay homage / to ancestors, samurai among them" (23). But in these poems, Japan is not his home. He remains, in his own words, "among / them [the Japanese he encounters] a tongue- / twisted alien" (12), despite his ancestral ties. This sense of being related by lineage and simultaneously an alien is an underlying preoccupation of Kiyooka's first book of poems, but one, "Coffee Shop," brings out this doubled positioning more explicitly.

In this poem, the poet enters the space of a coffee shop in Kyoto, a space that is marked by social and material particulars through which he reads his own perceptual boundaries. He immediately notices the "tremor of / cut glass," an effect he thinks may be attributed to the air conditioner or to the music—"Beethoven's / 7th"—both sounds that could have been familiarly encountered in Canadian (or western) contexts. But as he gets drawn further into the more microspaces of the coffee shop, he becomes conscious of his own distance from the scene:

> myriad colours
> reflected
> on each cut
> glass surface
> shimmer to
> the sound
>
> of voices,
> clattering
> cups, the music,
> all sounds
> other than
> my own (13)

"Coffee Shop" reveals a poet who is capable of the minute perception of particulars, even to the point of his own position in relation to what he encounters. Through the multiple lens of the "myriad colours" being reflected in surfaces made of glass is the "shimmer" of voices moving in synch with the clatter of activity and the sound of the music— "all sounds" except for his own voice. His own voice, in this sense, remains an alien presence in a Japan that is supposedly his inheritance as the son of issei parents. While this poem is highly adept in its handling of the perceptual moment, the recognition of the absence of his own sounds suggests that the space experienced in the poem is "foreign" to his own consciousness. He therefore remains an other in this space, despite his background as a Canadian of Japanese ancestry.

But from another perspective, Kiyooka's experience of alienation, of not belonging in Japan, was a gain for Kiyooka as a poet. Here, in the carefully composed language of his poems, he came face to face with the distances between his Canadian and his Japanese formations.

Wheels

A few years later, in 1969, Kiyooka would imagine Japan through a radically shifting lens. That year he was commissioned to create a sculptural installation alongside the Canadian pavilion for Expo 70 in Osaka. In being chosen as an artist to represent Canada at this auspicious international event, his identification as Japanese in his Canadian contexts, despite his birth in Canada, in a fortuitous twist made him an attractive candidate for the national artistic project. The assignment allowed him to spend the fall in Kyoto, commuting regularly to Osaka to construct his installation, the sculptural piece he called *Abu Ben Adam's Vinyl Dream*. It was during this intense time of concentrated attention to site-specific areas he visited in Japan that Kiyooka's critical awareness of his athwarted identity as a Canadian of Japanese ancestry came into sharper focus. Alongside the photos he took of the workman's gloves on the Expo site, photos that became part of a major exhibit and book of poems, *StoneDGloves*, he also took a lengthy road trip with his issei father and his Japanese friend, Syuzo Fujimoto, whom he calls "his intrepid guide" (141). Fujimoto would later join Kiyooka back in Vancouver in order to assist him on a major sculptural project, a series of cedar laminate sculptures.

It was during this pivotal trip that Kiyooka began to write what would eventually become *Wheels*, a major work that Kiyooka worked on for years during the 1970s and early 1980s. He published a handful of copies for private use in July 1985, but it would not be officially published until it appeared in *Pacific Windows: Collected Poems of Roy K. Kiyooka* (1997). In this long poem that shifts between poetry and prose, in this sense, mirroring the form of Basho's *Narrow Road to the Deep North*, the poet embarks on a journey around what he calls the "backcountry" of Honshu, setting out from Kyoto by train to Matsue, where they are to meet Syuzo.

During the journey, Kiyooka reflects not only on his troubling relationship with his father but also perceptively tracks his journey — the particulars of places he passes through — in the interplay of written texts and photographs. As he reaches the tourist site of Miyajima, on his way to Hiroshima, he begins to sense a growing apprehension in himself and in the landscape. Then, in a moment of exceptional clarity—a moment that opens up new spaces for Kiyooka and his ties to Japan —he encounters the relics of the bombing of Hiroshima in the Peace Museum. And as he snaps successive photos of the relics—click, click, click—the scene in the frame shifts to the 1940s and he comes face to face with his own traumatic past in Canada:

> i remember the RCMP finger-printing me:
> i was 15 and lofting hay that cold winter day
> what did i know about treason?
> i learned to speak a good textbook English
> i seldom spoke anything else.
> i never saw the 'yellow peril' in myself
>   (Mackenzie King did) (170)

This act of remembering on the poet's part is apparently spontaneous. He did not set out to write such a biographical account of his life, but here in Japan, while confronting the legacy of Hiroshima, he is reminded starkly of his identification by the Canadian state as an "enemy alien." Regardless of the vast distances between Hiroshima and the internment of Japanese Canadians, for the poet the association binds him to his parents' homeland.

So much of what Kiyooka carried in his imagined Japan came through his mother's nurturing in Japanese. In the quotation from Kiyooka's SFU papers that I cited earlier, Kiyooka acknowledges that his imagined Japan has been shaped by his childhood experience of speaking Japanese, or more specifically the "kochi-ben" of his parents. He goes on to acknowledge that "everytime i've gone back there [to Kochi] and walked the streets of that lovely city on the pacific, i hear the cadences of my own native speech: both nihongo and inglish subtly transmuted into an undialectical syntax" (*Pacific Windows*, 320).

Gotenyama

In the 1980s, Kiyooka made several extended trips to Japan in quick succession, including a month in Kochi with his mother in 1983, and several poetic sequences resulted from these trips. Of these, the one sequence that stands out for me—and is exemplary for my discussion here—is *Gotenyama*, based on a visit to Gotenyama, an area between Kyoto and Osaka, to see his friend, Syuzo Fujimoto, the "intrepid guide" in *Wheels*.[99] *Gotenyama* functions as an important text in Kiyooka's developing relationship to Japan. Tellingly, it is dedicated to "Syuzo / Satchiko / & Kana," as well as to a "Host of Friends scattered in Southern Nippon."

The central trope of the sequence, his "umeboshi-throat," as we will see, connects the text of the poems—its vernacular inglish—with his ancestral ties to Japan, only now, some two decades after *Kyoto Airs,* he moves beyond his estrangement by recognizing his own complicity in that condition. The specific occasion for such awareness on his part is the sudden onset of a painful "purple protuberance" (224) in his throat soon after landing in Japan. With a wry tongue-in-cheek seriousness, the poet immediately thinks that the growth has something to do with his denial of his cultural ties to Japan—signified in this instance by his failure to develop a refined taste for umeboshi, which in turn is associated with his failure to maintain Japanese as his mother tongue. He goes on to admit:

> divining exactly how
> his pucker'd throat felt on the back of
> his tied-tongue & wanting
> to nickname it—he promptly named it
> his 'umeboshi-throat' (224)

As he acknowledges his own "hubris" in estranging himself from the particulars of his visits to Japan and the friendships that he has formed over the years, he becomes highly conscious of the immediacy of his situation and the poetic "divining" process made possible by the growth in his throat:

> inexplicably—all the things i
> took for granted, begin, un-ravelling
>
> these words herald
> an unleavened world-of-things (226)

Once his consciousness is attuned to the moment, he begins to perceive
the minutest of particulars embodiments of living forms:

> out of
> hitherto (unrecognized) grit
> shredded paper
> scurrying ants pushing pebbles
> twigs dew & leafy
> runnels
>> an
>> ancient site
>> all the
>> seemingly haphazard
>> alignments
>> un
>> conceal
>> self (226)

Here, in the place Gotenyama, and here, in the poem *Gotenyama*,
Kiyooka undergoes a transformation that opens up the spaces of Japan
to his poetic consciousness. This process enables him to affirm and
renew the Japanese vernacular language that he had absorbed through
his mother's nurturing.

   Gotenyama celebrates Kiyooka's long friendship with Syuzo Fujimoto and ends with a note that the poem is a "sequel" to *Kyoto Airs*.
Perhaps Kiyooka saw *Gotenyama* as a direct response to the lone figure of the "tongue-/twisted alien" poet in that earlier text, a response
as well that answers to the Japanese Canadian trauma of alienation at
the heart of *Wheels*.

* * *

Among the documents left in Roy Kiyooka's papers when he died in January 1994 is a draft of a grant application in which he describes a fascinating writing project. He planned to live in Japan for a year, mostly in Kochi, but with trips down south to Kohama Island in Okinawa, where his close artist friends Isamu and Kazuko Akino resided, and up north to Sapporo, where his friend, the poet Yorifumi Yaguchi resided. Yaguchi was in the process of translating Kiyooka's *Pear Tree Pomes*, a book that was short-listed for the 1987 Governor General's Award for Poetry. By living through the seasons in Kochi, Kiyooka felt he would be able "to get in touch with the pulse of the place and wonder of wonders, re-discover whence I hail from and where that'll take me." His desire to live in Japan, he made clear, did not mean that he wanted to become Japanese. "I'm nothing if not a kanuck artist," he says, "and what I've accomplished is beholden to that fact." But having worked for decades in various Canadian contexts, and often against the exclusionary boundaries of Canadian nation-based cultural forms, he now (he is writing in the early 1990s) wanted to turn his attention towards Asia, and more specifically Japan, where he envisioned an alternate cultural possibility: "There's a barely inscribed Pacific Rim Dialogue —one borne of the time immemorial impact of Asians on N.A. that 'I' go on lending my voice to til all the racial epithets disappear into the flux of our multi-national discourse" (Roy Kiyooka Fonds, Special Collections, Simon Fraser University).

Kiyooka's imagined Japan, then, provides significant insights into the deep ambivalences that conditioned the lives of Japanese Canadians during and after the internment period of the 1940s. Uprooted in 1942, Japanese Canadians would not regain freedom of movement until April 1, 1949, the same year they were granted voting rights. To an extent, similar to Kiyooka, I grew up with a seemingly unresolvable tension between a perception of Japan as a cultural origin—through the influence of my issei grandmother—and a disavowal of Japan in the necessity to affirm my Canadian citizenship. The Japanese Canadian redress movement in the 1980s embodied the struggle to reclaim the integrity of Japanese Canadians as Canadian citizens whose rights were abrogated. The redress settlement of September 22, 1988 stands as a major accomplishment for them.

Today, we face the uncertainty of transnational and global forces that make it increasingly difficult to appreciate the deep emotional and cultural effects of the injustices endured by Japanese Canadians. In this post-redress era, Japanese Canadians need to no longer disavow their ancestral origins, but are able—indeed encouraged—to explore the multiple implications of such origins, not only as they were mediated in the past, but also as they call for new cultural possibilities. As this future unfolds, the work of Roy Kiyooka will no doubt be understood as an opening that is unprecedented in its scope and achievements.

Works Cited

Chu, Garrick and Gunn, Sean. *Inalienable Rice: a Chinese and Japanese Canadian Anthology.* Intermedia Press, 1979. Published online September 25th, 2013. https://issuu.com/ricepaper/docs/inalienable_rice_compiled.

Kiyooka, Roy. *Transcanada Letters.* Vancouver: Talonbooks, 1975.

----. *Pacific Windows: The Collected Poems of Roy K. Kiyooka.* Ed. Roy Miki. Vancouver: Talonbooks, 1997.

----. *Mothertalk: Life Stories of Mary Kiyoshi Kiyooka.* Ed. Daphne Marlatt. Edmonton: NeWest, 1997.

----. *Pacific Rim Letters.* Ed. Smaro Kamboureli. Edmonton: NeWest, 2005.

Kiyooka, Harry. *Roy Kenzie Kiyooka: Life / Times.* Calgary: Triangle Gallery of Visual Arts, 2001.

Miki, Roy. *Broken Entries: Race Subjectivity Writing.* Toronto: Mercury, 1998. Print.

Strands of Autoethnography:
Roy Kiyooka's Poetics of Locality in *Mothertalk*

Marisa E. Lewis

home is a thronging of voices —
home is a thronging of voices —
From *Wheels* (1985)

The Poetic Avenues of Mothertalk

Mothertalk: Life Stories of Mary Kiyoshi Kiyooka (1997) has been often discussed in the context of Canadian (auto) biographical writing. *Mothertalk* centres on Mary Kiyooka's 'life stories,' an intimate account that assembles complex imaginings of home, displacement and belonging amid the traumatic events of the Japanese Canadians' uprooting and interment. Posthumously published by NeWest Press in 1997, *Mothertalk* is the result of complex levels of translation, transcription and editorial intervention.

The project originates from Roy Kiyooka's recordings of his mother's stories. Matsuki Masutani also interviewed Mary Kiyooka in Japanese and then translated Mary's stories into English for Kiyooka, who rewrote his mother's account by adding his own poetic signature into a shared archive of remembrance.[100] Another level of complexity is added to the project as it is Daphne Marlatt's editorial interventions that defined the final version of the text. More specifically, Marlatt edited *Mothertalk's* numerous versions, re-organized the manuscripts chronologically, and added the poetry segments and appendices to the text.[101] *Mothertalk* identifies Roy Kiyooka as author, Mary Kiyooka as primary source, Masutani as translator, and Marlatt as editor, and is therefore critically received as a work of 'serial collaboration,'[102] reflecting the different roles each contributor had in the production of the text (Egan and Helms 48).

Considering the various levels of collaboration at play, *Mothertalk* poses critical questions about authorship, origin, and belonging, thus challenging many literary conventions by incorporating poetry segments, stories, footnotes, essays and photographs into the narrative. Critics such as Joanne Saul, Susanna Egan and Gabrielle Helms have argued that *Mothertalk*'s textual practices are integral for the text's politics of representing diasporic subjectivity and belonging. Saul's analysis in *Writing the Roaming Subject: The Biotext in Canadian Literature* (2006) establishes *Mothertalk* as a biotext.[103] Saul examines *Mothertalk*'s textual techniques of multiplicity as disruptive yet innovative, competing but at the same time appropriate for the text's poetics of difference in the contexts of race and ethnicity. It is thus *Mothertalk*'s stories, photos, footnotes, essays, and poems that mark the text as an ongoing site for story-telling, and break barriers by generating the effect of a continuous "blurring" of various voices and places (*Writing* 83). Yet, although these analyses consider the role of the poetic segments in *Mothertalk* as a technique that sustains hybridity, a critical analysis of the poetic segments in relation to the other aspects of the text (i.e the prose narrative) highlights the polyvalent ways locality is registered in *Mothertalk* and garners attention to the spatial arrangement of the text that reflects both Kiyooka's and his mother's complex relationship with Japanese and Canadian national and cultural spaces.

The poetic aspect of *Mothertalk* has an aesthetically prevalent and critically instructive role in our understanding of Kiyooka's effort to capture his mother's and his own experience with place. All six parts of *Mothertalk* open with poems that move beyond their epigraphic function. Each poem divides the text into different chronological and spatial transitions from Canadian to Japanese localities. Poems from various collections, such as *Kyoto Airs* (1964), *the Fontainebleau Dream Machine* (1977), *Gotenyama* (1985), *October Terrain* (1985), *Pear Tree Pomes* (1987), and an excerpt from Kiyooka's poetic essay "Pacific Windows" (1990) resonate with each part's thematic concerns, and as Saul argues, reveal the text's postmodern construction (*Writing* 83).

By incorporating these poems into an already diverse text, then,

Marlatt's editorial decisions are not only structurally-oriented, but they also reflect multiple and complex levels of *poiesis*, as they reinforce the text's poetic quality by generating a dialogue between Kiyooka's voice and his mother's stories. Marlatt's choice to place the poems at the beginning of each chapter, as Saul argues, "opens up the text" and further refracts Mary's stories (*Writing* 84). Most notably, Saul argues that the poetic segments affirm Kiyooka's poetic voice in a narrative that is comprised by many voices and loci, thereby further emphasizing *Mothertalk*'s plural authorship. It is safe to say then that the presence of poetry in the text does not simply reinforce the postmodern structure of diasporic writing, nor are the poems merely indexical headlines to a story about displacement. The poetic segments also invite an appraisal of the autoethnographic impulses of Kiyooka's poetic practice by confronting the reader with the creative friction between the text's different localities: Japan as a space of heritage, and Canada as a diasporic locus Kiyooka conceived as home.

My analysis turns to the poetic segments of *Mothertalk* in an effort to advance understanding about Kiyooka's complex relationship to locality. I focus on locality to describe Canadian and Japanese places and sites, for the local captures the unique ethnocultural inflections assigned to Canadian and Japanese spaces in Kiyooka's poetic practice. Locality thus advances a more intimate and personal understanding of place while it still reflects larger national spaces. Oscillating between Japan and Canada, the competing emotional shapes of both spaces are profusely visible in Kiyooka's poetry.

Through an investigation of the ways the poems interact creatively with familial, personal, and collective definitions of local and foreign spaces, I argue that Kiyooka's poems in *Mothertalk*—selected and added by Marlatt—become an autoethnographic medium that balances the tensions between belonging and non-belonging. The poems exhort the reader to critically assess the meaning of locality for diasporic subjectivity while they also reflect autoethnography's ongoing concerns about space and the writing *I*. That is, I conceive the poetic segments of *Mothertalk* as reflective of what James Buzard cites as "'problems of place and voice'" in his critical reading of autoethnography (60), a

problematic also undertaken throughout Kiyooka's work, which ultimately proposes cultural hybridity in the way Japanese and Canadian
localities interact in *Mothertalk*. Taking the poetic segments as my
point of entry while engaging with scholarship on autoethnography,
this essay attempts to explore definitions of the "local" in *Mothertalk* by
entering in a dialogue with a number of Kiyooka's poetic collections.

Institutionalized "Strangers":
The Japanese Canadian relationship with Locality

Born in 1926 in Moose Jaw, Saskatchewan, Kiyooka is known as a
photographer, painter, sculptor and poet. As a *Nisei* growing up in Calgary, Kiyooka was faced with the institutional failings of the Canadian
state at a time of sanctioned racism along with the "complexities of an
immigrant family," whose lives were "split," as Roy Miki mentions in
the Afterword to *Pacific Windows*, between "a working-class Calgary"
and a "distant Japan" (303). While Kiyooka grew up with his parents
in Canada, his sister Mariko was stranded in Japan because of the
institutional exclusions Japanese Canadians were faced with during
the war, a displacement that produced an acute sense of being torn
between national spaces and their complexities (305).

The epigraph of his first poetic collection, *Kyoto Airs* (1964),
evokes the family's displacement by imagining Kiyooka as reunited
with his sister, Mariko, in Japan: *"the sash you brought/ for my ukata is/
firm around my waist/ each time I tie it/ you are on one end/ & I am on
the other"* (*Pacific Windows* 9). The epigraph signals the trauma of
displacement by localizing both siblings in the same "ukata." The use
of the Japanese garment thus captures a nostalgic re-routing back to
the space of heritage by spatializing memory since Japan is not only
fraught with the emotional weight of diasporic stories, but with the
collective trauma of the uprooting of Japanese Canadians. And as Miki
argues, Mariko's presence in Kiyooka's poetry resonates with Kiyooka's
"struggle with the Canadian localisms that haunted the images projected in his writing, the ghosts of a splayed family history, the disappearance of a 'mother-tongue'" (*In Flux* 14).

Japanese and Canadian localities thus become intimately and problematically blended in the *Mothertalk* poems, assembling a complex picture of belonging. The poems and their following chapters produce an interplay between Japan as an emotionally conceived space of origins for Kiyooka and his mother, and Canada as a diasporic space of belonging, which abruptly disrupted the lives of Japanese Canadians by treating them as "enemy aliens" of the nation. In view of these complexities, I should acknowledge that a critical reading of place and locality in Kiyooka's poetry is immediately fraught with the difficult task of understanding what is considered local and what foreign in Kiyooka's poems. An attempt to engage an autoethnographic reading is an even more difficult endeavour, especially considering the traumatic history of the Japanese Canadian internment by the Canadian nation. But perhaps it is precisely the volatility and ambiguity through which Japanese and Canadian localities emerge in Kiyooka's poems that invite an analysis which considers how the writing self interacts, informs, and transforms place through the marginal position of the racialized former enemy of the nation. What does it mean for Kiyooka to blend Japanese and Canadian localities in a complex poetic *topos* while one is branded a stranger in the country of his birth then?

Kiyooka, as Roy Miki argues, was establishing his artistic career during particularly charged times, when Asian writing "came out of a climate of racism" and drastically affected notions of "Canadianness" (*In Flux* 2). Further, hostile "yellow peril" discourses institutionalized the social marginalization of Asian groups in Canada as the appeal to national security was shortly followed by the language of racialization. Yet, Miki reads exclusion as a formative juncture for Asian Canadian writing, arguing that the traumatic experience of legislative and social exclusion became an impetus for many Asian Canadian writers to bring injustice into light (*In Flux* 9). In order to concretize the conditions that shaped Kiyooka's treatment of local and foreign spaces, then, it is imperative to understand that the marginalization of Asian migrants along with the state's racist attitudes during the Second World War can be read as constructive experiences in the ways they signalled the production of texts that acted as testimonies and responded to Canada's institutional injustices.

"Athwarted" Selves, "Athwarted" Places

When asked to define his relationship with Canada in an interview with Miki, Kiyooka stated: "Growing up in this country and being beholden to the white culture, its institutions, I have nonetheless grown up *athwarted*" (*Broken Entries* 71; emphasis added). Kiyooka explains his sense of "athwartedness" as an "insider-outsider complex" (*In Flux* 15): "You are of it, and you are not, and you know that very well" (*Broken Entries* 71). Echoing a sense of confinement or even obstruction, the term "athwarted" signals Kiyooka's minority positioning as a racialized subject, but also a site for creativity as exclusion is treated as "a roadblock for Kiyooka which nonetheless did not prevent him from writing texts that outshined" (55).

Apart from his racialization, however, Kiyooka also reads his minority positioning in terms of language and articulation, issues that are prevalent in his poetic work (Saul *Writing* 84): "I wanted to claim some kind of articulation for myself," Kiyooka tells Miki (*Broken Entries* 64). If we are to understand the difficulty to articulate as a corollary of traumatic exclusion, "athwartedness" becomes a methodology Kiyooka adheres to and subverts in his poetic work, as he registers the difficulty to articulate the past, yet he assembles his own poetic testimony that brings injustice into light. In this context, his letter to Joy Kogawa and Tamio Wakayama entitled "We Asian North Americanos: An unhistorical 'take' on growing up yellow in a white world," which was read at the Japanese Canadian/American Symposium in Seattle in 1981 (*Mothertalk* 181), highlights his difficulty to articulate traumatic events of the past. In describing his problems with language and articulation, Kiyooka defines himself as "a white anglo saxon protestant, with a cleft tongue" (182). By "tongue," Kiyooka refers to his "mother tongue," the Japanese language, in which he was not fluent, yet he felt close to through his parents and their stories (Miki *Pacific* 303), but perhaps he is also hinting at the creative friction between one's mother tongue and an English mediated *I*, which defines his poetic work as heterogeneous. Belonging is therefore fraught with a legacy of trauma that travels through generations and permeates different localities, which are represented as creative sites where Kiyooka can reclaim his position in the Canadian nation in *Mothertalk's* poetic segments.

The branding of Japanese Canadians as "enemy aliens" by Canadian laws in its divisive politics ultimately presents us with an array of critical questions: *what* or *where exactly* is the local for Japanese Canadians? Can the local be identified in affective projections of Japan as the place of origins and heritage? Or, could we read the local as an "athwarted" term that becomes consistently contested because of the Canadian state's treatment of Japanese Canadians? As Miki argues, for Kiyooka locality is inscribed within the complexities of his own self-identification as a Canadian racialized artist (*In Flux* 14). Although trauma is intricately complex in his poetry, then, *Mothertalk's* poetic segments reflect a productive balance between what Irene Sywensky describes as "the space of silence" (346)—an expression of trauma and a trope of resistance—and the way Kiyooka explores the ethnographic textures of Japanese localities in a complex self-reflexive terrain. To attend to these questions, I turn to autoethnography as the theoretical framework that queries the relationship between writing *self* and place and signals locality as a creative yet not entirely stable site of belonging.

The "auto" biographical of autoethnography

Many critics of autoethnography point out the hermeneutical difficulties that arise from writers' representation of themselves *in place*. Autoethnography attends to the relationship between place and identity, individual and cultural community. Deborah Reed-Danahay argues that autoethnographic themes "break down dualisms of identity" (4), and as a result construct a multiple image of the self and the cultural or ethnic community it represents (4). *Mothertalk's* poetic segments project the anxieties inherent in diasporic understandings of belonging but also add an ethnographic quality to the narrativization of Mary's life stories. Since Mary's voice is filtered by multiple modalities of authorship, she transgresses the conventional qualities of a native informant, who is generally the cultural source or 'voice' of autoethnographic texts.

Saul contemplates some of the implications of the text's autoethnographic construction by discussing James Clifford's notion of auto-ethnography: "Once native informants begin to be co-authors and the ethnographer as scribe and archivist as well as interpreting observer, we can ask new, critical questions about ethnographies" (Clifford qtd in Saul 84). Kiyooka's poems complicate traditional notions of ethnographic discourses, since, as Saul continues, neither Kiyooka nor his mother are simply informants (*Writing* 88). Rather, both mother and son re-write themselves in what Smaro Kamboureli identifies as the "slip-page of the "auto" of autochthonous into the "auto" of autobiography (32), the creative combination of two exciting sites of cultural analysis, whose boundaries are consistently blurred by *Mothertalk*'s techniques.

Aside from asserting Kiyooka's authorial voice in the representation of his mother's stories, the poems included in *Mothertalk* complicate his understanding of Japanese localities, and signal a re-routing to a poetically recreated Japan, the place of ancestry that he knows through his parents but experiences for the first time in 1963 in Kyoto, a journey that inspired his first poetic collection, *Kyoto Airs* (1964). As an inter-disciplinary practice that emerged from the fields of sociology and anthropology, autoethnography is a field that challenges diasporic writing because of its unique modes of transgression in terms of textual practices. James Buzard defines autoethnography as "the study, representation, or knowledge of a culture by one or more of its members" (60). As a response to what Reed-Danahay calls "the changing conception of both the self and society" (2), autoethnography is characterized by "a double-consciousness" (3), merging self-reflexivity and ethnographic qualities.

The autoethnographic account disrupts conventional ethnographic and autobiographical practices and as Buzard notes, "occupies a curious position" as it responds to the "trope clusters of voice and place" (61). Departing from the press for objectivity that traditional ethnographies perpetuate, autoethnography grows out of "the problems of place and voice" at a time of mobility and cultural transference (61). As a genre, it maintains some aspects of traditional anthropological ethnographies, such as the native informant. Reed-Danahay writes:

[autoethnography] synthesizes both a postmodern ethnography, in which the realist conventions and objective observer position of standard ethnography have been called into question, and a postmodern autobiography, in which the notion of a coherent, individual self has been similarly called into question. The term has a double sense—referring wither to the ethnography of one's own group or to autobiographical writing that has ethnographic interest (2)

An autoethnographic text then is always in a continuous state of "the beyond," as Eleanor Ty and Christl Verduyn note in their critical study of autoethnography beyond conventional practices of ethnographic engagements in contemporary Asian Canadian writing (11). The account of the member of a culture/community marks autoethnography as an ongoing witnessing of different places, voices, and identifications, and therefore produces a text where many topoi and selves interact and often clash.

The reader's first poetic encounter in *Mothertalk* is an excerpt from "Pacific Windows" (1990), which captures the centrality of Mary's role and *place* in the spatial orientation of the text. Introducing the first part of *Mothertalk* entitled "My Heart's True Country," which, for Mary Kiyooka, is Tosa, Japan, the excerpt immediately links Mary with Japan and situates *Mothertalk* as the "joint effort" between herself and her son (Saul *Writing* 82). Mary's presence is registered as a confluence of different localities, mediating her sense of displacement through her relationship with place:

> And though it was never enough to simply sit and knit she would finish a vest for a son or a pair of slippers for a daughter, and when she felt like talking she invariably talked about all the family ties they had on both sides of the Pacific, and though she never mentioned it, they both knew she was the last link to the sad and glad tidings of the floating world. (*Mothertalk* 11)

This imagistic "floating world" signals the different localities at play in *Mothertalk*. Mary is registered as a source of mobile stories; stories that are in flux as they follow the movement of people from one place to another, complicating the "ties" she and her son have with "both sides of the pacific" (*Mothertalk* 11). As Saul states, Mary's story-telling "provides her son with the raw material for his own process of 'cultural recovery' as they enable him to move between private and public history, imaginative and physical geography, the local and the national" (*Writing* 82). Thus, it is in this intricate moving between cultural signifiers and memories that Kiyooka navigates locality through Mary's story of displacement, and in this process, he unravels his own understanding of belonging.

The passage from "Pacific Windows" reflects Kiyooka's idiosyncratic simplicity. It evokes his sense of displacement, the condition of being in-between different spaces without making "racialization or ethnocentric exclusion" the main problematic of the piece (Miki *In Flux* 75). Thus, the beginning of *Mothertalk* establishes both Kiyooka and his mother as diasporic subjects by subtly conjuring up various displacements rather than explicitly defining them. It is in this respect that Reed-Danahay reads displacement as central for autoethnographic texts, stating that "the most cogent aspect of the study of autoethnography is that of cultural displacement or situation of exile" (4). Through the figuration of his mother, Kiyooka explores multiple displacements and engages with what Saul describes as "the intense focus of the in-between" ("Auto-hyphen" 133). Interestingly, "Pacific Windows" is written in the third person singular: "Everywhere *he* walked that Fall pages from his past spoke of inchoate presentiments" (*Mothertalk* 11; emphasis added). The grammatical choice is intriguing as Kiyooka's distanced "he" soon joins a distinct "they," which speaks to the recollective tone of the essay. His voice and *person* gradually enter the text through an authorial "I" that hesitates, hides, and looks carefully at his shared memories with his mother, thus defining *Mothertalk* as a shared archive of recollection and signalling displacement as a common juncture that ties mother and son together.

Poetic Localities: The case of *Kyoto Airs*

Kiyooka's poetry interrogates localities as sites of belonging, proximity, and displacement. Responding to the tradition of *avant-garde* poetics, Kiyooka often employs what Fred Wah describes as "the poetics of the 'trans-,' methods of translation, transference, transition, transposition" (90), and it is the role Japan has in his poetic practice that most accurately reflects his transnational or trans-local affiliations. In his interview with Miki, Kiyooka emphasizes the impact Japan has had on his work:

> Something tells me, though I'll go on writing, that I think I've proven to myself that I had a writing to accomplish, and it had to do with being a Japanese Canadian. I didn't know this at the time I wrote *Kyoto Airs* [...] *Kyoto Airs* is my first book, and it's about Japan; the first long piece of *Transcanada Letters* is about Japan, and it's prefaced by the photograph of my grandfather with my mother. So all my texts have started in Japan. I don't know why that is so but that's true (*Broken Entries* 66)

Kiyooka's poetry, indeed, started in Japan. His 1963 trip to Japan resulted in his first poetry collection *Kyoto Airs* (1964). *Kyoto Airs* is an example of the explorative, imagistic tropes that autoethnographies use to capture the intimacy of place and self-narration, making Kiyooka, as Marlatt has noted, "a double citizen of language" ("From Eminence" 43). The poetry collection draws heavily on Kiyooka's impressions of Japan, connected to what Miki describes as an implicit representation of his own trauma of being labelled a stranger in the country he called home (*In Flux* 19). Kiyooka's witnessing of Japanese localities, especially Kyoto, moves beyond impressionistic understandings and produces a multilayered representation of Japan. Kiyooka hints at his intention throughout the collection, gradually defining his relationship with locality through his poetic vocation. In "The Room with a View," for example, he states: "I will flow these poems/to you 500 miles/away" (*Pacific Windows* 22), situating poetry as the means to bridge the distance between Canada and Japan. Poetry, then, creates a dialogical representation of locality by allowing Kiyooka to navigate his complex relationship with both spaces.

What distinguishes *Kyoto Airs* from Kiyooka's later poetic projects is that the locale of Kyoto is configured in an unprecedented confrontation with his own trauma as an "enemy alien." The local in this collection becomes a signifier for fractured kinships. Kiyooka is confronted with a locality that used to be imagined but is now known and this recognition brings forth his identification with both Canada and Japan in a pervasive witnessing. *Mothertalk* borrows two poems from *Kyoto Airs*. The first poem, "Burning Leaves," introduces the second part of the text called "No Notion of what was in Store for Me," which relates Mary's first encounter with Canada upon immigration. The chapter emphasizes Mary's intimate notion of community, especially between the *Issei* and the *Nisei* generations (*Mothertalk* 37). Mary's melancholic reflections in the chapter inform Kiyooka's relationship with Japanese sites. Placed towards the end of *Kyoto Airs*, "Burning Leaves" is a distinct poem in the collection as it weaves together individual and collective memory, exposing a witnessing of locality as dialogical rather than singular.

Resonating with Mary's first experiences in Canada, including her marriage to Shigekiyo Kiyooka, who is affectionately addressed as 'Papa' throughout the text, the poem visualizes the interplay between Japan and Canada by using the imagery of scattered leaves. While Kiyooka localizes himself in a broad "here," his sister Mariko is located at a distant "over there" (*Pacific Windows* 23), evoking the epigraph of the collection. Kiyooka's understanding of proximity is mediated through defining himself *in place*, hence the choice of verbs in the poem ("I am *sitting*," "I *know* where I am," "I *am* still here").

In relation to other poems from *Kyoto Airs,* "Burning Leaves" expresses the intensity of being in-between localities and their cultural significance. The poem "Itinerary of a View," for instance, explicitly articulates what Kiyooka implicitly refers to in "Burning Leaves": his hybridity. "Itinerary of a View" ends the collection with Kiyooka declaring his position both in Canada and in Japan: "I am a Canadian painter/ come home to pay homage/ to ancestors, samurai among them" (23). By pronouncing himself a "Canadian painter," Kiyooka subverts the discourses that constituted him a non-citizen or stranger in the place he sees as home, affectively reclaiming citizenship as he negotiates his status as a former "enemy alien," while his identity as "a Canadian painter" permeates Japanese localities and creates a multiple image of himself.

In relation to the chapters they introduce, the poems borrowed from *Kyoto Airs* arguably generate friction between Canadian and Japanese localities. This is visible in the chapter introduced by "Burning Leaves," where Canadian space contrasts with Mary's strong affiliations with Japan, her Samurai father, and her *Issei* identity. The same friction between localities is evident in the essay "We Asian North Americanos," added as an appendix by Marlatt, where Kiyooka connects his palpable relationship with place to his complex relationship with language and the figure of his mother:

> I've been talking of how my mother gave me my first language, a language I began to acquire even as I suckled on her breast, and what a motley mode of speaking it's all become in time. Need I say, that she couldn't save me from that fate. But I have seen a look on her face that told me she understood (wordlessly ...) the ardour of all such displacement. Thus it is that I always speak Japanese when I go home to visit her. More than that I can, for the time being, become almost Japanese. I realize that it's one of the deepest "ties" I have in my whole life (*Mothertalk* 183)

This excerpt reflects Kiyooka's and his mother's connection to Japan through language and story-telling. At the end of "Burning Leaves," it is his mother who collapses the distance between himself and his sister. The leaves can be read as metonymic of both himself and Mariko as scattered diasporic subjects and their mother as the agent who obliterates the distance between them: "I am still sitting here, and she/well she, is over there, both of us/watch falling leaves carried away on the inswept air./ o mother/ where is the rake?" (*Pacific Windows* 23).

Gotenyama *and* Kyoto Airs: *A Conversation*

Mothertalk also borrows a poem from *Gotenyama* (1985), an explorative re-orientation back to the issues of *Kyoto Airs*. Much like the other poems in *Mothertalk*, the poem "blithely" from *Gotenyama* reflects Kiyooka's autoethnographic impulse through an exploration of his "athwarted" relationship with language and place. Keeping both collections in view in this section, I read how their contributions to *Mothertalk*'s poetic segments create dialogues between Canadian and Japanese national spaces.

Like *Kyoto Airs*, the persistent emphasis on the difficulty to articulate language permeates Kiyooka's projection of locality in the *Gotenyama* poems. Gotenyama, a station in Osaka, Japan, becomes another "athwarted" space, allowing Kiyooka to contemplate his sense of displacement as key for his poetry's autoethnographic concerns (Reed-Danahay 4). Sharing *Mothertalk*'s preoccupation with articulation, the collection locates Kiyooka's perception of place in his mother's story-telling. As in *Mothertalk*, Mary Kiyooka provides "the raw material" for Kiyooka's poetic work (Saul *Writing* 87) as it is through her stories that Kiyooka navigates his hyphenated identity: the "Canadian Painter" (*Pacific Windows* 23) who is also a diasporic subject who returns to the place of heritage.

The poem "blithely" from *Gotenyama* introduces the third part of *Mothertalk* entitled "All Caught Up in our Canadian Lives" whereby Mary relates her experiences in Canada upon immigration. As in the two poems borrowed from *Kyoto Airs*, articulation becomes a central problematic in "blithely." The poem locates story-telling as an integral cultural site, registering Mary as caught between the Japanese and Canadian ways of living described in this chapter. Following the movement of "the azure & crimson paper carp/thru Gotenyama backstreets," "blithely" navigates the space of memory (*Mothertalk* 57). The "distant," open-ended "echo" Kiyooka experiences in Gotenyama brings him back to Calgary, his childhood home: "my mother/ taught me on the Saturday morning/ back porch/ of a long ago East Calgary/ circa 1930s" (*Mothertalk* 57).

The poem's ability to transgress national boundaries through memory reflects Kiyooka's complex relationship with language. Mary becomes a site of language in the collection, producing meaning through the intimacy of story-telling and thus corresponding with her representation in *Mothertalk*'s appendices. In "We Asian North Americanos," for instance, Kiyooka writes: "She reminds me of my Japanese self by talking to me in the very language she taught me before I even had the thot of learning anything" (182), thus collapsing the distance between Japan and Calgary and positioning Mary, much like in the excerpt from "Pacific Windows," as the reference point between different cultural spaces.

At this point, we are reminded again of the significance of Marlatt's editorial agency that defined the dialectic character of the text, constantly opening space for the interconnectedness between Japan and Canada, consistently signalling the autoethnography's textual intricacies. In an endeavour to create a dialogue between Mary's stories about Tosa, now Kochi City, Japan, in the chapter and its introductory poem, the choice of "blithely" arguably reflects the pervasive nature of story-telling, which spans across continents and consistently reiterates Mary's centrality to the narrative. And this careful attention to story-telling is consistently registered through Kiyooka's ambivalent relationship with the Japanese language. For example, in a letter to himself in the collection *Pacific Rim Letters* Kiyooka writes:

> almost all of what i came to know about Japan came thru translations of one sort and another, and so it is that my Japan is, among other things, an altogether habitable place in my mind: my callit duplicitous, ofttimes errant, mind. i take it that mind is itself grounded in language/s [...] the impulse to shape a viable word, one which i find voided in our political life, has driven me inside the labyrinth of language to gain for myself an articulation that could be said to include *both strands, or is it strains, of my Asian/American heritage* and now, more than ever, i simply want to proclaim its Pan-pacific resonances ("Letter to Myself" *Pacific Rim* 265; emphasis added).

Much like the letter, the rest of the poems in *Gotenyama* mediate Kiyooka's witnessing of locality through the difficulty of articulation. The collection reads like a long poem, tracing Kiyooka's experiences within the mystifying Japanese locale. In "Listening," for example, he contemplates his difficulty to articulate while witnessing the locale of Gotenyama, informing the reader that he possesses a "throat of no-meaning" (*Pacific Windows* 224). His navigation of Gotenyama consists of sensory and auditory understandings of the landscape, with his mother being a co-participant in a conversation between voices that struggle with articulation.

The collection's persistent emphasis on voicelessness reflects Kiyooka's cautious use of language. Like *Kyoto Airs,* many poems in *Gotenyama* mediate affective projections of locality while becoming media through which Kiyooka explores his fractured identity through the difficulty to articulate. And this complex mediation of place and language, or place through language is prevalent in *Gotenyama*. For example, the reference to the "ancient song" he hears in Gotenyama is reiterated throughout the collection and provides the landscape with a synaesthetic quality. Kiyooka's variant references to the "ancient song" he cannot fully articulate because of his "throat of no-meaning" marks Gotenyama as the space that is more likely fantasized or recreated than known (*Pacific Windows* 229). Like Kyoto, the place where he "pays homage to ancestors" (23), Gotenyama is both a local and foreign space for Kiyooka. The "ancient song" oozing out of the landscape becomes an invitation for Kiyooka to articulate "that irresistible/ raga-of-longing" (229), and therefore corresponds with *Mothertalk*'s emphasis on voice and language.

Kiyooka has characterized the way locality is projected through language, as he tells Miki, as a process of "osmosis" (*Broken Entries* 68). This process merges together different elements and implies a filtering of impressions and experiences through witnessing Japanese localities. In "Gotenyama Spring," for instance, his mother becomes a repository of his impressions and struggles with language, as well as a source of wisdom, being discursively close to *Mothertalk*'s postmodern construction. Like Mariko in *Kyoto Airs,* Mary Kiyooka becomes a co-participant in constructing the meaning of locality in *Gotenyama*. While his sister prompts him to speak in *Kyoto Airs* (21), Mary Kiyooka becomes a confidant and interlocutor in *Gotenyama*, as Kiyooka relates to his mother the various "echoes" he experiences in Gotenyama ("Gotenyama Spring," "blithely," "Listening"). At the end of the collection Kiyooka concretizes, as in *Kyoto Airs*, his understanding of himself *in place*. The last stanza of the collection defines Gotenyama as "the unsung/ Psalm" of his "cleft" or "fraught" tongue, and becomes "the erstwhile/ sequel/ to [his]/ Kyoto Airs" (232), reflecting the continuous exploration of locality and belonging that Kiyooka's poetry contemplates.

In *Gotenyama* and *Kyoto Airs*, Kiyooka's witnessing of Japanese localities signals the autoethnographic concern of writing the self through and in place. As Saul mentions in her discussion of *Mothertalk*, Kiyooka's poetic exploration of Japan is constantly shifting. "Japan comes alive primarily through the memories of his mother and his own rewritings" contends Saul, suggesting a degree of re-drafting of the autoethnographic *"I"* in the representation of locality (*Writing* 88). In this light, Fred Wah describes texts like *Mothertalk* as sites that mediate the complexities of hyphen: "The site of this poetics, for me, and many other multi-racial and multi-cultural writers, is the hyphen, that marked or unmarked space that both binds and divides," thus interpreting the plural character of localities in minority positioning (72). Reflecting a hyphenated identity, Kiyooka's complex affiliations with Canada permeate Japanese localities as the sites of ancestry and culture. His examination of locality is thus coloured by the emotional contours Japan and Canada have, rendering *Mothertalk* a text that sustains hybridity identity while making various statements about the problematics of place in diasporic life.

The Issei/Nisei *Relationship with Locality*

Attending to the poetic segments of *Mothertalk* also requires an examination of the generational tensions that figure in Kiyooka's appreciation of locality. The final section of my discussion attends to the

Issei-Nisei imaginings of locality projected by the poetic segments in *Mothertalk,* thus adding another level of complexity to our understanding of place.

Mothertalk is dedicated "To the Issei women of Mary Kiyooka's generation." Mary's presence and her intimate relationship with Japan permeate the text and become, as Marlatt mentions in her introduction, "the skeletal arc" of the narrative (*Mothertalk* 7). *Mothertalk* evokes various spatial, gender, and generational divisions. Responding to her role as "the last link" to Japan (*Pacific Windows* 298), Mary Kiyooka often sees herself as a site of cultural knowledge in *Mothertalk*, and as a result, her *Issei* identity is often juxtaposed to her children's understanding of locality and its cultural significance. For example, at the end of *Mothertalk* Mary laments: "They may look Japanese but they don't know that part of themselves because they're out of touch with the world their grandparents hail from" (172). At another instance toward the end she states: "When I pass away there wont be a soul left to tell how heart-of Tosa sang in our home behind an English facade" (172). Although this statement reflects anxieties inherent to diasporic understandings of space, culture, and subjectivity, the points of contact between the *Issei* and the *Nisei* in *Mothertalk* are registered as creative spaces of potentiality, thus validating Marlatt's decision to add the poems which, in turn, open a conversation between Kiyooka's connections with place and belonging vis-à-vis his mother's experience of space in the main narrative line of the text.

As Saul notes in her analysis of contemporary Canadian biotexts, Kiyooka cautiously navigates his mother's stories of place, and in this process, he re-drafts his terms of belonging, departing from traditional ethnographic native informants. In this regard, Buzard also argues that "the modern ethnographic imagination likened the physical territory inhabited by supposedly *immobile natives* to the iconic space of a cultural totality presumed to order and give meaning to every aspect of native life" (63). *Mothertalk*'s voices counter traditional ethnographies in this respect, that is, the fact that the native informant is an immobile figure rooted in a singular cultural location. *Mothertalk*, in contrast, creates a continuous dialogue between the *Issei* and *Nisei* generations through Kiyooka's retelling of his mother's story in a text where poetry creatively responds to the multiple divides with respect to Japanese Canadian identity and belonging.

Mary's understanding of Japanese localities is visible in the first chapter entitled "My Heart's True Country," which for Mary Kiyooka is Tosa, Japan. To a large extent, Mary expands on her nostalgic preoccupation with Japan by contrasting her experience in Canada during the Great Depression and the Second World War. Like Kiyooka, she also reads her different understanding of Japan in the context of language: "My kids will never know all that befell their Mom because she never learned to speak English well and they didn't learn enough Nihongo" (15). *Mothertalk*'s photographic sequence and the sections that follow this part represents articulation as a creative site in the interaction between the *Issei* and the *Nisei*. Kiyooka's re-telling of his mother's story thus produces what Saul cites as "an expanded text" that re-conceptualizes notions of proximity and distance in diasporic life (Clifford qtd in Saul 87). The variant levels of collaboration involved in the production of *Mothertalk* account for the pervasive theme of language in the text, as Kiyooka needed a translator for his mother's stories since his "brand of Japanese is previous both to the 2nd W.W. and television" as he humorously admits in "We Asian North Americanos" (*Mothertalk* 182), while his mother's English is characterized as "rudimentary" in the same appendix (182).

Articulation emerges once more as an anxiety that responds to the generational divides between the first and second generation diasporans, an issue Kiyooka consistently faces in his poetic perception of place. Language and articulation, however, are also persistent concerns in the poetic segments that introduce Mary's and her children's different perceptions of place and belonging. As in other autoethnographic texts, the divides between different generations of diasporans are deeply connected to variant reflections on place, local and foreign sites and identifications. In *Mothertalk*, Mary Kiyooka registers this gap regarding language by presenting herself as emotionally embodying Japanese localities: "Ah that's true I guess [...] but they didn't have a Tosa buried in themselves the way I have" (14) she remarks, thus reflecting not only the spatiality of memory, but the autoethnographic practice of recording what is perceived as an 'original' or native perception of place and culture.

It is ultimately *Mothertalk*'s form that best elucidates the autoethnographic concerns of Kiyooka's poetic project. A stanza from the long poem *October Terrain* (1985) introduces *Mothertalk*'s photographic sequence. The thematic concerns of *October Terrain* are discursively close to this part of *Mothertalk,* where Mary contemplates the trauma her family experienced during the uprooting by looking at the absences in the family photographs: "this line hops skips & jumps along—/ syllable by syllable it keeps falling back into a thronging/ (77)," writes Kiyooka. The emphasis on language and memory, of course, resonates with *Gotenyama,* where the "ancient song" (*Pacific Windows* 227) oozing out of the Japanese station becomes "a thronging" of meaning, a cluster or node that codes articulation within the complexities of self and location (*Mothertalk* 77).

For Kiyooka, the imagery of language clustering around locality corresponds with the function of the family photo album in *Mothertalk,* a site that presents us with a cluster of voices of both *Issei* and *Nisei* communities: "all all of your voices audible all/ breathing in the silent interstices between each letter ..." (77). Soon this thronging of voices becomes lived memory as Kiyooka remembers a phrase his father used to say: "no wisdom without laughter," an expression that he explains as "itself a tongue-tide language. mythos/mirth/ the girth of the whole rotund earth its ineluctable preamble/" (77). Kiyooka again connects articulation with the spatiality of memory, which transcends places and generations. The playful tone of the poem becomes a guide to read Mary and Roy Kiyooka's shared longing for finding meaning in localities, which are often connected to the trauma of exclusion and dislocation as the photographic sequence verifies. The photo album arguably serves the same purpose as the poem: to underscore the absence of voices as another creative way to read locality.

The final poems in *Mothertalk* reflect the connections between locality and intergenerational trauma. In an interview with Miki, Kiyooka emphasizes the difficulty many *Nisei* experience with articulating language. "I would say that most Nisei are [...] comparatively anonymous," states Kiyooka, contemplating an inherited silence that speaks to issues of intergenerational trauma (*Broken Entries* 64). As Sywenky argues in her discussion of the poetry of Joy Kogawa, the "space of silence" often becomes both method and thematic problem for *Nisei* authors (346), something also evident in the poetry of Joy Kogawa, who as another "enemy alien" of Canada is concerned with the meaning and problems of locality. In order to effectively assess the generational tensions present in *Mothertalk*, I will briefly compare the figuration of Japanese localities in Joy Kogawa's collection, *A Choice of Dreams,* and some of *Mothertalk*'s poetic segments, as they both reflect the ruptures the Japanese Canadian community experienced in Canada and present the reader with what Kiyooka has characterized as the *Nisei* authorial site of silence in his interview with Miki (*Broken Entries* 64).

Joy Kogawa's preoccupation with trauma and memory has been extensively discussed in critical endeavours, especially in analyses of her much celebrated novel *Obasan* (1981). Kogawa's poetic work shares Kiyooka's generational understandings and reflections on Canadian and Japanese localities. As *Kyoto Airs,* Kogawa's poetic collection *A Choice of Dreams* (1974) "builds on her three-month trip to Japan in 1969" (Sywenky 347), and similarly assesses localities dialogically, merging Japanese and Canadian affiliations in a multilayered witnessing of physical space.

Japanese localities are presented as palimpsestic in *A Choice of Dreams*; the poem "Zen Graveyard," for instance, engages with the same "haunted localisms" that Kiyooka struggles with in his poetry (Miki *In Flux* 14): "Mountainside, stone ghosts, graves/Rising in steps into the trees/Strange familiarity" (Kogawa 14). Here, Kogawa navigates memory through the hauntings that the locale of the graveyard produces. Localities are haunting sites in the sense that they are both unfamiliar and familiar to Kogawa, generating an uncanny or strange affiliation with Japan.

Like Kiyooka, Kogawa also experiences localities as "athwarted" sites that nevertheless balance the friction between proximity and distance. Although Kogawa pronounces herself a *"North American stranger"* in another poem of the collection (12), she still experiences a "strange familiarity" in "Zen graveyard" (14). Discursively alternating between proximity and distance, then, locality is never presented as singular or definitive in Kogawa's poetry. As in the poetic segments from *Kyoto Airs* and *Gotenyama* in *Mothertalk,* localities are always pluralistic as they reflect Kiyooka's *Nisei* subjectivity and his ambivalent relationship with Canada and Japan.

Nisei authors experience locality through the intricate interplay between proximity and distance, constructing a continuous and open-ended questioning of belonging in the place of ancestry, the place the *Issei* mediate through the intimacy of language and stories. One of the final poems of *Mothertalk* is a stanza from Kiyooka's much discussed long poem *the Fontainebleau Dream Machine* (1977), which engages with the spatiality of trauma, with which the last parts of *Mothertalk* are thematically concerned. The last two parts explicitly discuss the Japanese uprooting as a devastating experience, especially for the *Issei,* who had invested a life in Canada and were literally stripped of all affiliations they had cultivated. Tellingly, the stanza from *the Fontainebleau Dream Machine* locates trauma in Opal, Alberta, the small farming town where Kiyooka's family relocated themselves during the uprooting (*Pacific* 304). Titled *"l'aura of the Ukraine Opal Alberta the"* the poem haunts Mary's statements in the last parts of the text. Capturing the discrepancies between the "Coniferous sky over Europa" and "Asia," Kiyooka consistently complicates his affiliation with locality through the condition of "aphasia ..." in the poem (*Mothertalk* 133). Aphasia, in this excerpt, perhaps creates more questions than it answers; whether it offers resolution or if it signifies the disenfranchisement of the Japanese community during the war, aphasia reflects once more the text's autoethnographic preoccupation with fluidity and openness when it comes to place and cultural significance.

If we are to understand aphasia as a disruption or deferral of meaning, we must read Kiyooka's evocation of aphasia as related to the broader engagement with language and articulation in *Mothertalk's* poetic segments. The last part of *Mothertalk* mediates the uprooting as "A Bitter Pill to Swallow," as the name of the chapter informs us. In this chapter Mary reflects the abjection aphasia implies: "we were deprived of both freedom and livelihood. Twenty-five years after coming to Canada and becoming citizens we were stripped of everything. Boy it's been a bitter pill to swallow" (137). Mary's words reflect the trauma of the uprooting as a painful betrayal of the Japanese Canadian community. Even though Kiyooka's family was not interned, they were forced to relocate to Opal, where Kiyooka would stay until he pursued an artistic career after the war (Miki *In Flux* 15).

The uprooting was particularly devastating for the *Issei* generation, who, as Ann Sunahara states, were optimistic that there would not be extremities against them (27). Mary represents a generation's response to the uprooting, stating that "let's say we were scarred for life" (*Mothertalk* 139). Being in line with the final sections that discuss Mary's thoughts on the uprooting, *Mothertalk* ends with a poem from *Pear Tree Pomes* (1987), where Kiyooka addresses his mother in his own sense of "athwarted" articulation: "mother/ i am/ nothing but/ this pod-of-breath/nothing if not all/ the mud twig/ and spittle consonants/ mother the nests/ we feather at speech's behest" (157), understanding localities through a framework of emotional and intellectual difficulty, possibly close to the deferral of meaning aphasia suggests. Similar to the function of the excerpt from "Pacific Windows" at the beginning of *Mothertalk,* the excerpt from *Pear Tree Pomes*, located at the end of the collection, affirms Mary's position as the creative source of the narrative. Marlatt's choice of the poem along with her decisions regarding the chronology of the text add a cyclical reaffirmation of Mary's centrality both in Roy Kiyooka's life, and in the complex ways she defines his relationship with Japan.

Daphne Marlatt describes Roy Kiyooka as "an interrogative poet" and a "double citizen of language" ("From Eminence" 43). His poetic practice, indeed, reveals an ongoing questioning of localities as sites of recognition of belonging. Autoethnographic "strands" suggest a careful, conscious layering of different localities and literary practices when it comes to Kiyooka's poetry. The close examination of self and place in *Mothertalk*'s poetry does not simply illustrate localities as plural in the contexts of writing cultural difference; it also explicates the transformation of fraught spaces of exclusion and dislocation to spaces of potentiality for diasporic authors, producing new meaning about place and self. Ultimately, localities bring in the confluence between trauma and memory that becomes a kinetic site rather than a fixed space. And the poetry of *Mothertalk* reflects multiple moments of confluence, where Canadian affiliations and stories enter the representation of Japan, while concurrently Kiyooka explores his Japanese connections by reclaiming the identity obscured by his racialization. Despite the interpretative difficulty of approaching Asian Canadian writing and subjectivity, it is the "tropological," as Irene Sywenky puts it, methodologies of poetry (348), the open and flexible manipulations of language that construct new meaning out of the "enemy alien" and transform traumatic exclusion into a site of potentiality.

Works Cited

Buzard, James. "On Auto-ethnographic Authority" *The Yale Journal of Criticism* 16.1 (2003): 61–99.

Egan, Susanna, and Gabrielle Helms. "The Many Tongues of *Mothertalk: Life Stories of Mary Kiyoshi Kiyooka*." *Canadian Literature* 163 Winter, (1999): 47–77.

Kamboureli, Smaro. *Pacific Rim Letters: Roy Kiyooka*. Edmonton: NeWest Press, 2005. P. 265.

Kiyooka, Roy. "Gotenyama" *Pacific Windows: Collected Poems of Roy Kiyooka*. Ed. Roy Miki. Burnaby, BC: Talonbooks, 1997.

----. "Kyoto Airs" *Pacific Windows: Collected Poems of Roy Kiyooka*. Ed. Roy Miki. Burnaby, BC: Talonbooks, 1997.

----. *Mothertalk*. Edmonton: NeWest Press. 1997.

----. "Pacific Windows" *Pacific Windows: Collected Poems of Roy Kiyooka*. Ed. Roy Miki. Burnaby, BC: Talonbooks, 1997

Marlatt, Daphne. "Roy Kiyooka: From Eminence to Immanence" *West Coast Line* 38.3 (2005)

Miki, Roy. *In Flux: Transnational Shifts in Asian Canadian Writing.* Edmonton: NeWest Press, 2011. P. 1–30, 63–93.

----. "Inter-Face." *Broken Entries: Race, Subjectivity, Writing.* Toronto: The Mercury Press 1998.

Reed-Danahay, Deborah. *Auto/Ethnography: Rewriting the Self and the Social.* New York: Berg, 1997.

Saul, Joanne. "Auto-hyphen-ethno-hyphen-graphy": Fred Wah's Creative-Critical Writing. *Asian Canadian Writing Beyond Autoethnography.* Ed. Eleanor Ty and Christl Verduyn. Waterloo: Wilfrid Laurier UP, 2008. pp. 133–151.

----. *Writing the Roaming Subject: The Biotext in Canadian Literature.* Toronto and Buffalo: U of Toronto UP, 2006.

Sywenky, Irene. "Recovering the Voice of the Japanese Canadian Community: History and Private And Public Discourses in Joy Kogawa's Poetry and Prose." *Canadian Review of Comparative Literature* 36.3 (2009).

Ty, Eleanor, and Christl Verduyn. "Introduction." *Asian Canadian Writing: Beyond Autoethnography.* Ed. Eleanor Ty and Christl Verduyn. Waterloo: Wilfrid Laurier UP, 2008, pp. 1–31.

Man Dwells on Burial Ground:
Roy Kiyooka and Martin Heidegger [*StoneDGloves*]

Sergiy Yakovenko

Roy Kiyooka's work establishes the primary relationship between being and dwelling as defined by Martin Heidegger: "To say that mortals *are* is to say that in *dwelling* they persist through spaces by virtue of their stay among things and locales" (Heidegger, "Building Dwelling Thinking" 359). The concept of *dwelling in space* acknowledges a particular relationship that humans establish with things—things that constitute human space by virtue of being *ready to hand.* "The stone is worldless," says Heidegger (*The Fundamental Concepts of Metaphysics* 196), but the world-forming capacity of humans renders stones a part of the world. *To dwell* is also not the same as simply *to live.* For this reason, to juxtapose human's dwelling with "animal's poverty in world" (*The Fundamental Concepts* 271), Heidegger, following Hölderlin, specifies that "poetically man dwells"—and this is how one can imagine Kiyooka, transforming everything he touched as an artist and writer into poetry. Even his correspondence, published in *Transcanada Letters* and *Pacific Rim Letters*, in form is nothing short of a collection of free verses (with a prophetic anticipation of today's text-message spelling, or, as Kiyooka called it, "inglish"); likewise, his collected poems, *Pacific Windows,* is often indistinguishable in style from his letters.

Being essentially a transcanadian poet, Kiyooka *dwells,* nevertheless, at Pacific Rim, with his Pacific windows open to the country of his ancestry—Japan. Kiyooka's discourse, his use of signs (to avoid the list of genres he combines in his work), ranges somewhere between, historically, Matsuo Basho's travelogue *The Narrow Road to the Interior*, with its characteristic narrative interspersed with haiku (Kiyooka's *Wheels: A Trip Thru Honshu's Backcountry*), and, aesthetically, ekphrasis, a vivid verbal description of a visual work of art (*The Fontainebleau Dream Machine: 18 Frames from A Book of Rhetoric*). With his propensity to photographic travelogues, what looks like a piece of reality on the picture inevitably returns, in its poetical ekphrastic counterpart, to visionary art, turning the reality itself into Kiyooka's very own space, where the artist demonstrates—ecce homo—how to be the Heideggerian "man," who dwells poetically.

One of Kiyooka's most provocative and experimental collections, *StoneDGloves*,[104] which is the focus of this essay, helps to grasp the artist's view of human space in all its conflicting dimensions: the collection is too allegorical when it comes to the pictures of real physical objects, too condensed for randomly scattered things, too thingly for half-decomposed debris and garbage, and all too human for the deliberately dehumanized setting. Of course, the list of contradictions can go on endlessly. The point of my interpretation is to add one more controversy: Kiyooka seeks to bring up his modernist melancholies of art, memory, landscape, body, and word through the lens of an essentially postmodernist camera, which paradoxically gathers in its focus dissemination, depersonalization, indifference, and forgetfulness.

Along the lines of this duality, *StoneDGloves* can be read as not only Kiyooka's dialogue with Heidegger's ecology and anthropology but also as a defiance of a few Heideggerian concepts, such as hand, equipment, fourfold, and memory. The result of this defiance is a palimpsestuous effect of the double script: the implied gathering and memory can only be seen through dissociation and mourning, and the living breath of word and truth—through writing and supplement. To put it figuratively, Heidegger in *StoneDGloves* is constantly obscured by Jacques Derrida. To use Derrida's notion of *archive* as an allegory of memory's contamination by technology, from his book *Mal d'Archive*, we can say—playing with the double meaning of the French "mal"—that in Kiyooka's palimpsests the human sensibility for gathering, or "archive fever," is visible only through the lens of the "evil" or "sickness" of the archive's technological work of memorization.

The first contextual appeal of *StoneDGloves* is in its originally unofficial, double-shadowy character. Scott Toguri McFarlane, in his powerful interpretation of *StoneDGloves*, informs how the collection came about:

> In 1969, the Canadian government invited Kiyooka to produce a sculpture for the Canadian pavilion at Expo 70 in Osaka, Japan. Expo 70 was the first World Exposition in Asia. Protracted in the spirit of post-war globalization, it was celebrated as a "meeting of East and West." ... Kiyooka arrived in Osaka while the pavilions were still being built. Amidst Expo 70's promise of a global community, however, his attention was diverted to the un-ravelling assemblages—the clusters of twigs, stones and litter—that formed, reformed, and disappeared like hoarfrost on the construction sites. He was especially struck by the incredible number of gloves discarded by workers on the grounds. When not installing his sculpture, *Abu Ben Adam's Vinyl Dream*, Kiyooka meandered the Expo site taking hundreds of photographs of the gloves as they turned to stone. Far from celebrating the future architecture of Expo 70, *StoneDGloves* traces the un-ravelling archeology of its foundation. (118–119)

StoneDGloves was first presented as a series of exhibitions throughout Canada as well as in Japan and France. For the work, 40 black and white photographs out of 51 were chosen by Kiyooka, some of which were overlaid with free verse A catalogue published by Coach House Press in 1970[105] was produced concurrently with the exhibition. In Canada, the collection was exhibited in 14 cities. Both *Transcanada Letters* and *Pacific Rim Letters* contain multiple references to *StoneDGloves*, which illustrates how immensely important this collection was for the author himself. Complaining about the errors in the catalogue, Kiyooka sees the omission of some of his verses as "the Fate of [his] SG even tho they never expected a happy ending," yet already in a year he reflects on the *StoneDGloves*' exhibition at Dalhousie University in Halifax as "the best entire show [he's] ever put together," and in his letter to Noel Lajoie, Kiyooka calls the collection his "G(Loves"

(*Transcanada Letters* 89, 239, 247). In April 1978, Kiyooka refers to *StoneDGloves* as to his "TESTAMENT," which he would like to "re-avow": "the kinks" of the first catalogue edition were still bothering him a great deal, but they seemed to be just a pretext, as he felt more "into 'transformations' of everything" and wanted to re-issue the collection "BRAND NEW. that is the matter (photos) and (pomes) but re-invented" (*Pacific Rim Letters* 93). Six years later, in 1984, Kiyooka laments that he has misplaced "(ah precious!) negatives" of *StoneDGloves* having wanted "to reprint them, for the sake of their Omen" (*Pacific Rim Letters* 248).

Arriving in Osaka as a Canadian sculptor, Kiyooka sought to undermine his official occupation — by the shadowy art of photography. "Astonisht," to use one of Kiyooka's favourite words, by the view of discarded worker gloves amidst construction waste, he took hundreds of pictures, transformed by the focus of his camera from photographs into photoglyphs, which grew to overshadow his sculpture, *Abu Ben Adam's Vinyl Dream*, as an alternative exposition, revealing that which has been concealed, erased, palimpsested, overwritten and disposed of. Reporting in 1972 from Halifax, Kiyooka says that "even today theres 1000s of pairs rotting away just under the surface of rubble-mountain" (*Transcanada Letters* 247).

To go "under the surface," to uncover the true story of things, is akin to Heidegger's strategy of *Destruktion*, called upon to dismantle the metaphysical meanings of such ontological concepts as time, logic, history, body, matter, etc. by means of digging into their cultural etymology in order to reveal calcified layers they have accumulated in Western thought. As though through the new script of the Expo buildings, the palimpsest, Kiyooka sees the underlying text under the official construction, thus turning — by dint of the evidence collected in *StoneDGloves* — the Expo's construction into the Heideggerian de-construction.

The uncanny effect, created by the collocations of discarded gloves, caught in the focus of Kiyooka's lens, lies in a series of doubles that present themselves with surrealistic suggestiveness of fragments — of things, bodies, and bodies as things. As the only available ambience, this seemingly postapocalyptic landscape creates a new, deconstructed ecological philosophy—in Kiyooka's words, "glove ecology" ("StoneDG-loves" 73), which projects its uncanniness-unhomeliness ("unhomely" as literal translation of the German *Unheimlich*, "uncanny") onto the poetic word. This word, operating in the realm of language, which, according to Heidegger, is our "house of Being" ("Letter on Humanism" 217), intensifies the discordant effect of the unhomeliness. The transient status of construction debris is reversed into a permanent site for Kiyooka's new poetic building, in which humans, paradoxically, should not feel at home. The resulting effect as though indirectly mocks Heidegger's idealized concept of "dwelling": "Poetic creation, which lets us dwell, is a kind of building" ("... Poetically Man Dwells ..." 213). Being not a real building for dwelling, the gloves are nevertheless metaphorically "stoned" to defy the conventional "stone" dwellings, such as houses, temples, and tombs (the association of the Canadian pavilion at Expo 70, a pyramid, with a tomb is suggested by McFarlane (133)). At the same time, Kiyooka's collection allegorically (and metonymically) reflects the inherent parody of the Expo pyramid: a building intended in its conventional form as a dwelling for millennia has a transient status of exposition, located outside of the Canadian context, with a temporary purpose in mind, displaced in the global village where one dwells everywhere and nowhere.

Kiyooka's unhomely "glove ecology" (etymologically, also Heideggerian, "oiko-logy" — "dwelling-saying," as Hanspeter Padrutt insists in his "Heidegger and Ecology" (18)), is both an anthropological ontology and a philosophy of art. To address the latter first, *StoneDGloves* plays along with and at the same time derides the Heideggerian metaphysics of the work of art. As in Heidegger's "The Origin of the Work of Art," in *StoneDGloves* the work of art brings things into the open, makes them emerge as phenomena. Nowhere does a work of art resemble more literally and vividly the Heideggerian strife between the earth and world, producing the effect of "concealment-unconcealment," as in *StoneDGloves*.

In contrast to the protuberant official constructions, gloves never rise above the ground, dirt, earth, thus epitomizing the Aristotelian *arche*, the beginning, the ground, from which everything arises and to which everything returns. As a permanent zero point, or *nothing*, ground signifies a defiant difference between itself and the prominent thingness of pyramids and other object-like or symbolic constructions. In the preface to his treatise "On the Essence of Ground," Heidegger captures this differentiating negativity of ground: "The nothing is the 'not' of beings, and is thus being, experienced from the perspective of beings" (97). *StoneDGloves* can be read as a revelation ("the poem reveals" is one of the poems' titles) that is aimed at approximating this humble yet eye-opening perspective:

> the thumb pointing
> toward the shadow the glove
> throws across the dirt
> the dirt under your fingernails
> hard-bitten evidence ("StoneDGloves" 65)

The genealogical kinship between the pointing thumb and the dirt, or the substance to which it points, is *grounded* in the "hard-bitten evidence" of the dirt under the thumb's fingernail. Kiyooka's ecology is thus utterly anti-metaphysical, suggesting ground, dirt, or the foundation upon which men build their temporary dwellings, as their real and ultimate dwelling:

> glove ecology
>
> ground in—
> —to ground (73).

The defiance of Kiyooka's *arche* here is the re-cycling materiality, of which humans are reminded by the obsessive association of gloves and hands: ground is inside the gloves ("ground in"), and the gloves turn into ground ("ground in—/—to ground"), by means of which ecology is boiled down to the recycling of the ground, or ground returning to itself. The personification of the gloves makes it easier for the readers and onlookers to associate themselves with the gloves and the glove perspective of being: "this is a poem / for cotton glove, sad, worn out" (64). In the next line the glove is called "he" who has a "hand," which, playing with the possessive form of "it," creates the uncanny effect of the animate-inanimate double:

> ⋯⋯⋯⋯⋯⋯ if you put your ear
> to its cupt hand you'll hear
> his echo re-echo through the poem
> like a naked hand—reaching
> out for its own shadow (64)

The double of the hand and its shadow becomes figuratively involved in the threefold platonic shadow hierarchy, in which the hand casts the glove as its shadow, which in turn—already as a "naked hand" itself —reaches "out for its own shadow." Another instance of the threefold, which seems to be Kiyooka's preferable way of structuring images, is suggested by the palimpsestuous poetics of *StoneDGloves*. In what appears to be an unofficial revision (dated as summer 1970) of the above poem/inscription, Kiyooka intensifies the personification effect and reveals the layered structure of his poetics:

> re-visions
>
> after (palimpsest
> ⸺⸺⸺⸺⸺⸺
>
>
> ——if you put your ear to
> his cuppt hand
>   you will hear his pain
>   re-echo thru the pome
>
>   like a naked hand reaching out
>   for its shadow (*Transcanada Letters* 74)

If the official *StoneDGloves* refers to "poem" and "glove" in the first couple of lines ("this is a poem / for cotton glove, sad, worn-out"), the re-vision supplants them with "palimpsest" (apparently, the poem above the glove), which now is the antecedent for "his" hand and pain. The palimpsestuous poetics are also discernible on the level of the object itself, whose epistemological alienation from the subject, the author or the onlooker, just strengthens the unhomely effect of the image:

> even)
> my hand knows nothing
> abt *the dirt*
>
> > glove lies
> > gently
> >   under (*Transcanada Letters* 74)

The glove overwritten by dirt overwritten by the picture comprises the threefold that is structurally similar to the picture overwritten by the poem/inscription overwritten by the revision, which together come down to their dialectical synthesis: the object overwritten by the picture overwritten by the text. Kiyooka's later reflections on the aesthetics of photography confirm this threefold thinking. Years after the shooting of the gloves in Osaka, in his 1985 letter to Wilfred and Sheila Watson, Kiyooka comments on the aesthetics of photography as palimpsest: regarding a different collection, he mentions "*an actual Text that ought to accompany / these colour prints,*" yet a *stanza* below he says,

> *there is an actual Text that automatically wrote itself*
> *into the colour print, in the very moment of its*
> *actual taking. embossed upon the very texture of the*
> *things portrayed: the colour print is their pal-*
> *impsest* (*Pacific Rim Letters* 307)

In other words, the very automatism of the reality's turning itself into text, layered due to the palimpsestuous poetics of overwriting, is akin to what Derrida implied by the notion of *writing*, with the ensuing concepts of supplement, trace, and cinder standing in close proximity to the suggested imagery of *StoneDGloves*.

In this meaning of the automatic textualization of reality, *writing* does not yet differ from Heidegger's understanding of language that "speaks": "In its essence, language is neither an expression nor an activity of man. Language speaks" (Heidegger, "Language" 194). One can "seek" either "the speaking of language in the poem" (194), as Heidegger does with respect to Georg Trakl's "A Winter Evening," or the speaking of the language of things on a photograph. In either case, language presents itself as something more profound than an individual discursive activity, as "man" only "speaks in that he responds to language" (207). This rather passive response of an artist to what is already implied in the language of things is reflected in one of Kiyooka's multiple comments on *StoneDGloves*:

> i see them as a graph of a eye/mind in movement—
> grabbin' up life-signs as I've come upon 'em.
> they are in that sense 'relevance' stumbled upon (*Transcanada
>   Letters* 69)

Something that one stumbles upon cannot be properly owned or taken responsibility for, as one takes responsibility for a spoken word. The responsibility of an artist is limited to the Heideggerian *response* to the language that belongs to no one. That is why "'Copyrights' like worn-out / gloves are obsolete" ("StoneDGloves" 92):

> the glove
> flat-out on the page
> or found under-
> foot—the glove you said
> you found ...

all gloves
scratched in real dirt
fall from the lips
of fools—into the poem
'nobody' owns (77)

The linguistic nature of the glove collocations, stumbled upon by the artist, is reasserted by Kiyooka's equating of the gloves with words. In this conflated reality, objects, such as "1 pair of cotton gloves" or "1 pair of ghostly boots," can be found "among a heap of abandoned words" (72). "Found" is the word that Kiyooka himself uses with regard to both the photos and the poems in his "*postscript*" to the collection:

40 photo/graphs
and a brace of small poems:
from hundreds 'found'
on-site at Expo '70 (91)

To find and capture objects in their assemblages by way of the artist's camera is, as Heidegger says, stilling them. What Heidegger calls "dif-ference" is the dimension in which *things* appear as things in their intimacy, rather than in fusion with *world*—the dimension that allows things, thereby exalted into their own ontology, *to thing* themselves into the world: "The dif-ference stills the thing, as a thing, into the world" (Heidegger, "Language" 204). Reflected in *StoneDGloves*, this stillness is stressed several times as a condition of the very appearance of things as perceptible phenomena. Half-rotten or submerged in dirt, gloves are not an obtrusive object that imposes itself upon the eye. The language of things speaks only in the realm of "dif-ference," needed to still them into the world, and this "dif-ference" is brought about by the focus of the camera. Only thus *focused*, can the eye *listen* and *hear* the language of things: "Man speaks in that he responds to language. This responding is a hearing. It hears because it listens to the command of stillness" (Heidegger, "Language" 207). In Kiyooka's own metaphorical description, the artist's eye equals the camera's shutter, and the

captured thing, or image, *things* itself into the world due to the power
of the artist's imagination:

> PHOTOGRAPHY: as
> when the eye (shutter) opens
> and closes on each frame of a succession
> of images/ imaginings (*Transcanada Letters* 75)

In order to hear the language of things, that is, to maintain what Heidegger calls "dif-ference," Kiyooka makes sure to underscore the stillness
in the captured objects as well as in the ekphrastic poems: "the glove
falls down on the ground / in absolute silence" and "the words rise out of
the ground / absolutely silent ..." ("StoneDGloves" 75, 82). Heidegger
underlines that stillness is not merely the lack of sound—it is also mo-
tionlessness, a complete rest of things ("Language" 204), which is
echoed in the very stonedness of the *StoneDGloves*.

> (al-
> most
>   its own
> monument
> all
> most
>   s t o n e (85)

As an artist whose occupation is *to thing things into world*, Kiyooka
offers an interesting account of the conditions for both shaping things
through fabrication and exhibiting sculptures for aesthetic apprehension:

> ... the s-i-l-e-n-c-e at the core of
> our hapless desires that gives us the itch to
> shape things
> ...

s c u l p t u r e:
some thing shaped, placed
out there. together
with sky ground and air,
plus silence their
awesome partner ... (*Transcanada Letters* 299)

Silence as part of language's speaking is always oxymoronic, as is
Heidegger's assertion that "*language speaks as the peal of stillness,*" and
because man "is given to speech" rather than speaking himself, "the
peal of stillness is not anything human" ("Language" 205). Similarly, in
StoneDGloves, the language of things is supposed, oxymoronically, to
shout its stillness:

if—
the glove wont talk
    try stone. if
the stone wont—

    don't!
    shout!
            / stone!
            / glove! ("StoneDGloves" 83)

Kiyooka's ekphrasis betrays the artist's necessity always to stay attuned
to the generative aspect of his art because the emergence of things and
world and the emergence of the work of art are codependent: gloves as
waste aspire to the legitimacy of being the object of photography only
in photography that is the work of art, and, likewise, the work of art
qualifies for such and attains its aesthetic value only under the prem-
ises that the object is a *thing*.

    This originary element of art in Kiyooka is more acutely protuber-
ant than in Heidegger, although both conceptualize art as emerging
out of its basic material—a form rising from the earth. Heidegger illustrates "the happening of truth in the work of art" ("The Origin of the

Work of Art" 167) by way of two examples: a Greek temple at Paestum and *A Pair of Shoes* (1885) by Vincent van Gogh. In Heidegger's vision, the Greek temple is a special locus of energy, where "the world worlds," making all things appear out of the strife between concealment, the *earth*, and unconcealment, *physis*:

> The Greeks early called this emerging and rising in itself and in all things *physis*. It illuminates that on which and in which man bases his dwelling. We call this ground the *earth*. What this word says is not to be associated with the idea of mass of matter deposited somewhere, or with the merely astronomical idea of a planet. Earth is that whence the arising brings back and shelters everything that arises as such. In the things that arise, earth occurs essentially as the sheltering agent. (168)

This dialectics of arising things, that is, gloves, but also things suggested or represented by gloves and their return to dirt, seems to be the poetical essence of Kiyooka's "glove ecology" as the main technical device for conjuring up images of something that is always suspended in an interstitial space between *thing* and *no(-)thing*. The testimony and constant possibility of those things returning back from the state of appearance to the *earth* qua their "sheltering agent" is prescribed by the very subject of the images and fortified by the poetic inscriptions:

> the back of
> the hand invites
> the earth
>
> homely earth
> hearth
> haven / home ("StoneDGloves" 80)

The photographs themselves can thus be seen as bearing the quality of Heidegger's notion of "clearing," which in "The Origin of the Work of Art" is understood as "an open place" (178), "the openness of concealing and unconcealing, and is bound to the strife of 'world' and 'earth'" (Figal 40). Heidegger's later essay "The End of Philosophy and the Task of Thinking" confirms the "clearing's" interstitial status as the open space that invites the play of concealment and unconcealment: "It means... the place of stillness that gathers in itself what first grants unconcealment" (445). This invocation of "stillness," used in "Language," makes it also possible to think about "clearing" in terms of "dif-ference," the dimension that "stills the thing, as thing, into the world" ("Language" 204). Sharing this condition of stillness with Kiyooka's "photoglyphs," the notion of clearing may thus help to understand the *StoneDGloves*' aesthetics as the field of the taking place of *physis*, where the very appearance of things is posited as their essence.

With all their similarities in aesthetic philosophy, Kiyooka's palimpsests and Heidegger's work of art strike as incomparable when we place together the Greek temple and construction waste. This focus on the object is, of course, what makes the difference. Magnificent buildings, such as temples, are built with the use of worker gloves (hands), but, while the gloves are discarded, only the temple is positioned as a work of art. To disclose what lies beneath, in shadow, submerged in the dirt of insignificance is an act of aesthetic rebellion. Since, as we have established, *StoneDGloves* is the field of *physis*, where things appear in their essence-as-appearing, their *thingness*, the *world* that they laboriously bring about should be their own, full-fledged, independent world, which, naturally, as an aesthetic object can be made comprehensible only in relation to what is human. In this world of Kiyooka's palimpsests, there are landscapes, days and nights, the breath of life and tombstones, trees and bones. There is also a temple, although a Christian, not the old Greek one:

> trinity
> glove
> n
> gloveonglove (81)

An evocation of the Christmas tree immediately follows the palimpsest of the Trinity temple:

of children dancing 'round
    the Tree with
  one white glove nailed
    to its trunk (82)

Kiyooka's suggestion of the tree's bond with the ground, which makes "words rise out of the ground" and "fall" "into the mouths" of the children, dancing around "the Tree," is similar to Trakl's image of "the tree of graces," which, in Heidegger's interpretation, "call[s] the world-four-fold" "and thus call[s] world to the things" ("Language" 199): "Golden blooms the tree of graces / Drawing up the earth's cool dew" (198). Heidegger traces the fourfold of the sky and the earth and of the mortals and the divinities in several of his exegeses of various works of art, but the Trakl poem and the description of the Greek temple seem particularly suggestive of the *StoneDGloves* imagery. Against the backdrop of the night sky, Trakl-Heidegger's snowfall is mimicked by Kiyooka's glovefall: "The snowfall brings men under the sky that is darkening into night" (Heidegger, "Language" 197), and

  the glove falls
  down on the ground

  in absolute
  silence ...

  absolutely
  silent the sky enters

  the tip of
  the third finger ...

  as the moon
  rides the incoming tide ("StoneDGloves" 75)

The falling and fallen glove, viewed against the dirt-and-concrete background, is elevated in its environmental suggestiveness to Heidegger's Greek temple:

> ... the building rests on the rocky ground. This resting of the
> work draws up out of the rock the obscurity of that rock's bulky
> yet spontaneous support ... The luster and gleam of the stone,
> though itself apparently glowing only by the grace of the sun,
> first brings to radiance the light of the day, the breadth of the
> sky, the darkness of the night. The temple's firm towering makes
> visible the invisible space of air. ("The Origin of the Work of
> Art" 167–168)

A similar *thinging* of the fourfold evoked by the debased objects in
Kiyooka's photoglyphs questions the metaphysical magnitude of Heidegger's work of art, whose vocation, *physis*, or the emergence of
things as their essence, is often equated in the works of Heidegger with
aletheia, or truth.

Another of Heidegger's examples of the originary quality of the
work of art is to be found in *A Pair of Shoes*, painted by Vincent van
Gogh in 1885 (Van Gogh). These peasant shoes in Van Gogh's painting
present what Heidegger calls "equipment"—the term that places them
in close vicinity to Kiyooka's worker gloves. In Heidegger's view, Van
Gogh's "speaking" painting transfers us to the very ontological essence
of peasant boots, to its "equipmental quality":

> The equipmental being of the equipment consists indeed in its
> usefulness ... By virtue of this reliability the peasant woman is
> made privy to the silent call of the earth; by virtue of the reliability
> of the equipment she is sure of her world. World and earth exist
> for her ... only thus—in the equipment ("The Origin of the
> Work of Art" 160–161).

Having developed an elaborate story of the peasant woman based on
the pair of shoes, Heidegger claims that such a vision springs not from
"the observation of the actual use of shoes" but from the mere "near-
ness" of the work of art: "Van Gogh's painting is the disclosure of what
the equipment, the pair of peasant shoes, *is* in truth. This being emerges

into the unconcealment of its Being. The Greeks called the unconcealment of beings *aletheia*" (161).

Looking at the objects captured by Kiyooka's camera in *StoneDG-loves*, one may wonder: what kind of "truth" does the collection unravel behind those pieces of "equipment"? Also, recalling the vivid
description of the world of the peasant woman, who "is made privy to
the silent call of the earth" by dint of her "equipment," we may ask,
what kind of a world can be ascribed to those unnamed and invisible
workers who dropped their worn-out gloves in Osaka? The aesthetic
magnificence and ontological persistence of the shoes are warranted
by their reliability and usefulness, while Kiyooka's gloves are no longer
reliable or useful; they are disposed of, discarded equipment that have
forever lost their "equipmental being." Rather than taking part in the
creation of the human home of being, a space where humans can au-
thentically "dwell," the gloves as equipment serve as a constant sign of
displacement and homelessness.

Even the footwear in Walker Evans' *Floyd Burroughs' Work Shoes*
(1936) in its earthly, dusty backdrop and shabbiness, more closely resembling Kiyooka's glove assemblages than Van Gogh's peasant shoes,
does not strike with such a devastating alienation as those in Kiyooka's
StoneDGloves, regardless of being a part of the imagery of the Great
Depression. The shoes belong to Floyd Burroughs, they look thread-
bare yet reliable, and they are useful and meaningful. The anti-equip-
mental, in the Heideggerian sense, and rather existential, quality of
Kiyooka's stoned gloves is echoed in his other photo collection, which
shares its subject with both Van Gogh's *A Pair of Shoes* and Evans'
Floyd Burroughs' Work Shoes. In his letter to Sheila Watson, Kiyooka
noteworthily called this collection "the stoned footwear photos":

. . . . i
wish I had had the time to pair 'em with the stoned
gloves—dont black and write images (even—) of what
we encase our hands and feet in deserve each other—
as they slowly become the very dirt, imprint'd. (*Transcanada
Letters* 287)

This idea of imprint, appearing first in *StoneDGloves* in an ekphrastic inscription as "hand's shadow / foot's print," which are "intricately- / claspt" ("StoneDGloves" 79), falls back to what seems to be the real subject of those images—the two nether components of the Heideggerian fourfold, the mortals and the earth.

Human space, according to Heidegger, is a meaningful environment organized around things that are "ready-to-hand." The uncanniness of Kiyooka's worker gloves lies not so much in their alienated unreadiness-to-hand as in their doubleness-to-hand: being once equipment that was closest to hand and a unified whole with it, the gloves are now discarded doubles of the hand. Having lost their ability to co-create the world as useful equipment and things that are ready-to-hand, those shadows and doppelgangers of human extremities are full of ambiguity characteristic of Jean Baudrillard's notion of "remainder": "the shadow ... is a remainder par excellence, something that can 'fall' from the body ... But they are also 'metaphors' of the soul, of breath, of Being, of essence, of what proudly gives meaning to the subject. Without an image or without a shadow, the body becomes a transparent nothing; it is itself nothing but a remainder" (*Simulacra and Simulation*).

In this view, it is possible to assume that Kiyooka's gloves are called upon to preserve a sense of human hand. As hand's *shadow*—the appellation, repeated in the poetical part of *StoneDGloves* not once—gloves appeal to our apprehension of hands by dint of the ruse of estrangement, or defamiliarization. In one of his letters, Kiyooka claims that his *StoneDGloves* "have already / made a host of people take a hard look at even / their own hands" (*Transcanada Letters* 82). Two years prior to the publication of *StoneDGloves*, Heidegger, in his book *What Is Called Thinking?* had already attempted to defamiliarize the human hand as a bodily organ and present it as an organ of thinking. He argues that "the hand's essence can never be determined, or explained, by its being an organ that can grasp ... Only a being who can speak, that is, think, can have hands and can handily achieve works of handicraft" ("What Calls for Thinking?" 380). If we were to read Kiyooka's palimpsests as the realm of Heideggerian "dif-rerence," which stills things into world and where *"language speaks as the peal of stillness"*

("Language" 205), then following Heidegger's revelation would be, and to some extent really is, an insightful interpretation of *StoneDGloves*: "the hand's gestures run everywhere through language, in their most perfect purity precisely when man speaks by being silent" ("What Calls for Thinking?" 381). However, there is no meaningful "handicraft" in *StoneDGloves* to which the gloves as allegories of hands would point, and the "purity" of hand's gestures is always obscured by dirt and by the metamorphic suggestiveness of the gloves' shapes. Trapped in the limbo of concealment-unconcealment, or emerging-submerging, the gloves in Kiyooka's photographs never represent hands in their full Heideggerian glory—they are a permanent subject of metamorphosis, never a thing but rather

> all
> most
>
> a
> thing
>
> some
> thing ("StoneDGloves" 67)

The remainder of hand that gloves contain is suggested by the remainder of the gloves themselves, bearing likeness to "a naked hand—reaching /out for its own shadow" (64). This reaching for shadow is one of the representative "gestures" of Kiyooka's stoned gloves: being stoned and discarded as equipment, those gloves as allegories of hands lack the dexterity necessary for Heidegger's handicraft of thinking; they are ghosts reaching out for their unattainable bodies and as such are tragically split. One of the glove pictures, where the object shows disintegration to the degree of unrecognizability, is accompanied by a concrete poem (genre that is not rare in the collection), "glove's dream," which presents a visual pattern of disintegration, punctuated by the reiteration of the word "hands" with a centred yet barely recognizable against the predominant background appeal: "hold: held: help" (84).

Hands, evoked by such images, both on photos and in concrete verses, are only haunted by the spirit of the Heideggerian hand's glory but are not able to live up to the metaphysical marker of man as a being that is ontologically different from other species. As Derrida puts it, "It is precisely the play of presence and absence, the opening of this play that no metaphysical or ontological concept can comprehend" (*Of Grammatology* 244). The proliferation of hand's spectres in the variability of gloves and in the play of presence and absence mocks the integrity of the Heideggerian man, whom Derrida in "Geschlecht *II*" calls "the monster with a single hand": "when Heidegger writes: 'Man "has" no hands, but the hand occupies, in order to have in hand, man's essence' ... it concerns the difference between the plural and the singular ... What comes to man through logos or speech can be only one single hand. Hands, that is already or still the organic or technical dissipation" (182). Kiyooka's glove/hand, therefore, already qualified as Baudrillard's "remainder," can also be interpreted, by extension, with Derrida's notion of "supplementarity" (for example, education as a supplement of mother/nature in Rousseau)—something that in metaphysical tradition "constitutes the property of man: speech, society, passion, etc." (*Of Grammatology* 244) yet is marginalized by that tradition as privative, nonexistent.

Hand as man's essence in Heidegger ("What Calls for Thinking?" 380–81) is always opposed to hands as bodily organs or prehensile extremities because the latter represent "technology"—something that contaminates the purity of speech, memory, Being, etc. and that for Derrida is epitomized in the most characteristic "supplement" of Western metaphysical tradition—in *writing*. That Kiyooka's *StoneDGloves* represents writing and *is* writing as such is clear from the very palimpsestuous poetics of its visual and verbal appearance; it just consists of supplements, like the glove on one of the first photos in the collection that covers dirt and concrete debris and faces the viewer with hand's "supplement," palm, also covered, in its turn, by the pun inscription: "palimpsest / palm poem" (63). Moreover, the *writing* quality of *StoneDGloves* is also indicative of a particular form of memory, which, due to its "technological" tools such as monuments and material inscriptions (the glove is "its own monument," reads one of the palimpsests (85)), represents what Heidegger calls memorization (*hypomnesis*), as opposed to living memory (*mnesis*), not contaminated by "the art of writing" (Derrida, *Memoirs: For Paul de Man* 107). The introduction of the stoned gloves as their own monuments, with their characteristic technological attributes such as memorization, (over)writing, inscription, reiteration, and fragmentariness, dismantles the purity of the Heideggerian place of clearing, where the truth of Being is gathered together by the gravitational forces of the fourfold.

Heidegger's man, as Derrida points out, "*calls himself* man only by drawing limits excluding his other from the play of supplementarity ... The approach to these limits is at once feared as a threat of death" (*Of Grammatology* 244). To Heidegger's purity of hand, memory, thinking, and Being, devoid of any spectral traces or supplements, Derrida juxtaposes the work of mourning, which is always inhabited by writing, or technology, threatening to substitute death for the living essence; and so does Kiyooka in *StoneDGloves*, where the interchangeable pair "breath"/"death," playing with the duality of presence and absence, is one of the leading motifs:

> Deeper
> than death
> the breadth
> of breath (78)

> after that death 'breath'
> breaks into s-i-l-e-n-c-e—("StoneDGloves" 85)

The whole collection reads as hardly anything short of eulogy with a photographic report from the burial ground: "words continue on long / after the burial of the last glove" (85). This ground is haunted by the spectral appearances and disappearances of gloves and words, which bury and overwrite each other:

> if out of the air—
> a piece of cloth falls into your hands
> wipe your eyes with it
>
> if out of the ground suddenly—
> a pair of gloves suddenly appear on your hands
> use them to bury these words
>
> then ask your breath 'where' words come from
> where StoneDGloves go (62)

In this metamorphic dialectics, mourning works through mutually reversed directions: the living breath of words and tears mourn the stoned gloves, which, in their turn, may fall from the air as pieces of cloth to wipe the tears or appear from under the ground to bury the words of mourning.

In 1969, the same year when Kiyooka was preparing his sculpture for Expo 70, Heidegger wrote an essay "Art and Space," which he etched onto lithographic stone to be printed together with collages by the sculptor Eduardo Chillida. If for Heidegger sculptures open space and "gather in," for Kiyooka the reverse might be true. It is not the official sculpture but the remainder, the lithographic stone of *StoneDGloves* that becomes the site of unconcealment.

As McFarlane testifies, the designer of the Canadian pyramid of mirrors "Erickson-Massey repeatedly emphasized the pavilion's ability to *reflect* the constantly changing sky—under which lies the whole world" (132). Thus, as such, the Canadian pyramid at the Expo 70 seems to manifest an ideal Hedeggerian thing, which in the fourfold gathers together the earth and the sky, the mortals and the divinities. However, the fact that Kiyooka stays with the shadow and the remainder, with the stoned gloves rather than with the sculpture, points to the aesthetics and the ontology of space alternative to that of Heidegger.

As totally inhuman space, devoid of all essence, the photographed construction site suddenly appears as a site of liberation, a potentiality of new space. The discarded gloves become an undisposable remainder of Expo 70, the Expo's shadowy double, and, to some extent, and following Baudrillard's figurative description, its "soul." Contrary to the overt symbolism of the pyramid, mourning that is at work in *StoneDGloves*, with its concurrent effects of technology—both of the camera and of the palimpsestuous writing—as well as with the play of presence and absence, of hand and its double, of remainder and supplement, is consistent with the rhetorical figure of allegory. According to Paul de Man, allegory "designates primarily a distance in relation to its own origin, and, renouncing the nostalgia and the desire to coincide ... establishes its language in the void of this temporal difference" (207). Kiyooka's "allegories" defy the Expo qua a "global intellectual project" (McFarlane 132), as Heidegger's "symbolic ... self-mystification that conceals death itself beneath the joy of homecoming" (Latimer 184). If, as Roy Miki states, "it is the aura of the 'bereft' that becomes a constituting moment of liberation in *StoneDGloves*" (315), then it may as well be liberation from the grand narratives and metaphors of Modernism, including the expressive quality of its painting.

Kiyooka's palimpsests of photos and inscriptions embody what Linda Hutcheon calls "photographic 'fringe' constructions," which "combine the visual and the verbal" and represent "the typically postmodern border tension between inscription and subversion, construction and deconstruction—within the art itself" (118–119). The images of waste, which can proliferate endlessly, point to something beyond their fortuitous associations—to the alternative of expressivity, to copies without the original, or simulacra. It is not a coincidence that Frederic Jameson notes the preponderance of photography over painting in postmodernism (9), and, as Miki testifies, it was the year when "the gloves fell that marks the beginning of the period when writing and photography, no long[er] painting, assume centrality" (316) for Kiyooka. It was a change of aesthetic paradigm, designating the self-deception and the lack of truth in pyramids, sculptures, or peasant boots as expressive symbols that have lost their subject. Being snapped from reality rather than purposefully created, the associative images that the poet reads into the photographs undermine the modernist hermeneutics, which always looks for a bigger psychological truth behind a painting as the individual expression of the artist. *StoneDGloves* may very well fit into Hutcheon's description of postmodern photography, which "interrogates and problematizes, leaving the viewer no comfortable viewing position. It upsets learned notions of the relations between text/image, non-art/art, theory/practice" (119).

Without refuting Heidegger's elevated "poetically man dwells," Kiyooka in his collection makes a point that such purified, metaphysical human dwelling is haunted by the spectres of homelessness and invites the viewer and the reader to join him in mourning—to overcome their bedazzling hubris and to peep into the ground and under the pyramid, where stoned gloves, as their own monuments, are buried in absolute silence.

Works Cited

Baudrillard, Jean. *Simulacra and Simulation*. University of Michigan Press, 1994. http://mysite.du.edu/~tweaver2/ artd2355/schedule/baud_sim.pdf.

De Man, Paul. "The Rhetoric of Temporality." *Blindness and Insight: Essays in the Rhetoric of Contemporary Criticism*. 2nd ed., revised. Introduction by Wald Godzich. U of Minnesota P, 1983, pp. 187–228.

Derrida, Jacques. *Archive Fever: A Freudian Impression*. U of Chicago P, 1995.

----. "Geschlecht II: Heidegger's Hand." Translated by John P. Leavey, Jr. *Deconstruction and Philosophy: Texts of Jacques Derrida*. Edited by John Sallis, U of Chicago P, 1987, pp. 161–196.

----. *Mémoirs: For Paul de Man*. Translated by Cecile Lindsay, Jonathan Culler and Eduardo Cadava. Columbia UP, 1986.

----. *Of Grammatology*. 1976. Corrected edition. Translated by Gayatri Chakravorty Spivak. The Johns Hopkins UP, 1997.

Evans, Walker. *Floyd Burroughs' Work Shoes*. 1936, The Metropolitan Museum of Art, New York, and Dome: MIT Libraries, https://dome. mit.edu/handle/1721.3/25280.

Figal, Günter. "Phenomenology: Heidegger after Husserl and the Greeks." *Martin Heidegger: Key Concepts*. Edited by Bret W. Davis. Acumen, 2010, pp. 33–43.

Heidegger, Martin. "Bulding Dwelling Thinking." Krell, pp. 343–364.

----. "Language." Hofstadter, pp. 185–208.

----. "Letter on Humanism." Krell, pp. 213–66.

----. "On the Essence of Ground." Translated by William McNeill. Pathmarks. Edited by William McNeill. Cambridge UP, 1998, pp. 97–135.

----. "... Poetically Man Dwells ..." Hofstadter, pp. 209–27.

----. "The End of Philosophy and the Task of Thinking." Krell, pp. 427–49.

----. The Fundamental Concepts of Metaphysics: World, Finitude, Solitude. Translated by William McNeill and Nickolas Walker. Indiana UP, 1995.

----. "The Origin of the Work of Art." Krell, pp. 139–212.

----. "What Calls for Thinking?" Krell, pp. 365–92.

Hofstadter, Albert, translator. Poetry, Language, Thought. By Martin Heidegger, Harper Perennial, 2001.

Hutcheon, Linda. The Politics of Postmodernism. Routledge, 1989.

Jameson, Frederic. Postmodernism, Or, The Cultural Logic of Late Capitalism. 1991. Duke UP, 2001.

Kiyooka, Roy K. "Notes Toward a Book of Photoglyphs." The Capilano Review, 1990, pp. 76–94.

----. Pacific Rim Letters. Edited and with an afterword by Smaro Kamboureli. Newest Press, 2005.

----. "StoneDGloves." Pacific Windows: Collected Poems of Roy K. Kiyooka. Edited by Roy Miki. Talonbooks, 1997, pp. 57–92.

----. Transcanada Letters. Edited by Smaro Kamboureli, afterword by Glen Lowry. Newest Press, 2005.

Krell, David F., editor. Basic Writings. By Martin Heidegger, Harper Perennial, 2008.

Latimer, Dan. Contemporary Critical Theory. Harcourt Brace Jovanovich, 1989.

McFarlane, Scott Toguri. "Un-Ravelling StoneDGloves and the Haunt of the Hibakusha." All Amazed for Roy Kiyooka. Edited by John O'Brian, Naomi Sawada, and Scott Watson. Arsenal Pulp Press, Morris and Helen Belkin Art Gallery, Collapse, 2002, pp. 117–49.

Miki, Roy. "Afterword: Coruscations, Plangencies, and the Syllibant: After Words to Roy Kiyooka's Pacific Windows." In Pacific Windows by Roy K. Kiyooka. Pp. 301–20.

Padrutt, Hanspeter. "Heidegger and Ecology." *Heidegger and the Earth: Essays in Environmental Philosophy*, edited by Ladelle McWhorter and Gail Stenstad. 2nd ed. U of Toronto P, 2009. Pp. 17–44.

Van Gogh, Vincent. *A Pair of Shoes*. 1885, Van Gogh Museum, Amsterdam, and National Gallery of Art, Washington, D. C., www.nga.gov/exhibitions/gogh/html/rotate/009.htm.

Revisionings:
Form and History in Roy Kiyooka's
"the 4th avenue poems"

Jason Wiens

I n issue 11 (1969) of George Bowering's long poem magazine
Imago, Roy Kiyooka published "The 4th Avenue Poems,"
a series of sixteen poems with a dedication that reads: "for John, &
Jos., more than friends." These names refer respectively to John Newlove and the artist Marken Joslin, with whom Kiyooka had been living
earlier that decade in the Kitsilano area of Vancouver. This intimate
second person address continues throughout the serial poem, both
through explicit dedications of specific poems (i.e. the dedication to
'10': "for Jos, somewhere, in the world") and by frequent turns to an
epistolary or journal form, as we see in the second and eighth poems
of the sequence:

> Dear John: I threw out all your dirty socks
> foul tin cans and lousy pulp. You left a month ago ...
> your women even the fat one doesnt come knocking.
> the mice have gone after other crumbs. John
> you still inhabit the other room, I can hear you
> mumbling obscene syllables, strung on a Grave rosary (Kiyooka
>   1969, 4)

. . . .

Jos has left.
John too. Others
before them
left by the back door.
I am still here
tied, to what they
left behind. What I have made
I will also leave
when that time comes (10)

"What I have made / I will also leave": "The 4th Avenue Poems" can be read as poetic leavings produced in a particular historical time and place. Addressed as they are to departed friends, the poems offer Kiyooka's "farewell to Vancouver," as Roy Miki notes, "before moving to Montreal where he would teach (1965–69) in the Fine Arts Department at Sir George Williams University" (Miki 1997, 308). Kiyooka's note to the poems informs us that the sequence was written "winter 64 / spring 65" and "revised in Montreal winter 68" (Kiyooka 1969, 18). The poems would again be revised by Kiyooka in the 1990s as he was preparing, in collaboration with Miki, to publish his collected poems under the title *Pacific Windows*. Kiyooka would unfortunately and unexpectedly pass away[106] before the editorial and revisionary process was completed, leaving Miki, as was the case with many of the other texts collected in *Pacific Windows*, with a 'computer version' from which to work. The collection was published, with capitalization removed from the title, as the second sequence in *Pacific Windows*: between *Kyoto Airs* (Periwinkle, 1964) and *Nevertheless These Eyes* (Coach House, 1967). Even though "the 4th avenue poems" were not published until 1969, this sequencing in *Pacific Windows* recognizes the earlier stages of their composition. Coming from a poet working out of a "desire to be more attentive to the mundane particulars of daily life," for whom the "practice of revision inevitably became a re/vision in which a new text was produced" (Miki 1997, 302), the re/visions between the *Imago* version and the *Pacific Windows* version tell us much about shifts in avant-garde poetic practices from the late

60s to the early 90s. Archival investigations in the Roy Kiyooka *Fonds* held at Simon Fraser University's Special Collections, however, reveal a proliferation of versions of the poems, or textual witnesses, further destabilizing the text. These textual witnesses include typescript drafts, audio recordings, Kiyooka's artwork, digital files, and even a poem by a different poet. I want here to read through this unstable textual proliferation, understanding that, as D.F. McKenzie puts it, "[t]he ostensible unity of any one 'contained' text—be it in the shape of a manuscript, book, map, film, or computer-stored file—is an illusion. As a language, its forms and meaning derive from other texts; and as we listen to, look at, or read it, at the very same time we re-write it" (McKenzie 60).

A close examination of these various iterations of "the 4th avenue poems" provokes questions about reading poetry as a formal textualization or documentation of history, and the problems posed to scholarly interventions and re-readings of this textualization. As Jerome McGann has observed, "Literary documents bear within themselves the evidence of their own making ... and those evidentiary marks solicit an interpretation of their meaning and significance. Historical patterns are literalized in the interpretation of a transmission history's documentary record" (McGann 84). In comparing the different versions of the poems, in light of the significant historical gap between the mid-1960s and early-1990s, we are essentially considering a comparative social history of forms. The historical knowledge the poems transmit is embedded in the social text of these forms. I read the different versions of "the 4th avenue poems" as indexing the shifts in poetic practices in the west coast poetry scene from the 1960s to the 1990s, from the spontaneity of a poetics reflective of the poets included in Donald Allen's 1960 anthology *The New American Poetry*, to the more disjunctive poetics associated with Language Poetry. We need to consider the implications of formally revising poems, which seemed written to address not just "the mundane particulars of daily life," but also Kiyooka's immediate responses to major historical events such as the 1964 Alaska earthquake or the assassination of U.S. President John F. Kennedy. If history is inscribed into the poem through its formal strategies, how is history differently inscribed when those strategies change? If "the 4th avenue poems" are poetic responses to a particular place and time, and thus consistent with the emphasis on the local circulating in Vancouver poetry at the time (most famously around *Tish*), how might the local details—or what Louis Zukofsky called "historic and contemporary particulars" (Zukofsky 12)—be rendered differently when the formal strategies of their rendering change?

As mentioned, the documentary archive of these poems extends beyond the two publication venues of *Imago* and *Pacific Windows*. Examination in the Kiyooka *Fonds* reveals inchoate versions of "the 4th avenue poems" in multiple media, including audio. On March 26, 1963, Kiyooka read with John Newlove in Vancouver at the "2nd Annual Poetry Session." In prefatory remarks to one suite of poems, Kiyooka comments, "About four months ago I wrote several poems about this little room that I [unclear] in. Mr. Newlove lived in this room before I did. It has pink walls. I want to read you three little poems, that I call 'Pink Room Poems.'" The first of these "Pink Room Poems" he read was an early manifestation of what would become the third poem of "the 4th avenue poems." Here is my transcription of what Kiyooka read, from a reel-to-reel recording of the event held in the Roy Kiyooka *Fonds*:

fourteen nails
with nothing on them cast
thin shadows on the pink walls
bent   this way
and that
into the wall   bruised
from the missing blow
no point wondering
who hung what from which nail
even nails are useless
unless used
to look up without necessity
to see even one bent nail
is to hang a coat from it

My transcription here of course introduces the crucial formal element of line breaks, an editorial intervention that moves beyond transcription and into both creation and interpretation. In deciding where to place the line breaks, I take into consideration two main factors: Kiyooka's breath pauses on the recording, and the line breaks he employs in a later version of the poem. On top of this, my own aesthetic preferences inform these decisions. This reminds us of the fraught relationship between the audio and print archive, particularly in the kind of genetic exercise I am engaged in here.[107]

In "the 4ᵗʰ avenue poems" version published in *Imago*, the poem becomes revised and winnowed down to this:

> thirteen nails,
> bent this way and that in-
> to the wall
> cast thin shadows
>
> no comfort knowing who
> hung what from which nail,
> even nails are useless
> unless used (Kiyooka 1969, 5)

The most immediately recognizable substantive variant from the audio recording to this published version would be the shift from "fourteen" to "thirteen" nails—suggesting numerous possibilities: that Kiyooka miscounted, that a nail was removed during the revision process, or that he decided that "thirteen" somehow worked better—the "unlucky" number being more suited to the somewhat sombre tone of the poem, for example. Kiyooka's breaking of the word "into" and enjambing it between the second and third lines could be read as a formal extension of content: that is, the breaking of the word "into" into its component parts seems to more accurately depict the nails being driven into the wall —what Charles Olson might have called "the kinetics of the thing" (Olson 387). The closing lines of the poem are also interesting, not only in the alliterative and assonantial sound patterns, but in the paragrammatic play with "useless / unless used." All of this is to say that, far from the spontaneous and unmediated representation that the poem might appear or aspire to be, it is rather a carefully constructed aesthetic object.

The poem would undergo further revision before it appeared in *Pacific Windows*:

> bent this way and that
> thirteen nails
> throw thin shadows on
> the wall
>
> no comfort knowing
> who hung what from which nail
> even nails are useless
> unless they're used (Kiyooka 1997, 25)

To me, this is a weaker version of the poem, as the revisions eliminate or attenuate the two formal features of the poem I just discussed. In suggesting that the revision process is not always in the direction of improvement, I realize that "improvement" carries evaluative freight. But the editing process—and indeed the compositional process itself—is a fundamentally evaluative one, and one of the goals of a genetic criticism is to map out the different possibilities considered in various drafts of a text, and, through juxtaposition, invite a consideration of their implications. As Daniel Ferrer puts it, "The earlier documents, the more inchoate traces, are as interesting as the ultimate corrections; or rather, they are interesting *in relation* to the late variants, the 'final' text and all the intermediary stages, because they mark the course of the genetic sequence" (Ferrer 49). For Ferrer, a genetic approach is like psychoanalysis, because it "rests on the assumption that it is impossible fully to understand the present state of an utterance without knowing the previous states it has gone through" (49). We can better understand what a poem is doing by comparing it to versions of it doing something else.

The Roy Kiyooka *Fonds* present an interesting case study of Ferrer's theory. Although there does not appear to be any extant collection of drafts of "the 4th avenue poems" in the *Fonds* (certainly there is nothing listed in any of the finding aids), a perusal of "Packet 2" — a collection of what appear to be miscellaneous drafts — does turn up early versions of the 11th poem in the series, a kind of homage to Walt Whitman. The "original order" — more on this below — of the drafts in "Packet 2" suggests the following sequence of development:

> Leaves of Grass grow in
> the crackt pavement of the parking lot where
> my comely daughter sings
>
> these words lie under her tiny feet
> in the back alleys the tenements and temples
>
> these words found in the back alleys
> the tenements and temples
> lie under her tiny dancing feet
>
> Walt! She dances weightlessly on
> your eye-lids
>
> Walt she dances
> weightlessly
> on your eye-lids
>
> these words
> are pasted on her brow

In this draft we see Kiyooka working — improvisationally; riffing, really — through a pair of different stanzas. In the next draft in "Packet 2," he collapses the stanzas into a shorter, more condensed version:

Leaves of Grass grow
in the crackt pavement of the parking lot where
my comely daughter sings. these
words 'found' in back alleys, the tenements and
temples lie under her dancing feet,
Walt can you feel her tip-toe across your
eye-lids weightlessly

respond!
respond!

He then returns to multiple stanzas in the following draft:

Leaves of Grass grow
in the crackt pavement of the parking lot
where my comely daughter sings

These words 'found' in backalleys
the tenements and temples
lie under her dancing feet --- Walt!

She dances weightlessly
on you [sic] eye-lids. These words are
pasted on her brow

The archive therefore provides written textual witnesses to at least part of Kiyooka's process in writing the poem. A genetic critical approach would examine the various drafts not through an attempt to reconstruct "intent" on Kiyooka's part, but rather, through juxtaposition of the witnesses, read the poem through the material conditions of its production.

I have been using the term "archive" in the common sense of a repository. But if we expand the definition of archive to include the broader written record, then the publication venues could also be seen as archival iterations of the poems. The poems that are published are conventionally granted more authority—the author "authorized" their publication, after all. They are also conventionally considered more stable and fixed. But the existence of multiple published versions of the poems undermines that authority and stability, moving the published texts onto a more equal footing with the archival materials held in the repository. And so we could—indeed should—continue to read the evolution of the poem through the published record. The *Imago* version maintains much the same imagery, but arranges it differently:

Walt, we dance

    leaves of grass grow
    in the parking lots, in the small cracks
    of the pavement   where
    my daughter sings

weightlessly

    this poem lies
    under her feet in the backalleys,
    the tenements and temples of
    her dreams

on your eyelids (Kiyooka 1969, 13)

In this version, Kiyooka has chosen to use spacing and variable margins to create a kind of column-poem effect, undermining the linearity we see in the earlier drafts. In other words, "Walt, we dance / weightlessly / on your eyelids" bears an ambiguous relationship to the rest of the poem: at once an extension of and separate from it. In the *Pacific Windows* version, these parallel poems and ambiguity are removed in a return to a more linear structure:

    Walt
Leaves of Grass
grow in the parking lots in
the small cracks
of the pavement where my
daughter   sings

> weightlessly
> this poem lies under her feet
> in the backalleys
> the tenements & the temples
> of her dreams
>   dancing
> weightlessly
>   on your eyelids (Kiyooka 1997, 27–28)

If the 11th poem in the sequence is not only an homage to Whitman but is addressed to him, providing the details of a particular time and place, the accumulation of different versions of the poem means that "the poem lies" in a double sense of the word, not only in terms of location, but in terms of relative sincerity and accuracy.

The poem also "lies"—or rather, its archival record does—in another way. I mentioned above that the "original order" of the documents in the file suggests this particular sequence—that is, that I as a reader assume a linear temporality from the sequencing of the documents. And yet, as a researcher, I can't necessarily make the assumption that the papers as gathered into the file—by Kiyooka, by a family member after his passing, by an archivist, by a fellow (perhaps irresponsible) researcher, or by anyone else—represent such a sequence. Ferrer argues that genetic criticism

> is at the same time a more and a less material pursuit than textual criticism. It is more abstract because its final object is not a printable text but a movement, the process of writing, that can be only approximately reconstituted from existing documents and only imperfectly represented, be it by a narrative, a "genetic" edition, or a hypertextual presentation. It is also more concrete, insofar as it does not go beyond the existing documents towards an ideal text that never existed anywhere, but instead strives to reconstruct, from all the evidence it can muster, a historically attested chain of events. (Ferrer 49)

The archive itself, as well as the narratives and readings it enables, is also an imperfect representation in its historical witnessing. But even if we cannot with any certainty reconstruct a linear sequence to the drafts, much less arrive at any conclusions about the scriptor's "intent," reading the drafts through juxtaposition further opens the text, revealing Kiyooka's work to be characterized by process and indeterminacy. This approach seems especially suited to Kiyooka's poetry, marked as it is by "the openness of a textual attentiveness that is always in process" (Miki 2002, 75) that Miki links to "subjectivities coming into formation in and through the traumatic effects of racialization and minoritization" (74).

The "4th avenue poem" that most directly addresses history in the broader public sense would be the fifth one, which references the Alaska earthquake of 1964, and the assassination of John F. Kennedy in 1963—tumultuous events in both literal and figurative senses. The references to these events arise in the opening stanzas of the poem. Here is the opening to the *Imago* version:

> the color of
>
> Death, is black and white,
> puked-in to a million homes. His death
> no more colorful than
> harvey lee oswald's or jack ruby's
>
> when the quake struck Alaska
> the eskimos didnt know what hit them.
> without t.v. they didn't know
> how he got it. it was not their way. (Kiyooka 1969, 7)

This is not simply a poetic response to historical events, however; it appears indebted to, or even a response to, a section in the "Thing Language" sequence of Jack Spicer's *Language*, published in 1964:

> Smoke signals
> Like in the Eskimo villages on the coast where the earthquake hit
> Bang, snap, crack. They will never know what hit them
> On the coast of Alaska. They expect everybody to be insane.
> This is a poem about the death of John F. Kennedy. (Spicer 221)

I suppose it could be possible that both Kiyooka and Spicer coinciden-
tally referenced the Alaskan earthquake and the assassination of JFK
in poems written in the same year, but it seems more likely there is a
relationship of influence and response here. It is clear that Kiyooka was
not only familiar with Spicer's work but appeared to admire and draw
from it. I would go so far as to say that Spicer's poem presents another
"variant" of Kiyooka's text, expanding the social context that the documents are witness to.

Beyond the direct echo of Spicer's "Thing Language," the "correspondences" (to use Spicer's term) between Spicer's and Kiyooka's work
here are multiple: the disjunctions; the serial form of the poems as a
whole; the ambivalence towards technologies of mass-communication.
Other documents attest to this relationship of influence and response.
In a letter to "Michael" of October 5, 1966, for example, Kiyooka
acknowledges Spicer as the source of a quotation: "embrace an absolute
geometric circle—the naked loss stays with you like a picture echoing"
(Kiyooka 2005, 7). And another poetic draft entitled "among the heaps
of the uncollectable" in "Packet 2" not only references Spicer, but appears to engage with Spicer's notion of a poetic inspiration arriving
from an "outside":

> among the heaps of uncollectable papers
> the mildewed piles
> a scrap of blue floral wallpaper with a phone number
> scribbled across it   *dead or alive*
> jack keeps dialing that number   he lets it ring
> four or five times   hangs up and after
> another beer   dials it again
> dead or alive he has that number ringing

in his head, it will ring in his head long after
the numbers have died. dead numbers dont lie
dead poets cant sleep forever with their numbers
imprint'd in their rotting heads.
among the uncollectable papers of jack spicer a scrap
of blue floral wallpaper with a phone number
of a long dead boy friend who took his number with him

This unpublished poem located within Kiyooka's archive is itself meta-archival: a rumination on and among "the uncollectable papers" found in Kiyooka's collected papers—and a reminder that the archive excludes through the very process of inclusion. The papers may be "uncollectable" because of material damage to them, "the mildewed piles." But they may also be uncollectable because no one recognizes them as having historical significance. The determining factors of what are and are not significant archival materials are historically contingent, after all. And the "uncollectable papers" invoke the archival anxiety that so much of the material archive is lost, unrecoverable. Derrida alludes to this anxiety when he writes, "right on that which permits and conditions archivization, we will never find anything other than that which exposes to destruction, and in truth menaces with destruction, introducing, *a priori*, forgetfulness and the archiviolithic into the heart of the monument. Into the 'by heart' itself. The archive always works, and *a priori*, against itself" (Derrida 12).

The fifth poem of "the 4th avenue poems" invites closer scrutiny in part because it demonstrates some of the most significant formal transformations from the 1969 version to the 1994 version, but also because it engages with the broader historical and social context of 1960s North America. Here are the remaining stanzas of the version published in *Imago*:

The storm was static on t.v. with
the power gone, the lights all-over-town
snuffed out, one after another.
Judy's father got it, his way, that night.

His way was not theirs. Death, like a set
with burnt-out tubes emits weak signals.
Death, John is no avenger. Vengeance is 3D-
technicolor. Are you alive? Why dont you write? (Kiyooka 1969, 7)

Considering the fifth poem as a whole, what immediately strikes me is
the degree to which the repetitions, linebreaks, ambiguous pronouns,
and discontinuous sentences produce a disjunctive, rather than projective or associational, poetics. Meaning, or reference, in this poem is
established within the collision of various contextual frames: while it
appears immediately clear that the occasion of the poem is the assassination of John F. Kennedy, the reference to "His death" is not so much
determined by our awareness of the historical context as it is overde-
termined by the references to "harvey lee oswald," "jack ruby" but
especially by "puked-in to a million homes." A poem ostensibly about
the death of JFK quickly transforms into a critique of the flattening
effects of mass communications: "His death / no more colorful than."
Kiyooka's misprision here in the naming of Kennedy's assassin ("harvey
lee oswald" rather than "lee harvey oswald") may be an extension of
that critique — between him and "jack ruby" there were a lot of killers'
names to remember, not to mention the proliferation of names involved
in conspiracy theories — or it could possibly signify a refusal to "properly" commemorate Oswald.

    In the second quatrain, the focus shifts to another major historical
event: the devastating Alaska earthquake of 1964. The stanza demonstrates a growing consciousness of the replacement of immediate, material experience of the real with a technologically mediated re-con-
struction of that experience. 'the eskimos' here introduces a plural
pronoun, 'they,' which will as the poem proceeds undergo a similar
referential slippage to what we already see happening in the second
quatrain with 'he.' "it was not their way" further introduces an element
of cultural difference, an element which appears threatened by the
"Vengeance" of "3D- / technicolor." "it" in "it was not their way" lacks
a definite referent, thus invoking the multiple contexts of the collision
of traditional Indigenous practices with mid-twentieth century technologies, as well as a supposedly pacifist culture, alien to the political

violence which would result in the assassination of a U.S. president. The last line of the third stanza, juxtaposed with the first of the fourth ("Judy's father got it, his way, that night. // His way was not theirs"), reveals a common thematic of death threading across all four stanzas: when "Judy's father got it, his way," it was not a mass-media event dealing with death, as was the case with Kennedy and the Alaskan earthquake. "His way was not theirs," however, also returns attention to the occasion of the poem—the assassination of JFK—and invokes the suspected political conspiracy behind the assassination. Within the immediate context of "the 4th avenue poems" as a whole, the "John" who is addressed in the final quatrain and asked "Are you alive? Why dont you write?" would appear to be the same "John" to whom the series is dedicated; however, given the occasion of the poem, "John" here could also refer to the dead U.S. president. The production of multiple and overlapping contexts demonstrates at the formal level what might be termed the poem's paraphrasable content: a comparison of differing experiences of death, and how those experiences are differently medi- ated "Vengeance," as an act of violence which occurs posterior to a previous act, is closer to 3D-technicolor than to death (3D-technicolor being posterior to "black and white"), but also to the events which it records and re-constructs.

Here is the 're/visioned' version of the fifth poem of "the 4th avenue poems" as published in *Pacific Windows*:

> the color of Death is black & white puked
> into a million livingrooms. his death no more colorful
> than Harvey Lee Oswald's. or a Jack Ruby's.
> when the big quake struck Alaska the Inuits didn't know
> what hit them. without t.v. they didn't know
> how JFK got it. it wasn't their way. the big storm was
> static on t.v. with the power down the lights
> all over town snuffed out one by one. Judy's father got it
> his way that night. his way wasn't their way.
> Death like a burnt-out t.v. set emits weak signals. Death
> John is no avenger: vengeance is 3D-technicolor.
> are you alive? why don't you write? (Kiyooka 1997, 26)

The most striking difference between this and the earlier version of the poem is of course the collapse of the more lineated, stanzaic verse into the prose poem form. There are important changes in diction: "eskimos" becomes "Inuits," for instance; even allowing for the 'mistake' of putting into plural an already plural noun (Inuit), this reflects a historical shift in the naming of Indigenous peoples (and, were the poem revised today, "Inuits" might be replaced with another name). A perhaps more significant change would be the replacement of the indefinite pronoun "he" in 1969's "he got it" with a specific reference to "JFK," the effect of which is to—once again—actually reduce the ambiguities which I note in the previous version.

The shift from lineated verse to prose also shifts the correspondences of the poem: whereas in 1969 the text's disjunctions correspond for the most part with the devices and strategies of, say, Spicer's work, in the newer version the text seems most closely to approximate 'new sentence' practice. This would place Kiyooka's work in an aesthetic continuum that reflects broader transformations in avant-garde poetic practices in Vancouver over the 25 years between the two versions of the poems: from a poetry inflected by the poets represented in *The New American Poetry*, to a poetry inflected more by language writing, and embodied in the Kootenay School of Writing. In Kiyooka's case, rather than later poets re-working inherited strategies from their precursors, we have a poet re/visioning his earlier work to correspond with new poetic strategies, reading practices, and communities. To return to a point I made earlier, the change of form in the poem between 1969 and 1994 is not simply a question of aesthetics: the formal changes also register the shifting social text of the poem.

This prompts the question: if the form of the poem changes in the twenty-five years that pass between the re/visions, does its paraphrasable 'content' change as well? Kiyooka has written that the series, along with his "Zodiac Series" of collages which accompanied the publication of George Bowering's *The Man in Yellow Boots / El Hombre de las Botas Amarillas* as a special issue of *El Corno Emplumado* (1965), "embodies my own cantankerous sixties politics" (Miki 311). How, then, is a politics differently 'embodied' in the later poem? Moreover, given the increased historical distance from the occasion of the poem's composition, how do we understand the re(con)textualization of history which the poem produces?

One immediate effect of the removal of stanzaic divisions is to collapse the multiple contexts invoked by the poem even further into one another. In the 'original' version, the stanzaic divisions at least separate several different contexts (the assassination of JFK, the Alaska earthquake, a more localized 'big storm' and an enigmatic reference to 'Judy's father'). In the new version the focus shifts from the quatrains 'down' to the more discrete level of the sentence. To be sure, the sentence is very much an important unit of composition in the earlier version; however, here it appears to be the *primary* unit of composition, with the paragraph acting, in proper new sentence fashion, as a unit of quantity. If we accept Fredric Jameson's analysis of new sentence practice as symptomatic of a "schizophrenic" experience of temporality, in which, "[w]ith the breakdown of the signifying chain ... the schizophrenic is reduced to an experience of pure material signifiers, or, in other words, a series of pure and unrelated presents in time" (Jameson 27), then Kiyooka's re/visioned work might be read as demonstrating an increased fragmentation of experience and an inability to re-construct this experience into a meaningful narrative. If the text's paraphrasable content is a critique of the levelling and de-humanizing effects of mass communication, changes in the poem's form seem to mirror precisely those effects. The earlier poem thus offers an anticipatory glance at a 'black and white' death which loomed, in 1964, 1965 and 1968, across the North American landscape. In 1994, this death returns with a vengeance, not only in "3D-technicolor" but (to step 'outside' the poem for a moment) in the emergence of a real-time, interactive communications network, the profound ambivalence of which is most clearly articulated by the term "World Wide Web."

As I mention above, Kiyooka regarded "the 4th avenue poems" as a companion piece to his "Zodiac Series" of collages, introducing another documentary witness to the social context of the poem—and, like the audio recording I discuss above, a textual witness in a different medium. The collages consist of twelve black and white oval frames of juxtaposed-heterogeneous content. Here we find images of unidentified figures, crowds, violence (a nuclear explosion, a bleeding man being attended to), what appear to be expressive "amorphous scrawls and blotches" (Kröller 37) and language which ranges from the referential ("Do you have to be asked") to discontinuous and handwritten text, to arbitrary letters resembling sound or concrete poetry (RRSSSSTTTT-TUU). In her illuminating discussion of Kiyooka's collages in relation to Bowering's poetry in *The Man in Yellow Boots*, Eva-Marie Kröller sees the "focus and perspective" of the collages changing "with the dizzying frequency of a television image" and that the piece as a whole "suggest[s] both an eye mournfully reflecting impending catastrophe and an angry rent in the dense verbal and visual fabric of propaganda" (37). Thus the politics of the "Zodiac Series," as Kröller describes them, would seem to correspond with those of "the 4th avenue poems," at least as I have read those politics in my arguments above.

Kiyooka also published an explanatory poem to accompany the collages in the issue of *El Corno Emplumado*:

> if some one should ask
> how they were made
>
> tell them he made them
> from a handful of paper & paste.
>
> if they should want to know what
> they are about   tell them
>
> they are about things waiting
> to reveal them-selves;
> a wanting to conceal him-self.
>
> if they should persist
> and want to know more   tell then
>
> his hand is waiting
> to reveal them, too. (Kiyooka 1965, 94)

If we accept the poem as a rhetorical 'explanation' of the collages, the lines that they are "about things waiting / to reveal them-selves" could suggest a productive role for the reader, or perhaps the need for historical distancing. Moreover, if the series is also about "a wanting / to conceal him-self," we could read this as a poststructural effacement of the artist as locus of creative authority—although given the drive to re/vision Kiyooka's earlier work as early articulations of a racialized subjectivity, these lines could also remind us of the effacement of that racialized subjectivity throughout the 1960s, both in terms of the reception of Kiyooka's work as well as his own insistence that he was a "Canadian artist." And within the context of the archival explorations I am undertaking, we could see the various substrata of materials relating to "The 4th Avenue Poems" as textual witnesses waiting to reveal themselves, and throw further light upon the poems.

A more comprehensive exploration of Kiyooka's archive would need to include the "computer versions" which Miki used in editing *Pacific Windows*. According to Miki, "[t]he term 'computer version' refers to the texts inserted on the Macintosh computer by RK. This electronic text is part of the RK papers in the Estate of Roy Kiyooka" (Miki 1994, 318). The electronic texts are stored in more than 60 floppy disks held in the SFU collection, some annotated and dated, but many others not. These diskettes are not yet inventoried, much less examined for what they contain. Accessing those files—and transferring them to a more secure digital platform—will at some point be necessary, if it is even possible at this stage. And that will require finding a working Macintosh from that era—perhaps Kiyooka's, though it is not part of the Kiyooka collection at SFU. As Matt Kirschenbaum has pointed out, "[o]ur best Representation Information is, one could argue, *embodied* in the working hardware we maintain for access to the original media" (Kirschebaum para. 27). According to Kirschenbaum, archival practices—both from the perspective of archivists and researchers—are only starting to confront the implications of what he terms (in an homage to McGann) "the .txtual condition":

What separates digital media and practices of digital archiving radically from the spatial organization of the conventional archive (embodied as physical repository) is the so-called "time-criticality" of digital media, the inescapable temporality that accounts for observations such as Duranti's about the errant ontology of digital documents … On the one hand, the avant garde nature of the material is such that traditional procedures of appraisal, arrangement and description, and access must be challenged and sometimes even overruled. On the other hand, however, the media and data objects that constitute the born-digital elements of the Collection are themselves obsolescing at a frightening rate. This ongoing oscillation between obsolescence and novelty, which manifests itself constantly in the workflows and routines we are evolving, is characteristic of the .txtual condition as I have come to understand it … (Kirschenbaum para. 28)

What Kirschenbaum means by the "time-criticality" of born digital documents is the fact that every time a file is opened it is, in a sense, created anew. This would be the "novelty" sphere in the oscillation between novelty and obsolescence he describes. For all the technocratic rhetoric celebrating the digital turn, our digital platforms obsolesce "at a frightening rate." We have paper records dating back many centuries; our digital records will survive a fraction of that, at best. But the most important implication, for the purposes of archival research and genetic approaches, in the shift from analog to born-digital modes of composition, would be that the word-processor allows for the editing of documents without leaving a trace of what is edited. In the various iterations of the eleventh poem in "The 4th Avenue Poems" that I discuss above, we can trace the development of the poem in different stages, and assign or infer some significance to the variations, which throws light on the "completed" version of a text, because there remain material traces of that process. But those material traces are lost in the process of born-digital composition. The word processor has been a boon to writers because of the ease with which it permits editing, but something of a bane to textual and genetic scholars, at least those employing more traditional methods of textual scholarship. Were we to access the digital files on Kiyooka's floppies, they would certainly be of scholarly interest. But they would also serve as reminders that traces of the composition process are forever irretrievable.

Yet the same could be said about any archival investigation. As is so often the case, McGann puts it most clearly and elegantly:

> The records we have expose the absence of the records we
> don't have, or records that never passed beyond an immediate
> (perhaps oral, in any case ephemeral) experience. Our problems
> with the meanings of the extant records are bound up, are sealed
> with, those that are not extant. They tell of relationships that,
> as we glimpse their absent presences, now reveal the presence
> of a dizzying network of further relations. (McGann 56)

The very instability of Kiyooka's texts that I have tried to demonstrate and discuss here demands an archival approach to his work. The "dizzying network" in which the texts are situated mirror the social networks and historical conditions—construed both broadly and narrowly—in which Kiyooka was himself embedded. While we can never fully recover lost social context around the poems, lost among "the uncollectable papers," we can read the poems as encoding that context within themselves. If literary documents bear the evidence of "the history of their own making," they also bear witness to their historical and social context, not only in their referential indexing, but in their formal structures as well.

Acknowledgements

I would like to acknowledge the assistance of Tony Power and the staff at the Simon Fraser University Special Collections.

Works Cited

Derrida, Jacques. *Archive Fever: A Freudian Impression*. Translated by Eric Prenowitz, U of Chicago P, 1995.

Ferrer, Daniel. "Production, Invention, and Reproduction: Genetic vs. Textual Criticism." *Reimagining Textuality: Textual Studies in the Late Age of Print*, edited by Elizabeth Bergmann Loizeaux and Neil Fraistat, U of Wisconsin P, 2002, pp. 48–59.

Jameson, Fredric. *Postmodernism, or, the Cultural Logic of Late Capitalism*. Duke UP, 1991.

Kirschenbaum, Matt. "The .txtual Condition: Digital Humanities, Born-Digital Archives, and the Future Literary." *Digital Humanities Quarterly*, vol. 7, no. 1, 2013. Online.

Kiyooka, Roy. Reading at "2nd Annual Poetry Session." March 26, 1963. Audio recording. *Roy Kiyooka Archival Audio*, Simon Fraser University Special Collections, item 11.

----. "among the heaps of the uncollectable." Undated TS draft, *Roy Kiyooka Fonds*, Simon Fraser University Special Collections, MsC 32.4.11.

----. "Packet 2." Undated TS drafts, *Roy Fonds*. Simon Fraser University Special Collections, MsC 32.4.11.

----. Untitled poem. In *The Man in Yellow Boots*, by George Bowering. Ediciones el Corno Emplumado, 1965, p. 94.

----. "The 4th Avenue Poems." *Imago* no. 11, 1969, pp. 3–18.

----. *Pacific Windows*. Edited by Roy Miki, Talonbooks, 1997.

---. *Transcanada Letters*. Edited by Smaro Kamboureli, NeWest, 2005. Kröller, Eva-Marie. George Bowering: Bright Circles of Colour. Talonbooks, 1992.

McGann, Jerome. *A New Republic of Letters: Memory and Scholarship in the Age of Digital Reproduction*. Harvard UP, 2014.

McKenzie, D.F. *Bibliography and the Sociology of Texts*. Cambridge UP, 1999.

Miki, Roy. "Afterword." *Pacific Windows: Collected Poems of Roy K. Kiyooka*, edited by Roy Miki, Talonbooks, 1997, pp. 301–320.

----. "Unravelling Roy Kiyooka: A Re-assessment Amidst Shifting Boundaries." *All Amazed: For Roy Kiyooka*, edited by John O'Brian, Naomi Sawada, Scott Watson, Arsenal Pulp, 2002, pp. 69–83.

Olson, Charles. "Projective Verse." *The New American Poetry*, edited by
    Donald Allen, Grove Press, 1960, pp. 386–397.

Spicer, Jack. *The Collected Books of Jack Spicer.* Black Sparrow, 1975.

Zukofsky, Louis. "An Objective." *Prepositions: The Collected Critical Essays.*
    UP of New England, 2000, pp. 12–18.

With Roy Kiyooka

Wednesday, September 16, 1970,
At The University of Alberta

On The Relationship Between Painting And Poetry:

It was Jean Arp, I believe, who said, painting and poetry go together. The one activity complements the other and both together give me a context for articulating more than either discipline per se ... that's all and I feel that way about it. Painting ... Poetry ... <u>Art is where you're in it</u>. I don't know if I'm going to develop that theory ...

On Mixing Painting And/Or Photographs And Poetry:

Yes, I've just completed a 40–page photo-book called *The Eye in the Landscape*. It's a photo-study of part of Hornby Island and combines photographs and words, the words are definitely subordinate.

In *StoneDGloves*, photos and words grew apart together. I mean I was working on this big sculpture for the Canadian Pavillion at Osaka and taking photographs of gloves at the same time. Then I would go home and make notes concerning the day's happenings and I would take the day's roll of film into the processors and pick up the previous day's photos and in that way just accumulate material—with then no thought of combining them. That came later when I got back.

On Reasons For Writing Poetry Or Making Paintings:

I was simply one of those people who had no choice of vocation. I was an artist per se from that time when to have an identity was synonymous with vocation—it's that long ago. I've always been an artist ... at eighteen or so I didn't go thru that anguish of 'what am I going to do with my life?—shall I be this or that or some other thing?' ... the question never occurred to me.

About 'Description' In Poetry:

I've written a number of poems about paintings and about painters. Most of them are for me now, too descriptive to be good poems ... To describe as I've done in some of these poems, is to situate oneself somewhere outside of the experience and look at it, rather than, making in-the-language an equivalent—something equal to the painting. I continue to describe though because I don't know how else to deal with some experiences. In that white poem I've just read, which I feel is a good poem, it's no longer just descriptive—it is its own thing. I suppose what I would like to be able to do is to make a poem that is its own thing and simply takes its place beside a painting also its own thing, in its place ...

Concerning The Relationship Between Painters And Poets:

Well there was Baudelaire who told us how great a painter his contemporary Delacroix was and then there was e.e. cummings who I for one remember as both painter and poet and there's Vincent van Gogh whose letters to Theo and to others say at least as much as his paintings do and you've all heard of Wyndham Lewis, painter and writer, buddy of Ez Pound and others, and it's been said of R.M. Rilke that he never really got off the ground until he came to Paris and worked for a while as Rodin's secretary and in that context learned literally learned how to see a thing and recently Peg Atwood did the illustrations for her book of poems called I think *The Journals of Susan* (sic) *Moodie* and as you can see the list can be extended ... It would include Robert Duncan's drawings for his own poems and Henry Miller's naïve watercolours. Miller once upon a time wrote a sentimental thing called 'to paint is to love again.' — ya, that's the title of the book. I feel my position in some ways is awkward simply because I'm mostly a painter who writes poems and most of the people I've mentioned are the other way around and I don't necessarily see eye to eye with them.

Has Black Mountain Influenced The Painting On The West Coast As Much As The Poetry?

I'd say very little in the sense of any painter from say Vancouver having studied with any painter affiliated with B.M. (Black Mountain). It was during the late fifties that I taught at Regina College that the first direct influence by which I mean the actual presence of the painters was felt in Canada. At that time a number of famous NY painters came to lead a workshop in Saskatchewan and that contact and later seeing their paintings (for me) was the first sense of it. It was then and later in the early sixties that B.M. poets started coming up to Vancouver and it was then at that time that the first paintings of their contemporaries began to be seen here but no one knew the painters as such. The stimulus in that sense was less for the painters than the poets — how the B.M. poets grabbed the imagination of poets — those who wanted to be poets.

What Charles Olsen had to say for verse in 'projective verse' had its parallel in what some of the painters (at about the same time) were saying about painting — it's more than mere coincidence ... something more like how the alert members of the same generation came to a similar sense of possibility, in each art form ... it's something like that, like the idea in the air to be grabbed by whoever ...

Has Cage Had An Impact On The West Coast?

Oh yes—incredible, I'd say: most of the young musicians I've met know Cage.[109] Those with a conservatory background who get into electronics know Cage. And those who came to music by simply making sounds on whatever instrument was available and going on from there know Cage. I'd say he's been central to a lot of the sounds that are in the air and in our ears. I feel it's a lovely eclectic period we're into ... most of the musicians I know give me an anthology of 'all' sounds, the jazz thing, the rock 'n' roll bit, the whole gush of western music plus the lovely oriental drone ... all of it combines in their particular way. ya.

Has Cage Had An Influence On Poetry As Well?

I think that Cage is important ... the quality of the man coming thru the prose is affecting ... he's a superb theoretician and a lovely storyteller, his books are full of both. There are all those lovely people Cage has had something to do with and how he has them doing their thing there on the page—ya, the man's quality shines thru ... and that's important. I suspect that both bp and Bissett have been into him ... and I know a great number of others also.[110]

How Much Of Your Work Comes Spontaneously?

It all comes out—one way or another ... but 'it' has to be formed. The thing occurring as a possibility is something easy enough ... but to give it form, that form that it is, is for me an arduous process. The StoneDGloves exhibit, the organization of it from 500 photos, and the writing of the poems from all kinds of notes represent five/six months of continuous work ... I mean everyday for several hours including Sundays and all your holidays: each day I would examine the photos and then re-examine them—to find a context for the best of them, and each day I would write and rewrite the poems—and it's not in my nature to let a thing go until I've got thru with it, completely. Taking the images from white thru to black is something that occurred as a possibility when I was working with Bob Cain at Focus Prints. We would make several tests of each image to be enlarged, at different exposures to ascertain what exposure would be the right one for a particular image of a particular size. It was while doing these tests that I thought, ya why not take the image thru from white to black at precisely measured intervals, why not do that to show how the image can and does appear and then finally disappear, into black ... so that's what we did.

The Probability Of Oriental Influence On Your Work – Its Relevance

Like most people who have done the oriental thing my access has been thru translation ... so that in my late teens I was reading say Arthur Waley's numerous translations from the Chinese and Japanese classics ... but then I also had my immediate family and what that gave me ... it's all very complex, this thing of influences. I've recently been as they say, taking stock of myself—thinking of where I did come from, what I've done, and all the different places I've lived and the people multitudinous people I've known and do know ... and only now I've been trying to fit it together. For instance, I've never been to Europe, I've never had the compulsion to go there. I've never once said to myself, my life is going to be incomplete unless I go to Europe. When I lived in Montreal Europe seemed only a stone's throw away and I thought, one nice weekend I'll just hop on a plane and go to London—you know the British Museum, the Tate, Carnaby Street and all that—for a start, but I did not accomplish that either. As a matter of fact what I did was to go straight to Japan from Montreal ... it has to do with roots, source, feelings and correlations...

You Were Born In The Prairies. Is That Important To You?

Yes, I was born is Saskatchewan, Moose Jaw, Saskatchewan. I don't think it unfair to ask an artist about his background. I'm not sure how useful it is. Most of what we grab from the past, particularly the remote past as literature, comes without author. About a large number of beautiful things that have been made we know nothing about who made it and it doesn't seem important. What we do know is conjecture. What is relevant about them comes thru the work they left behind ... I think perhaps that biography insists too much upon the idiosyncratic—and I'm not sure how useful that is in what gets done. I've never been much interested in the kind of art that is personal in the sense of a kind of existential stance towards life. That isn't my sense of art ... I'm much more interested in disappearing into the thing I make, getting lost in it completely. I don't want my poem or painting or piece of sculpture or even photos to say, 'hey, look at him! look at him!' I want to become the made thing and nothing but that, that thing.

More Relating To Things Made

In painting, to come upon a configuration that truly excites me and to realize that—is for me to disappear into it. And my sense of poetry is, if I come upon a sequence of words, with each word truly there ... placing before my eyes and my ears, an image or sequence of images, then I've disappeared into that also. In either case if I've not accomplished what I have said above then it's less than satisfactory ... I haven't made a thing that is simply and transparently there.

I've had this sense for a long time. The kind of paintings I have been doing do not allow the usual signature to be scrawled in the lower-right hand corner of the canvas. I place it on the back because it always looks a little grotesque up front, insisting on a name too much.

I feel that a lot of poetry gets terribly abstract—the words don't point to things and to the relationship that obtains between things. There are words that for me don't do anything. I like the words there, a substantial thing believable as say a block of wood is.

How Come You're Interested In Anonymity?

It's as old as your neolithic cavemen, your Alley Oop. Or medieval guilds. Or that tradition in the Orient of basic anonymity that persisted thru until recent times. The great temples like Ankor Wat and Konorak represent phenomenal imaginative and physical labour yet are anonymous ... as erotic sculpture cum architecture they've never been excelled—never will be, I feel ... that whole ambience. And closer to home no one knows who authored those magnificent totem poles.

Canada – Canadian Art And All That

I'll sort of preface this by saying that I think one of the tyrannies of what happens in Canadian kulture is that a lot of generalities are at work trying to convince us of how self-conscious we ought to be about Canadian culture ... and I've had this exposure for most of my life and it's always been a drag. I've simply never had the sense of Canadian or artist or poet as something separate from human—I've never had that sense of identity or vocation. Most of the people in this country I know and respect are not quote Canadian unquote. They don't feel 'more' or 'less' so—they are human beings, given to do particular things and doing that as well as they can. For me there isn't any argument vis-à-vis the qualitative thing. There have been and continue to be incomparably lovely things made-in-Canada. That however doesn't mean these things have a priority over things made elsewhere.

Canadian, for me, is a complex possibility. It (at least) has to include the obstinate, the weird, the recalcitrant, the bizarre and the fanciful—at least, that much.

Then there's the Canadian Group of Seven. You have seen lousy silk-screen repos of their paintings every time you stood in line at a Canadian bank to cash a cheque. Their paintings, some of their real paintings are among the great visionary landscapes of anytime/anywhere. My point is that they were often superb painters who happen to be Canadians—in the way that I am also.

If you live in say Northern Ontario all your life your sense of geography is not going to be the same as if you had grown up in the rain forests of British Columbia. My sense is that geography does get into everything, everything I do ... it really does and it can't be helped. It's never a deliberate searching for ideas—it is more like osmosis the way it gets into your system. The Mediterranean was the birth flare of that whole Indo-European culture. For me a constant aspect of the Medi is its light—how it suffuses everything from Homer to Matisse. It got into everything made there. The light that obtains in any given place permeates what is made there. Light is in this sense I suppose, a permeation... through and through—I don't know how else to put it.

The light here in Edmonton is different from light in Vancouver and the light on the west coast—like WOW! The clarity here knocks your eyes out. It's not as intense now as say in the middle of winter when it's twenty below out and you have six inches of snow and a dazzling blue sky—that really knocks my eyes out.

Proximity To Centres Of Culture

I don't know if say Edmonton is further away than another place. I don't think it matters now. I've lived in every province except the Maritimes[111] and I've lived in most of the big cities in them and I've never felt that I couldn't be at home ... to be at the centre is to be where the ideas are, that is, in your own head, wherever you are. Right now I'm in Vancouver and that feels like the centre. One of the useful things about art is that you literally take it with you wherever you go ... you don't have any choice—you can't choose to leave it all behind.

If Art's That Important, Where Is There Room For People?

Well for almost 25 years I've spent most of my days making things, things like a painting, a poem, a piece of sculpture, or a photograph ... and then in the evening I would always go out and it would then be the people thing. Yes that's part of it ... people are important, of course they are ... I have a wife and three lovely daughters. I have countless numbers of friends ... we form an incredibly intricate configuration. There is involvement, together. I can't really separate my art, from people ... really I can't. People do wear gloves, you know ... some people wear gloves.

Can You Live Off Art And Other Matters

My art has never supported me. Well, let's see, I guess I could give you a resume of the different things I've done ... for whatever that's worth. I've dressed store-windows, written copious copy for underwear and sundry goods, done show cards ... worked on the killing floor of the Swift Canadian Company in Edmonton during the war years ... I've worked in logging camps and sawmills in Northern Alberta ... I've farmed, farmed badly a quarter section of land that was virtually all sand, good only for rye we were told ... I designed and built the entire guts of a store modelled after the five and ten, then stocked the shelves, even managed the place for a while ... Let's see, I spent five summers on the Great Slave Lake in the Northwest Territories as fisherman and fish processor ... I learned how to navigate, taking boats out on a large body of water under diverse conditions and bringing them back ... I learned how to set nets and pull them in and dress the fish and all that, it was an incredible experience. That's part of what I've done ... I've taught art for almost 15 years at several institutions ... all of these things have been useful ... they add up I suppose to one man's life, the shape of it. I don't regret any of it, not a bit. I'm glad in fact that that's the way it was. I've had very little formal education ... my sense of the possibility of art grows largely out of this varied life experience ... I'm not too interested in argument, particularly the kind that wants to argue aesthetics, not that I'm not involved there but simply it's not where my head is most of the time.

Do Creative Artists Survive In Academia?

I think most c.a. survive badly. They're schizophrenic, they feel this obligation to contexts incompatible with their sensibilities, what in fact they do do. The strong persist like that all their lives, they somehow manage to survive. They might even get a few things made.

I think good teachers are those that recognize that there is nothing to be taught other than what the occasion at hand allows. I have my own obsessions, they get into everything I make. They will surely get into what I teach. Whatever is in my head at that moment seems important ... it's where I've always started from ... it's how I've taught for a long time. My varied involvement includes literature — all the different senses of it that I've had time to know ... teaching, for me is that occasion for outering that, that's what it is.

About Students And Their Teachers

My sense of the relationship insists that 50% of the job is up to the student and his job, as mine, is to bring whatever insight he has to the occasion. That student should know what his needs are and go find the man/woman teacher who's going to teach him something to fulfill that need. For me, that's the best sense of a student — simply a person who has that awareness of himself and the awareness of where to go to get it. I'd say the best art teachers and the best students have always related in this manner. They've simply found each other.

Concerning Universities

I've never been interested in them except as occasions for sitting down and rapping with a group of students. In fifteen years of teaching at several institutions it would seem that I could and did remain only as long as it took a student to get through four years and then 'both' of us would leave. There seemed no point in staying on and doing it again, at that place.

I think of the aftermath of the computer bust at Sir George Williams [112] and I was there then and simply want to say that is was a very tense time ... I mean there was a lot of poison in the air, then, it was incredible. Well, after that and other matters, universities seem to be slithering backwards towards those tight structures that prevailed before it all happened ... and for me, that's counter to my sense of possibilities — which is towards more mobility. Professorial staff, particularly the real good guys should not be the private preserve of a particular institution and its students but ought to be accessible to students all across the country, one way or another ... and the means are there, to do it. Parallel to this is greater mobility for students — across disciplines and across institutions. I'm interested in this as a definition of what 'education' could be.

Literature In Universities

If you happen to be studying 'literature' and don't try to write it yourself then I'd say that your education is both academic and incomplete. And I don't mean carrying out those assignments that enable your teacher to tick off what you may have picked up on ... but to do something in the language because words are all round you. They occur in our books and in our press and in the mags and they occur in these in a multitude of languages and all of us can talk and there are those of us who are given to talk a great deal and then there are people who can and do read, write and talk in several tongues and isn't 'words' one of the ways we constantly give shape to our life and isn't literature all about this, this fact of, the shape of our lives. What I am trying to say is that you won't know literature unless you've tried, in your own way, to give yourself that shape that words enable. Literature is our shapeliness in words. ya.

More On Teaching Art And Looking At It

It's really useless to talk about different painters, what they did, go into thorough analysis of their work, and how both painter and painting relate to the general history of the time, etc. without having a student put in as much time making 'his' own painting, however awkward. You want to find out ... Well, years ago I gave a class the project of doing a painting, of a painting of a Rousseau. I said to them, "spend some time going through all the art books you can get your hands on and all the repros (sic) you can also grab and examine, really examine all the different Rousseaus you come across and then, if you find one, for whatever reason grabs you—I want you to paint it and I want you to make an exact replica of it and you can spend up to six months doing it."

"Well," they said, "that's a bum trip ... jesuschrist, what's all this about—'me' copy someone else—I wanta be original, I don't wanta copy anyone, yah, yah, yah!" I insisted and this lovely thing happened—they were really called upon to examine a painting carefully ... in a way that they had never done before, which was the real intent of the project ... and each of then did a really commendable painting—despite the fact of their copying a Rousseau. Some of the old man's magic rubbed off on all of them. You can see it in their work to this day as all of them are painters today, each in his own way. Just to get in there and really look 'look' at a painting ... you simply can't put a time limit to that sort of activity. Paintings, as well as other things, need to be looked at carefully ... there's no other way of getting at it—for a painter, anyhow. To paint is to make 'space' and the time to build up to that is part of the business of looking. I've spent several months looking at a painting say the size of that blackboard and sometimes days would go by before a discreet change was made, a change that you might not even notice as having occurred ... and then, to go on looking, just looking, at it. It's impossible to tell anybody about that, that looking, and what it reveals, unless you have also done it.

About Making Poems And Reading Them Aloud With Body Gestures

It's part of the act of making a poem for me ... I mean I mumble words over ... mumble arrangements of words over and over. One wants the poem 'concretely' there, on the page and one wants it there so that it is also a notation for the voice. The tension between syllables between word-s, for me, is a very body thing—it's not just off the top of my head. I feel the energy of a poem as a very physiological one ... I have to feel it in my body, somewhere down here—not just on the tip of my tongue.

I feel the advantage I can bring to the possibilities of poetry is a highly developed visual sense. A poem or a drawing, anything diagrammed on a two dimensional surface. Visibility in this sense, is for me as important as say 'content' is, whatever 'it' is. For me content takes-care-of-itself, if the rest of the matter works.

I have no sense of my poems as property. I don't feel that I own poems after I've made them. I simply don't believe in poems, in those senses that obtain say in real estate—though I know that's part of the literary game. I don't have any faith in senses other than a poem as a gift, something received and then given away.

More About Reading And About Poetry

Stan Persky is a well known west coast writer. He is a frequent contributor to *The Georgia Straight* and an incredibly active man on the scene there ... well Stan and I along with others gave a reading and Stan read for about half an hour and what he read was what he had written that morning about the events in his life the previous day—and then I got up and read and said, "well that was interesting really interesting because Stan read to you what obtained the previous day in his life and in the act of re-creating that he used perhaps three thousand words and I'm going to read to you something that started with perhaps that many words but now several months later there might be, if I counted them, three hundred words." To date nothing that has happened to me surfaced as poetry except weeks, months, years later ... it simply doesn't come out that way for me. For both of us hopefully, all the words we use are real, very real there on the page and off the tip of our tongues. I suppose that each of us represents distinct possibilities, two senses of what's about.

... Kurt Schwitters was one of the most inventive makers of collages. He walked the streets of the cities of Europe in the 20s and 30s casually picking up paper cupons (sic), theatre tickets, handbills, trinkets, wrappers, postcards—you name it and Kurt had it, he had it stuffed in all of his pockets, all of them stuffed with this debris ... and he would take it all home and sort it out into this box for these things and this other box for something else and sometimes later perhaps years later he would take a thing out of its box and place it beside another thing from a different box and in this way he would put together in the most loving fashion, his collages. Kurt Schwitters was never too far from my mind as I prowled the site at Expo looking for and photographing these gloves, all of these gloves. What I was doing was what he did, both of us walking about kicking up debris ... there's fascination there, underfoot. There surely is.

I had the lovely experience walking the site one day—looking for gloves when from three stories up a grey tattered glove came tumbling down ... plop against the side of my face. That experience later led to the preface of *StoneDGloves*.

On The Use Of One's Contemporaries For The Sake Of Poetry

... When I had completed the MS for these poems I sent them to three poets that I respect and I said to them I want you to pick the poems to pieces and send it back so that I can put them together again with those senses you have given me. And I sent the poems to Victor Coleman, John Newlove, and George Bowering and got back three utterly distinct critiques. Victor, it would seem sat down one evening and re-wrote all of my poems ... he simply restructured them on the page without changing a word or even the sequence of words, in such a way that other relevancies were revealed. John gave me an incredible insight into

seemingly small things like should there be a comma here at this juncture and if so does the emphasis of the rest of the line change. Again,
I found this a most useful insistence. And George Bowering's insistence
had to do with the oral possibilities of the poem. I had written the
word 'clasped' ... c-l-a-s-p-d and he said if you say it over and over
again, to yourself, it comes out c-l-a-s-p-t. And I did say that word over
and over and yes that's how it does sound so I did change the spelling
of it, to that. You go over the comments and you include the relevant
ones into the matrix of what you're making—and hopefully it comes
out a better thing. I've got great faith in that sort of help as an extension of my own limits.

Afternoon in the Students Union Building University of Alberta, Wednesday, September 16, 1970

... Well, I'm willing to sit here for a couple of hours and not say a thing...
(a long pause)
It's a nice view from here...all these lovely flowers...
(another long pause)
What have we to talk about? ... What have we in common? ...
(an even longer pause)
Why didn't you let the photos speak for themselves?

It might appear to you as the most idiosyncratic gesture but let me
assure you it's just the most contemporary form of a tradition that is very
old. In the orient for instance, there is painting and there is poetry and
there are those forms in which both co-exist ... that's just one possibility.
All around you is provocation, call it photo-journalism ... all those
pictures and all those words and all their endless combinations—I
don't see that what I've done is anything new... at least I didn't feel I
was doing something that was brand new.

And What Will You Be Doing Next?

I am one of those artists who is as interested in a quantitative universe as much as any qualitative one. A characteristic of artists like myself is what I'd call our fecundity—we have to keep making things because for us there is a lot we want to make and in the act of making things we tell how the shape of our lives shapes the things we put our hands to.

Before sitting down to put this show together I was in Japan to make a piece of sculpture for the Canadian Pavilion at Osaka. I took these photos there in the time left-over. And before that in Montreal I made a number of fiberglas (sic) sculptures. I also did a few paintings and continued to write poetry. There is simply no end of giving form to our lives, our visions.

How Did It Start? Did You Know You Would Put This Show Together?

No, I didn't. I think one happens upon an idea as one happens on things... for me it is rarely a premeditated thing.

I'll see you all for an hour or so ... then we'll all disappear. I may never see you again, and then again I might and I may even remember your face. At least for a short while we will have been together.

The gloves and I have spent about eight months together. There was the four months spent photographing them, and then several months spent looking at them, just looking at them and asking questions about them, about their size and how light or how dark they should be and in what sequence they should occur and so on. My ideas, I would say are in the air—they're just 'up' there somewhere.

How Does Your Approach To Photography Differ From Someone Else's?

The simplest answer I can give you is that what I see through the eye of a camera (which is an extension of my eye) would not be what anybody else looking through the same camera is likely to see or even want to see. I assume that my approach is different but I can't give you a simple rationale of my difference except by what I am telling you at this moment, right? How anybody uses language, shapes it say in conversation, is in fact how they do think ... the sequence of words from instant to instant shapes perceptions which could be another name for thought ... and that's what I think I thought at this moment, out loud.

Did You Do Your Own Processing?

No—the processing into these large formats was done in a photo-lab by an expert at that. It was collaborative ... there's that sense in which all art is of course a collaboration, it comes from source and it goes thru a transformation that's partly your doing and partly this involvement with other people and their skills which you need to add to your own to complete the thing. Sometimes there's a multitude of people involved in your art in complex ways.

Photography is as distinctive an art form as any of the other so-called art forms. It's a medium you push your vision through, as say words are also a medium to push vision through. I suppose that the impossibility of seeing that photography is an art form has something to do with the sheer accessibility of it—everywhere you turn there's another goddamned picture! And there could be the same problem with words—everywhere you look there's fucken words! We all have this excess to deal with but it is still possible to make art from either. I don't believe in secret formulas for making artifacts. There aren't any secrets ... it's there to be read about, looked at, examined, talked and wondered about. There aren't any secrets, none. No one has a privileged access to the multitudinous forms of art—not more than anybody else.

Questions Relating To Talent, History And Progress

I don't think talent means much today... it may have at one time. Certainly if it means anything today it has to do with the young. It's of no consequence to a middle-aged man. Blake said that energy was the only life, energy was the life divine.

That sense of it, that energy, the sheer abundance of it and the artifacts that are its issue ... is what I find most compelling. Talent is nothing. The energy given off by one of Blake's poems or etchings or the combination of both, to me is as much 'the content' as any of the other things extricable as such.

And I want to say that History, as a yardstick or say whip, is not my sense of it. I'm not interested in literature say if it is insisted that I worship at the feet of William Shakespear (sic) or Blake—such fatuous esteem can divest you of your own articulation, 'articulation' could be another name for history. No, history/ literature/ tradition, you name it, as bully boy to put you in your place, is nonsense. It's the wrong use therefore abuse of it. And you can usually tell if some teacher is laying the godalmightyhewasgreatbit on you because it tends to give you that s-h-r-i-n-k-i-n-g feeling ... no, that ain't my sense of it.

And have you ever looked at a painting, an old painting, looked closely at it, for a long time and then as you were about to get bored with it—you tell yourself, wow the magic is all there, it's really all there ... and yes, a hand has done that and yes even my hand could do something like that. It would make similar marks however inept and if I stick to making marks on canvas I am going to make a painting and it won't be what his hand has done. Has this ever happened to you? If it has and you would most certainly know if it did you might become a painter or something ...

We don't have more ability to set down a compelling image of the world than primitive man had—the cave paintings in Lascaux are evidence. I don't believe in progress, it's mostly bullshit ... we have been talked to across generations and it's my sense of it that it's also our capability ... it could be 'all' that we really possess, that articulation I spoke of earlier, here and now. I call that capability, Art. Articulation equals History. Ya.

(long pause)

The interesting thing about this microphone is it is meant to extend the voice ... you would think therefore that it out to be shaped like an enormous tongue, but doesn't it look more like some other aspect of the male anatomy ...

The thing about photography, and the thing about the visual arts overall is you must not confuse the verbal extrapolation (in front of it, or whatever other way you look at it) with the visual image. It has its own relevance, its own language, and is not transferable, in its uniqueness, its exactitude. It's like making a translation. It has its own experiential dimension, that you simply grab, and walk away with—mute. And there is the fact that we all spend a goodly third of our lives in silence. At least that much time silent. And again, we all know that s-i-l-e-n-c-e talks. It says things, lovely, lonely beautiful things ... For me, the picture talks.

The Difference Between StoneDGloves On The Wall And In The Book

It's a different photographic experience. After all some of the photos on the wall are sixty inches by forty inches whereas the book will be eight by ten inches. Then, because of the difference in size the means of reproduction is different and therefore the value scale e.g. tones will be different. I'm interested in scale—what a big thing does experientially and what a small thing also does. The same subject matter e.g. gloves say, is not the same experience big and small despite the fact of ... Part of the artist's trip is to 'diagram' the equivalent of what he senses, in terms of his artifacts. He wants the artifacts to exist in a complex relationship to his complex sense of a very complex universe ... : there's the experience of finding the gloves and the experience of photographing them and the experience of looking at hundreds of contact prints (thru a magnifier) and the experience of seeing the selected photos larger and then larger and there are a number of other steps we will skip ... all the way over to like this occasion, as part of it.

   ... if you are looking for neat demarcations like pigeon holes, categories that are Kantian, places to put things ... you're not going to get anywhere near me because that isn't what I'm about. And it's not what most artists are about.

By Silence Do You Mean When We Sleep,
Or Do You Mean The Absence Of Words?

Both.

I'm Sitting Here And I've Got Millions Of Words Goin' Through
My Head—If I See A Picture 'Words' Inevitably Follow ...
I Can't Help Thinking In Words

Why not just pictures? If you are a painter which is what I am, you could sit for hours and not a word will pass through your consciousness. You would have a sense of im-a-ges, pictures that move through your mind—and they-re not word-s.

I Still Don't Understand How You Can Have Pictures
Without Words Coming In

I understand that and I do that too. Like I come to a street corner and I see the lights and they say 'red' and almost like a Pavlovian dog I stop! Then when it turns 'green' I step off the curb on my way across the street ... I am obedient to those kinds of signals—they require minimal energy, they help me stay alive.

I read various kinds of art criticism which argue pro and con particular senses of art. They are all interesting if you're interested in that kind of thing—there's that old contention between 'the classicist' and 'the romantic' and what was peculiar to each ... but I would like to remind you that it is only us humans who create categories and then proceed to dump things into them. Categories are useful to get-ahold-of-something but they are not useful if you just stay there and don't want to stay there, like a bathroom fixture, forever. I'm not too interested in the kind of painting some painter has done and simply be left with that because I know that the next time around that painter might astound me—leaving me (sic) wordless! This has happened and I know that I will continue to be confounded ... and hopefully will even confound myself.

I was known as a hard-edge painter for a number of years and it would make me boil when some soft critic threw his pablum-prose in my har-dege (sic) face ... blah, blah, blah, it all became a bore because imperceptibly I was getting soft-er (laughs) ... painters aren't interested in labels.

And I have no faith in comparative literature, I don't believe in all these and those comparative hooks ... and I don't believe in comparative criticism. It's the particularity of a given thing that grabs me ... it's the simple insistence that you take 'the thing' and 'look' at it, as intently as the occasion enables, then ask yourself what about it? That's for me. For me it's the kind of particularity that is interesting. Look at any Thing ... looking at any Thing and asking yourself now what does it resemble reminds me of the boys sitting around having a beer and one of them says "well you know so-and-so isn't bad but compared to so-and-so she hasn't got anything, etc." What does that mean? ... I'm not interested in dealing with a woman that way. I want my life there, where. I deal with what is immediate, as substantial fact ... but it's not that simple.

It's very useful to have taught painting in a studio or classroom where people are actually making paintings. What you do is you simply go from one to the next, observing the particularities of each painting and dealing with that. It's the intense scrutiny of each painting at whatever phase it's in and what might be said about it then.

Do You Find It Easier To Express Yourself In Painting Or In Words?

Well, without trying to avoid the question I'd say that I am awkward in both of them, in different ways. I don't know ... I don't think of it in those terms but I do recognize my awkwardness within the context of each form, definitely. And that is my answer. Franz Kline, the American painter, once said about painting, of course, when you're young you do everybody else's painting, but your own. When Franz was a young man he was infatuated with the particular kind of light that he found in Vermeer's paintings and he worked very hard to see if he could get it ... then, much later he realized, ok, that was useful but it isn't my thing, and so it goes. He tried a lot of different things and then all of a sudden he found he was not doing anything, in the manner of anyone else but what he could do.

I think that 'imitation' is a more actual and important aspect of the learning process, particularly when one is young, than anything else. To me, imitation is more interesting as a concept than say originality — I'll throw that out for whatever it's worth! Like how a child learns to speak ... imitation as the process of coming to articulation has a lovely naivete about it. There are none of those insistences, hard-nosed facts, etc. That comes later. The child immersed in a babel of sounds will none-theless find his own voice. What I'm getting at is that all good poets and painters tell me that the trip through life vis-à-vis being an artist, is to come back to the incredible simplicity, that joy, the naivete of simply making things — zip, zipzip, zip, zipzipzipzip, zip! — that's Matisse at eighty-three cutting out his paper collages. I think it is im-portant — the possibility of a man or a woman having kept intact some of the sensibility which some of you, not too long ago, did in fact have, or even continue to have, as over against those senses of, quote, sophis-tication, unquote. I think it is deadly to art.

I have three kids, 14, 12, and 9. What an occasion — WOW — to see what happens in the imaginative life of a human being: like where it comes from, where it's going, and all the things feeding in. My youngest daughter is a real magical child. She is an artist, she instinctively knows that a ball point pen and a piece of paper is the act of transformation. She knows this in a very real way. She knows that language is also an act of transformation ... and she does not call the end product in either case 'poetry' or 'art'... but what she does has the attributes of both.

Do You Attempt to Influence Her?

Leave it alone ... You simply accept several things: that your house is going to be messy and that you provide the things that are necessary. I've given my children tape recorders, cameras, and endless coloured crayons, pencils, paints, piles of paper and clay, and yards of cloth and sewing machines and you name it. That's it. I don't think about it too much. I've never sat down and said, 'Well now let's look at what you've done, you've got four fingers on that hand and five toes on that foot,' or whether the eyes are straight, or whether you've crossed your t's and dotted your i'—I think they'll come to that soon enough without me doing that to them. Incidentally, I don't have much faith in 'education' departments cum pedagogy. I don't know what anyone can teach you that will make you a teacher with the limited senses of the sciences or the arts you will have in three or four years. I don't understand a methodology of communicating that, that thinness of information. I don't think that you can make a teacher out of everybody, though there is that larger non-institutional sense in which 'everyone' is both a teacher and a student in whatever context. I think it is possible to have a gift of communicating ideas and methodology it's just that—how we tell another about something so that information is passed on.

I'd like to find out from you and your friends what you think a thought is. What is this, a thought? What is an idea? Have you ever asked yourself what a thought is? Or a letter is? I don't think it is very useful to assume you know then go on to fabricate a lovely fantasy about it, if in fact you have not asked yourself very basic questions about it. Part of the business of the artist is to ask himself these questions. You make photographs partly to find out what photography is all about. And part of the business of writing a poem is simply to rediscover what a poem is all about. And you do it over and over again because there is no simple answer for anything including a poem. I have obsessively painted a particular kind of ellipse for many years ... and part of that trip has to do with nuances, ramifications, qualities of elliptical forms. Yes, that's a large part of it, for me. You cannot do a painting without wanting to find out what, in fact, it is. A lot of things like that happen in contemporary science and philosophy. Do you know Ludwig Wittgenstein? And what he was trying to do in philosophy? He did not get around to creating a comprehensive picture of the universe because he could not get beyond asking himself, what is philosophy. We all know that there is no simple answer to that. That old bogey 'progress' has nothing to do with starting with A-B-C and then going on to write say a sonnet. If you wipe progress out of your mind you can understand how it is possible to write a sonnet and continue to be fascinated by A-B-C's all of your life.

George Braque spent fifty years painting pots and pans, little knives and white clay pipes — all that domestic stuff. He never took any of it for granted. And I've spent over forty years using the twenty-six letters of the alphabet and find it an inexhaustible source of vivacity. I am not about to take the language for granted, particularly when I write a poem. You keep your dictionary beside you, you have your etemylogical (sic) dictionary and your other books, source books, you're involved in the texture, the whole study of the language ... ya, you're interested in all of it. I don't think you can write poems without a sense of the roots of words. You simply don't get the resonance across unless you are aware of the changes words do go through. Have you ever spent ten hours say on a given occasion reading the dictionary — what a mine of incredible human, imaginative, information. Picasso, one time, was included in one of those very large expensive art books that include half a dozen other masters, in their environment. He was photographed in his studio and in his garden and as he took a walk and as he sat and ate and as he stood proudly beside a huge stack of so called priceless canvases and he was also asked if he would like to contribute a preface to his part of that book and Pablo got out a pencil and a sheet of paper and scrawled all twenty-six letters plus a few numerals and other marks and then he cut out each letter, numeral and mark and put it all into an envelope with a note that read, here are the letters of the alphabet , why don't you use them to write a preface for me ... I don't have time. Kind of witty, or perhaps opting out, but it makes a point in terms of what I've been saying.

What do you think of Rock and Roll? What do the Lyrics of Bob Dylan or Leonard Cohen or Gordon Lightfoot say to you?

I'm sure that most of you have listened to them more frequently that you have listened to poetry. Why isn't Bob Dylan taught in a grad English seminar? Why isn't his work examined, as say Robert Frost's work is. Isn't the fact of all you and perhaps twenty million others who know his songs by heart a factor?

On Zappa

I think he is incredibly inventive. He is an artist and has done as much as anybody can: he has changed the way we hear sounds and changed them in such a way that any young musician coming along will have to know the Zappa-sounds as part of his vocabulary of sounds, out of which he will himself grow. No man can do more than that. Zappa is one of those musicians who can make my ears wiggle!

I think that the line between high and pop culture is as thin as this curtain wall. It might be useful to talk about high culture, in the senses of it that are the backbone of the humanities at any university... it might be, but, let's talk about popcult, that other thing out there that's making all the noise. You can day or night see it on your telly or hear it on your radio or see it again in larger format whenever you go to the movies ... and it has its own folk heroes, its own mythology and is inseparable from whatever sense we have of ourselves. A few days before coming here I went to hear Ornette Coleman at The Cellar. He is one of the big guns, someone who puts a buzz in your ear that you can't forget—ya, that is what is meant to be an artist.

Some of the young people I know in Vancouver have decided that the only context in which they can become a poet, musician, or painter is to be in the world where it is all happening. They have not gone to the universities or conservatories or art schools to study because the intellectual milieu they belong to enables them to learn from each other and their peers. And all of this occurs where the poem and the music and the painting are alive, 'they' are being made. And they know the people who make it. Out of this menage these young people piece together bit by bit the information they need to make what they will. This way of learning is like a collage rather than any lineal rational approach.

For myself the collage is the how of what we do with information, today. We collage information ... we can't make those lovely rational constructs of it because of its plenitude, its sheer collaborativeness. We take this, we take that, and we lay all together ... and that kind of organization has been insistent at least since the early nineteenth century.

Concerning The Flowers Mentioned At The Beginning Which In Fact Are David Samila's Paintings

David perhaps started with small drawings. He would do many of them. Then at some time he would decide upon one or several of them, as a basis for a painting or paintings. He might at this point go a step further in drawing by enlarging the small drawings so that they were the size they would be as a painting. After transferring the drawing to a piece of plywood the size the painting is to be he would cut along all the indicated lines with a Skilsaw. The separate pieces would look like pieces from a giant jigsaw puzzle. The next step would be covering all the separate pieces with canvas, taking care that the canvas be taut and properly stapled down at the back of each piece. While doing this David could be thinking about colours. Then he would paint each piece and perhaps re-paint it several times until he felt right about it and all the other pieces and their colours. After all that he would put it together. It is only then that you will see what is, in fact, in front of you now. My description will of course leave a great deal out but it will give you as sense of 'how' David may have done them.

The 'why' and 'what' of it I will leave to you.

What Kind Of Subjects Are You Interested In?

All kinds. My philosophy leads me to believe in 'the challenge of' the homely aspects of everyday life. I am interested in the commonplace world and all the commonplace things in it. I'm as interested in the space-s between us, the spaces our arms and legs make as I am interested in the fact of your head and all its varied features. If you're a sculptor you're always thinking about form, 3D form and how it articulates space. And if you are a poet you're interested in talking, about words, out there in the air or flat out on the page ... it's all part of a configuration—I'm interested, of course, in configurations; for instance the deep blue carpet beneath us makes the space between all of us more insistent than say any grey carpet could. That blue does give the spaces between us an insistence it would not otherwise have—and that's worth looking at. Wondering about.

I've found that you simply can't make any 'thing' if you try to account for who it is likely to appeal to. I don't think it is one of the factors involved. It's certainly not one of my concerns and as far as I can see, the only thing that can be made is money ... and we all know the shit that is sold in the name of what they think we oughta have. I can't account for the circumstances in which you may happen to see one of my paintings, or read one of my poems—I simply can't account for that. I should imagine though that your response is as much your responsibility, as the fact of my having made it, with, equal responsibility. I don't really care if you do or don't like my show. I will listen to you if you want to tell me why, but that, all that, is after the fact of, making it. And I can't account for that, simply can't deal with it.

This interview was conducted in 1970 by Sheila Watson at the University of Alberta. The responses were taped and transcribed by Stephen Scobie and Douglas Barbour and were edited for the first issue of White Pelican *by Roy Kiyooka.*

Biographic Chronology
—Roy Kenzie Kiyooka

Early Family Life

Roy Kenzie Kiyooka was born January 18, 1926 in Moose Jaw, Saskatchewan, Canada to Harry Shigekiyo Kiyooka and Mary Kiyoshi Kiyooka (né Oe). He was one of seven children: George, Mariko, Roy, Harry, Joyce, Frank and Irene. Mary Kiyoshi Kiyooka came to Canada from Japan in 1917 to join her husband Harry Shigekiyo Kiyooka (Kiyooka, *Mothertalk*, 1). The Kiyookas' oldest child, George, was born in Victoria, British Columbia. Mariko was born in Kochi after Mary returned for a family visit. Mary remained in Japan for two years after which time she reluctantly left George and Mariko with her extended family to return to Canada. George lived in Umagi with his father's family (29). Mariko lived in Kochi with her mother's family (67) until she was six years old and was taken to live with her father's family in Umagi (114). George was able to return to Canada at 13 years old (116), but Mariko remained behind during and after the war, eventually coming to Canada to join her family as an adult (116).

A few years after Roy's birth, the family moved to Calgary, Alberta. In the early 30s they ran a vegetable stand across from the old City Hall (118). They remained in Calgary for over a decade: establishing a home, secure employment and schooling for the children. The Kiyooka family lived in the working-class neighbourhood of Victoria Park.

In the years leading up to WWII, systemic racism and racist government policies directed at Japanese Canadians made for difficult living conditions. On December 7, 1941, a military strike on Pearl Harbor by the Imperial Japanese Navy Air Service killed 2,403 Americans (2,335 military personal and 68 civilians). At this time, Canada declared war on Japan and implemented The War Measures Act, Order-in-Council P.C. 9591. This required registration with the Registrar of Enemy Aliens for all Japanese nationals and citizens naturalized after 1922 with a deadline of February 7th. ("Japanese Canadian History" n.p.)

Beginning February 26th, the Canadian government began a campaign of mass evacuation of Japanese Canadians from a 100–mile-wide zone along the coast of British Columbia including the confiscation of property and belongings. By November 1942, over 21,000 individuals had been interned in road camps, internment camps and prisoner of war camps. Property was liquidated without consent and the money used by the government to fund the camps.

The evacuation and internment campaign was not implemented within Alberta-based Japanese communities. However, owing to widespread racism towards issei and nisei populations, Roy's father, Harry Shigekiyo Kiyooka was dismissed from his job at a hotel. In 1942, the Kiyooka family moved to a subsistence farm in the small town of Opal, Alberta (Kiyooka, *Mothertalk*, 1). Roy and his family were also fingerprinted and registered by the RCMP. Roy had to abandon his education at 15. He never returned to high school.

Opal was northeast of Edmonton and had about a dozen homes and three grain elevators. The Kiyooka family moved to a one-room log house (without water or electricity) until Roy's father was able to buy a quarter section farm. Once there, Roy and his father built a two-room log house. Harry Shigekiyo Kiyooka was employed as a logging camp cook. In addition to working on the farm, Roy worked a number of manual labour jobs to assist in supporting the family including working as a fish processor in Great Slave Lake, Northwest Territories.

Roy Kiyooka, Chronology and Career Trajectory

1946–49

Returns to Calgary to attend the Provincial Institute of Technology and Art where he studies with Jock Macdonald and Illingworth Kerr.

1949–50

Lives in Toronto for nine months. Paints.

1950

Wins the O'Keefe Award for Painters Under Thirty.
Moves to Calgary.
Begins teaching at Coste House while working as window trimmer and sign painter at Hudson's Bay.

1951

His work is featured in the National Gallery of Canada's Biennale.

1953–55

Obtains full-time teaching at the Institute of Technology and Art in Calgary.

1954

His painting *Pastoral* wins the Calgary Golden Prize.

1955

Exhibitions in Calgary, Edmonton, Winnipeg, Ottawa and Toronto.
Marries Monica Dealtry Barker, architect.
Wins a scholarship to the Institute Allende in San Miguel de Allende, Mexico. The couple moved there together. He studies under James Pinto.

1956–1960

Obtains full-time teaching at the Regina College of Art. His daughters, Mariko and Fumiko, are born in Regina.

Participates in 5–6 major exhibitions a year in galleries, museums and
 touring exhibitions throughout Canada. During this time, he teaches
 summer school classes at Emma Lake preceding the celebrated Emma
 Lake Workshops and participates in the Workshops themselves.
 Sponsored by the University of Saskatchewan, he and Art McKay
 suggest that New York artist Barnett Newman lead a workshop on
 abstract expressionism.

1958

His work is featured in the Walker Biennial exhibition at the Minneapolis Art Gallery.

1960

Obtains a teaching position at the Vancouver Art School (now the
 Emily Carr University of Art and Design). His daughter Kiyo is born
 in Vancouver.

1963

Travels to Japan where he reunites with his sister, Mariko. Visits the family
 farm in Kochi-ken Shikoku (Kiyooka, *Roy Kiyooka, 25 Years*, n.p.).
 Attends the Vancouver Poetry Conference.

1964

Kyoto Airs is published by Periwinkle Press (printed by Takao Tanabe
 who also designed the book).
 He is awarded the Senior Art Fellowship from the Canada Council.

1960-1964

He participates in 6–7 major exhibitions a year in galleries, museums
 throughout Canada in addition to his participation in the Northwest Annual at the Seattle Art Museum in 1961, 1962 and 1963.

1965

Moves to Montreal with the family to teach at Sir George Williams
 University (now Concordia University) where he teaches until 1970.

Represents Canada at the Eighth São Paulo Biennial and received the
   Silver Medal.
His hard-edge paintings are featured at Galerie de Siècle, where Quebec's
   most celebrated contemporary painters are represented. He is ex-
   hibited annually as part of their roster of artists for the next 4 years.
Solo exhibition at Grippi-Waddell, New York.
Made a member of the Royal Canadian Academy of Arts

1966

Roy Kiyooka and Vicki Tansey's dance / performance art piece at Sir
   George Williams is part of Montreal's first "happening."

1967

"NeverthelessTheseEyes, For Stanley Spencer" is published by Coach
   House Press.
Begins work on cedar laminate sculptures.

1968

His work is featured in a group exhibition entitled *Seven Montreal
   Painters, Molinari, Barbeau, Tousignant, Goguen, Kiyooka, Hur-
   tubise, Juneau* that was featured at the Washington Gallery of
   Modern Art and the Hayden Gallery at M.I.T. Boston.

1965-1969

He participates in 7–8 major exhibitions a year in galleries, museums
   throughout Canada and the United States including in San Francisco and New York.

1969

He moves away from painting to pursue a variety of other media including photography and sculpture.
He is awarded a commission to build a sculpture for the Canadian
   pavilion at Expo '70 in Osaka, Japan. He produces "Abu Ben Adam's
   Vinyl Dream." Onsite for the installation in Osaka, he takes photographs of discarded workers' gloves. These images later evolve

into a large series of photographs and a book of poetry entitled *StoneDGloves: Alms for Soft Palms.*

He returns to Vancouver and continues work on cedar laminate sculptures.

1970

StoneDGloves: Alms for Soft Palms is published by Coach House Press. The work is exhibited by the National Gallery of Canada in Ottawa as a touring exhibition that travels to fourteen cities from 1970–1.

He is represented by Bau Xi Gallery from 1970–1983 and has a solo exhibition in Vancouver in November 1970.

He teaches briefly at the University of Calgary. Here he makes *Ottoman/ Court Suite* (a series of silkscreen prints).

He is one of 15 West Coast Canadian artist / photographers involved in *bc almanac(h) cb* which is co-produced by Michael de Courcy and Jack Dale for the National Film Board. (de Courcy, n.p.).

bc almanac(h) cb is shown at the Vancouver Art Gallery, the Edmonton Art Gallery and the Museum of Modern Art, New York.

1971

Solo Exhibition at Bau Xi Gallery, Vancouver from May 18–June 12 entitled: "16 Cedar Laminates."

He begins to move away from work as a studio artist choosing to focus on work of a more time-based and improvisatory nature.

artscanada/afloat, a collaborative, site-specific performance is documented through photography and a collaged version is submitted to *artscanada* as a letter to the editor. It is published in August / September 1971. The work is captioned, "COPACIFIC, wash—out—there."

He is hired to be head of the painting department at NSCAD (Nova Scotia College of Art and Design). He remains there for one year. This time is well documented in *Transcanada Letters* (Talonbooks, 1975).

While at NSCAD he organizes the Vancouver/Halifax Exchange (March 6 to March 11, 1972). 11 Vancouver artists are invited to

Halifax to present art, performance, poetry and film. Events take place at NSCAD, Dalhousie and other venues along with a series of panel discussions. Halifax artists travel to Vancouver where they are hosted in simultaneous events at the Vancouver Art Gallery.

1972

StoneDGloves: alms for soft palms is featured in an exhibition at Centre Culturel Canadien, Paris.

"letters purporting to be abt tom thomson" is published in the February / March 1972 issue of *artscanada* as a letter to the editor Anne Brodzky. It will eventually become the basis for his novel, *The Artist and the Moose: A Fable of Forget.*

1973

He is hired to teach at the University of British Columbia. He remains in this position until his retirement in 1991.

He is invited to exhibit at the Kyoto Museum of Modern Art as part of "Japanese Artists of the Americas."

1974

He is invited to exhibit at the Tokyo Museum of Modern Art, as part of "Japanese Artists of the Americas."

Artscanada/afloat is published as an entire issue of *BC Monthly* in January 1974. From this project, he produces 125 gelatin silver prints. The work is purchased by The National Gallery of Canada in 2000. The Morris and Helen Belkin Gallery also owns prints from this work.

1975

Transcanada Letters is published by Talonbooks. It includes many of Roy Kiyooka's letters written between October 1966 and February 1975. It also includes a brief summary of works made during this time and where they are located.

The Vancouver Art Gallery hosts a major retrospective exhibition of his work entitled "Roy K. Kiyooka: 25 Years." It travels to University

of Calgary Art Gallery, Windsor Art Gallery and the Robert
McLaughlin Gallery.

1977

The Fontainebleau Dream Machine: 18 frames from a book of rhetoric
is published by Coach House Press.

1978

He is named an Officer of the Order of Canada in recognition of his
painting and teaching.

Kiyooka and de Courcy co-produce an updated version of the *bc
almanac(h) cb* project, collaborating on the initial proposal for the
National Film Board stills division for the west coast photographic
exhibition/collective publishing-initiative which will ultimately
become *13 cameras/vancouver*. This is a collaborative project
(conversation with Michael de Courcy, 2018).

An exhibition of *13 cameras/vancouver* is hosted at Vancouver Art
Gallery and the exhibition catalogue is published by the National
Film Board. Dates in the catalogue read "Oct. 77/ April 79."

1979

13 cameras/vancouver is featured in an exhibition at the National Film
Board of Canada, Ottawa.

1980s

Kiyooka hosts events, exhibitions and performances at "Blue Mule,"
his gallery/studio on Powell Street. He self-publishes over 10 chapbooks during this time.

He begins meeting New Music composer Don Druick weekly for an
"apprenticeship" in music/sound. He is not interested in learning
musical skills or tuning, rather he wants to focus on improvisation
and experimental sound by playing his zither and recording each
session.

1981

Trip to Kohama, Okinawa, Japan. He begins learning to improvise on the jamisen.

1982

Wheels, a trip thru Honshu's Backcountry (manuscript version) is published by Coach House Press.

Solo Exhibition at University of Toronto Scarborough Art Gallery (now Doris McCarthy Gallery). Vicki Tansey performs.

1983

60–day trip to Japan (8 cities). His mother travels with him for the first half of the trip.

Music improvisation and recording continues. Begins to collaborate with Howard Broomfield and Trudi Rubenfeld.

1984

Two month trip to Japan (4 cities).

1985

Solo Exhibition at Richmond Art Gallery entitled *In/Around/My Japan: A Canadian-Japanese Artist's Color Prints taken between 1969–1984*

Performance with Howard Broomfield and Trudi Rubenfeld at Coburg Gallery.

Trip to Japan, 4 cities.

Weekly collaborative improvisation at Blue Mule Gallery with Rhoda Rosenfeld and Maxine Gadd.

1986

Trip to Japan (Kochi City).

1987

Pear Tree Pomes illustrated by David Bolduc is published by Coach House Press and short-listed for a Governor General's Literary Award.

1989

His work is included in the group exhibition *The Flat Side of Landscape; Emma Lake Artists' Workshops* at the Mendel Art Gallery.

1990

Solo Exhibition at Artspeak Gallery and Or Gallery.
Pacific Windows is published in *Capilano Review*.

1990-91

His work is part of a touring exhibition entitled *The Yellow Peril Reconsidered* featured at Galerie Saw, Contemporary Art Gallery (Vancouver), Eye Level Gallery, Plug-In Inc., Gallery 44, and Oboro.

1991

He retires from University of British Columbia.

1992

Solo Exhibition at the University of British Columbia Fine Arts Gallery.
His work is included in the group exhibition *The Crisis of Abstraction in Canada* at The National Gallery of Canada.

1993

Bypass surgery.

1994

On January 4, 1994, Roy passes away at his Keefer Street home in Vancouver, British Columbia.

Works Cited

Canadian Writers, Faculty of Humanities & Social Sciences at Athabasca University, Roy Kiyooka. http://canadianwriters.athabascau.ca/english/writers/rkiyooka/rkiyooka.php Accessed October 10th, 2017.

de Courcy, Michael. Email Correspondence with Juliana Pivato, July 2018.

Kiyooka, Fumiko. *The Bulletin: A Journal of Japanese Canadian community, history + culture*. Remembering Roy Kiyooka: 1926–1994, http://jccabulletin-geppo.ca/remembering-roy-kiyooka-1926–1994/, accessed March 4th, 2018.

Kiyooka, Kiyo. Email correspondence with the author, August 10, 2018.

Kiyooka, Roy. *Mothertalk*, edited by Daphne Marlatt, NeWest Press, 1997.

---. *Pacific Rim Letters*, edited by Smaro Kamboureli, NeWest Press, 2005.

---. *Roy K. Kiyooka: 25 Years*. Vancouver Art Gallery, 1975.

Marlatt, Daphne. "Roy Kiyooka: From Eminence to Immanence." *West Coast Line*, 38.3, Winter, 2005, 39–47.

The National Association of Japanese Canadians. Japanese Canadian History, http://najc.ca/japanese-canadian-history/, accessed April 29th, 2018.

O'Brian, John, Naomi Sawada and Scott Watson, editors. *All Amazed for Roy Kiyooka*, Arsenal Pulp / Morris & Helen Belkin Art Gallery / Collapse, 2002.

Sava, Sharla. "Roy Kiyooka: photographing the local from the inside out," *C Magazine*, 60, Nov 1998–Jan 1999, 26–32.

Selected Bibliography
—Roy Kenzie Kiyooka

Publications:

Kiyooka, Roy. *The eye in the landscape: photo/graphs of the point, Hornby Island*. National Film Board of Canada, 1970.

----. *The Fontainebleau Dream Machine*. Coach House Press, 1977.

----. *Kyoto Airs*. Periwinkle Press, 1964.

----. *Nevertheless These Eyes*. Coach House Press, 1967.

----. *Pear Tree Pomes*. Coach House Press, 1987.

----. *Roy Kiyooka*. Edited by William Wood, Artspeak Gallery / Or Gallery, 1991.

----. *Roy K. Kiyooka: 25 Years*. Vancouver Art Gallery, 1975.

----. *StoneDGloves*. Coach House Press, 1970.

----. *Transcanada Letters*, Talonbooks, 1975 (reissued in 2005, edited by Smaro Kamboureli).

----. *Wheels* (manuscript edition). Coach House Press, 1982

Posthumous Publications:

----. *The Artist and the Moose: A Fable of Forget*. Edited by Roy Miki, LINEbooks, 2009.

----. *December/February '87 '88 Roy K. Kiyooka*. Illustrated by David Bolduc, Coach House Press, 1995.

----. *Mothertalk*: *Life Stories of Mary Kiyoshi Kiyooka*. Edited by Daphne Marlatt, NeWest Press, 1997.

----. *Pacific Rim Letters*. Edited by Smaro Kamboureli, NeWest Press, 2005.

----. *Pacific Windows: Collected Poems of Roy K. Kiyooka*. Edited by Roy Miki, Talonbooks, 1997.

----. *Transcanada Letters*. Edited by Smaro Kamboureli, NeWest Press, 2005.

Self-Published / Chapbooks:

----. *A February Postscript to OCTOBER'S PIEBALD SKIES & Other Lacunae/s*. February-March, 1989.

----. *All Amazed in the Runnels of His 60 Winters*, January, 1987.

----. *An April Fool Divertimento*. June, 1986.

----. *G O T E N Y A M A: A Sequel to Kyoto Airs*. December, 1985.

----. *a june skylark for kai's birthday air*. May, 1987.

----. *The Long Autumn Scroll*, (mid-1980s).

----. *MARCH: PROSE: WORK/S: A Concatenation of Pacific Rim Vernacular/s*

----. *OCTOBER'S PIEBALD SKIES & Other Lacunae/s*. September-October, 1988.

----. *Struck from the Heat of a Cold December Sun*. December, 1983.

----. *Three Nippon Weathervanes: Kumo/Cloud/s, Toksuka Topiaries, Kohama Skies*. (mid-to-late-1980s)

----. *Wheels: A Father & Son Trip Through Honshu's Backcountry*, w/ Photographs. July, 1985.

Collaborative projects:

Kiyooka, Roy and Michael de Courcy. *13 Cameras*, National Film Board of Canada, 1979.

----."artscanada/afloat" *BC Monthly*, January, 1974, Vol. 2, Issue 1, Web.

----."COPACIFIC, wash-out-there." *Artscanada*, no. 158–9, August / September 1971, 72.

Illustrations:

Bowering, George, *The Man in Yellow Boots / El Hombre de Las Botas*. Illustrated by Roy Kiyooka, Mexico Ediciones El Corno Emplumado, 1965.

Livesay, Dorothy, *The Unquiet Bed*. Illustrated by Roy Kiyooka, Ryerson Press, 1967.

Other Published Work, Magazines & Periodicals:

----. "the 4th avenue poems." *Imago*, edited by George Bowering, 1.1, Talonbooks, 1969, 3–18.

----. "The Fontainebleau Dream Machine." *The Long Poem Anthology*, edited by Michael Ondaatje, Coach House Press, 1979.

----. "From Roy Kiyooka." *White Pelican* 1.1, 1971, 35–40.

----. "from *The Artist and the Moose: A Fable of Forget*." *Dandelion* 29.1, 2003, 127–139.

----. "letters purporting to be abt tom thomson." *artscanada*, 164–5, Feb / Mar 1972, 25–34.

----. "Mutualities: A Packet of Word/s." *Vanguard*, October 1977, 11–13.

----. "Notes Toward a Book of Photoglyphs." *The Capilano Review*, 2.2, Spring 1990, 76–94.

----. "of seasonal pleasures and small hindrances." *BC Monthly*, November 1978, np.

----. "Pacific Windows." *Capilano Review* 2.3, Fall 1990, np.

----. "[The Women Say What I Like]." *boundary 2*, 3.1, A Canadian Issue, Duke University Press, Autumn 1974, 121.

----. "Two excerpts from *Wheels*." *Paper Doors*, edited Gerry Shikatani and David Aylward, Coach House Press, 1982, 89–102.

----. "We Asian North Americanos: An unhistorical 'take' on growing up yellow in a white world." *West Coast Line*, 24.3, Winter 1990, 116–18.

----. "*Wheels* (a journey in process)." *Descant*, 12.1–2, 1984, 25–50.

Special Issues:

"A Celebration of Roy Kiyooka." *Brick: A Literary Journal*, 48, 1994, 13–33.

(This one is for Roy Kiyooka and Warren Tallman) *West Coast Line*, 16.29/9, Spring/Summer 1995, 7–28.

"The O Issue." *Dandelion*, 29.1, 2003.

Books on Roy Kiyooka:

O'Brian, John, Naomi Sawada and Scott Watson, editors. *All Amazed for Roy Kiyooka*, Arsenal Pulp / Morris & Helen Belkin Art Gallery / Collapse, 2002.

Essays and Interviews on Roy Kiyooka:

Barbour, Douglas. "Roy Kiyooka: Writing the 'trans' in *transcanada letters*." *West Coast Line: A Journal of Contemporary Writing and Criticism*, edited by Roy Miki, 29.1, 1995, 11–23.

Barnholden, Michael. "Under the Logos of the Blue Mule: Self Publishing the Serial Poems of Roy Kiyooka." *Dandelion* 29.1, 2003, 171–177.

Bök, Christian. "Oneiromechanics: Notes on the Dream Machines of Roy Kiyooka." *West Coast Line,* 29.1, 1995, 24–28.

Butling, Pauline. "Poetry and Landscape, More than Meets the Eye: Roy Kiyooka, Frank Davey, Daphne Marlatt, and George Bowering." *Writing in Our Time: Canada's Radical Poetries in English (1957–2003).* Eds. Pauline Butling and Susan Rudy. Wilfrid Laurier University Press, 2005. 89–101.

Chivers, Sally. "'This is my memory, a fact': The Many Mediations of *Mothertalk: Life Stories of Mary Kiyoshi Kiyooka.*"*Auto/Biography in Canada: Critical Directions.* Ed. Julie Rak. Wilfrid Lauirer University Press, 2005. 69–88.

Danyluk, Paul. "'everything wants to hang together': Re-imagining Roy Kiyooka's Academic Subjectivities." in *Retooling the Humanities: The Culture of Research in Canadian Universities.* Eds. David Coleman & Smaro Kamboureli. Edmonton: University of Alberta Press, 2011

Dragland, Stan. "The Fire That Breaks from Thee Then." *West Coast Line,* 29.1, 1995, 7–10.

Egan, Susanna, and Gabriele Helms. "The Many Tongues of *Mothertalk: Life Stories of Mary Kiyoshi Kiyooka*." *Canadian Literature* 163, 1999, 47–79.

Fisher, Susan. "Japanese Elements in the Poetry of Roy Kiyooka and Fred Wah." *Canadian Literature* 163, 1999, 93–110.

Fong, Deanna. The Roy Kiyooka Audio Assemblage. *The Capilano Review blog, The Capilano Review.* https://www.thecapilanoreview.ca/roy-kiyooka-audio-assemblage/

Gilbert, Gerry. "Laughter: Five Conversations with Roy Kiyooka." *artscanada,* 32.4, no. 202/203, Winter 1975–76, 11–21.

Goellnicht, Donald C. "Asian-Canadian, Eh?" *Canadian Literature*, no. 199, 2008, pp. 71–99.

Halebski, Judy. "Japanese Elements in Contemporary North American Poetry as seen through Roy Kiyooka's *Pear Tree Pomes*." *Dandelion*, 29.1, 2003, 70–80.

Kim, Christie. "Ephemeral Publics and Roy Kiyooka's *StoneDGloves*." in *The Minor Intimacies of Race: Asian Publics in North America*. University of Illinois Press, 2016.

Kiyooka, Fumiko. "Remembering Roy Kiyooka: 1926–1994." *The Bulletin: A Journal of Japanese Canadian Community, History and Culture*. Feb. 7, 2014.

Kiyooka, Fumiko. "Inner Passage: roy kiyooka." *The Canadian Literary Society of Japan*, 21, 2013, 15–31.

Kröller, Eva-Marie. "Roy Kiyooka's 'The Fontainebleau Dream Machine': A Reading." *Canadian Literature*, 113–114, 1987, 47–58.

Lee, Tara. "Representing the Body in Roy Kiyooka's *Kyoto Airs*." *Dandelion*, 29.1, 2003, 142–161.

Lowry, Glen. "Roy Kiyooka's *Transcanada Letters*: Re: Reading a Poet's Prose." *West Coast Line*, 36.2, Fall 2002, 16–34.

Marlatt, Daphne et al. "A Celebration of Roy Kiyooka." *Brick, a literary journal*, 48, 1994, 13–34.

Marlatt, Daphne. "Roy Kiyooka: From Eminence to Immanence." *West Coast Line*, 38.3, Winter 2005, 39–47.

McFarlane, Scott Toguri. "'Kiyooka' and the Desert of Living in General." *Dandelion*, 29.1, 2003, 14–31.

Miki, Roy. "Can I See Your ID?: Writing in the 'Race' Codes That Bind." *West Coast Line*, 31.24, Winter 1997, 85–94.

Miki, Roy. "English with an 'i': Imagining Japan in the Poetry of Roy K. Kiyooka." *The Canadian Literary Society of Japan*, 21, 2013, 3–13.

Miki, Roy. "Inter-Face: Roy Kiyooka's Writing, A Commentary/Interview." *Broken Entries: Race, Subjectivity, Writing*. Mercury, 1998. 54–74.

Miki, Roy. "Roy Kiyooka: An Interview." *Inalienable Rice: A Chinese and Japanese Canadian Anthology*. Powell Street Revue and the Chinese Canadian Writers Workshop, 1979. 58–64. https://issuu.com/ricepaper/docs/inalienable_rice_compiled

Miki, Roy. "Roy Kiyooka." *Dream Elevators: Interviews with Canadian Poets*. Ed. Beverley Daurio. The Mercury Press, 2000, 73–85.

MillAr, Jay. "Portraits of Kiyooka." *Dandelion*, 29.1, 2003, 65–68. Print.

Moruzi, Kristine. "Re/Turning Home: Renegotiating Identity in *Wheels*." *Dandelion*, 29.1, 2003, 40–55.

Morton, Stephen. "Multiculturalism and the Formation of a Diasporic Counterpublic in Roy K. Kiyooka's StoneDGloves." *Canadian Literature* 201, Summer, 2009, 89–109.

Mount, David. " Mr. Kiyooka, That Dangerous Supplement: Picture Brides, Photographs and Misrepresentation in *Mothertalk*." *Dandelion*, 29.1, 2003, 164–7.

Munton, Ann. "The Long Poem as Poetic Diary." *Proceedings of the Long-liners Conference on the Canadian Long Poem: Open Letter* 6th. S, 2–3, Summer-Fall, 1985, 93–116.

Saul, Joanne. "Ghost Selves: The (Auto)biographical Voices of *Mothertalk*." *a/b: Auto/Biography Studies*, 17.2, Winter 2002, 221–244.

Sava, Sharla. "Roy Kiyooka: photographing the local from the inside out." *C Magazine*, 60, Nov 1998–Jan 1999, 26–32.

Wah, Fred. "PEARAGRAPHS: On Roy Kiyooka's *Pear Tree Pomes*." *Capilano Review* Series, 2.2, Spring 1990, 95–97.

Wah, Fred. "Is a Door a Word?" *Mosaic: An Interdisciplinary Critical Journal*, 37.4 Dec. 2004, 39–70.

Watson, Sheila, "Interview with Pierre Coupey, Roy Kiyooka and Daphne Marlatt." *The Capilano Review*, 8.9, Fall 1975 - Spring 1976, 351–60.

Watson, Sheila. "With Roy Kiyooka." *White Pelican*, 1.1, 1971, pp. 18–35.

Watson, Wilfred. "Born in Moosejaw: The Letters of Roy Kiyooka." *NeWest Review*, 1, 10 May 1976, p. 8.

Woo, Mandy, "Doing the Ottawa Pretzel: Form and Language in Roy K. Kiyooka's *The Artist and the Moose*." *West Coast Line*, 44.3, Fall 2010, 40–43.

Books featuring content on Roy Kiyooka:

Dobson, Kit. *Transnational Canadas: Anglo-Canadian Literature and Globalization*. Wilfrid Laurier University Press, 2009.

Kamboureli, Smaro. *Making a Difference: Canadian Multicultural Literatures in English*. Oxford University Press, 2007.

Miki, Roy. *In Flux: Transnational Signs of Asian Canadian Writing*. NeWest Press, 2011.

Saul, Joanne. *Writing the Roaming Subject: The Biotext in Canadian Literature*. University of Toronto Press, 2006.

Films on Roy Kiyooka:

de Courcy, Michael. Roy Kiyooka VOICE, 1998, 39.39min.

Kiyooka, Fumiko, *Reed: The Life and Works of Roy Kiyooka,* 2012, 94 min.

Contributors

Veronica J. Austen is an Associate Professor specializing in Canadian and Post-colonial literatures at St. Jerome's University (within the University of Waterloo). She came to the study of Roy Kiyooka when she encountered *Pear Tree Pomes* in a Canadian Poetry course in her first term of her M.A. and has been looking at his work on and off ever since then. Her current research explores how the visual arts are represented by or incorporated into contemporary Canadian literature as a means of exploring experiences of racialization.

Deanna Fong is a poet and scholar who shares her time between Vancouver and Montreal. Her doctoral studies in English at Simon Fraser University focused on the intersections of event theory, auditory media, literary communities, and affective labour. She is a member of the federally funded SpokenWeb team, who have developed a web-based archive of digitized sound recordings for literary study (http://spokenweb.concordia.ca) and the Poetry Okanagan Sound Archive at the University of British Columbia (Okangan campus). With Ryan Fitzpatrick and Janey Dodd, she co-directs the audio/multimedia archive of Canadian poet Fred Wah (http://fredwah.ca), and has done substantial cataloguing and critical work on the audio archives of Roy Kiyooka. She is the author of *Butcher's Block* (Pistol, 2008) and her critical work has most recently appeared in *Amodern*, *Digital Humanities Quarterly*, and *The Capilano Review*.

Max Karpinski is a doctoral candidate in the English Department at the University of Toronto, where he holds a Joseph-Armand Bombardier Canada Graduate Scholarship. His dissertation analyzes contemporary Canadian poetry that redeploys the pastoral mode to probe the connections between the degradation of the environment, the unequal relationships between land, labour, and profit, and the ongoing enclosures and appropriations that define settler colonialism. He has previous publications in *Canadian Literature* and *Lemon Hound*.

Marisa Lewis is a PhD student at the University of Ottawa. Much of her research explores Canadian cultural memory, civic identities, and processes of colonialism. Her doctoral research examines what the formation of transnational solidarities between Canada and other nation states reveals about conceptions of citizenship, anti-racism and ethical engagement.

Roy Miki grew up in Winnipeg and moved to Vancouver in the late 1960s. He is the author of many books, including *Redress: Inside the Japanese Canadian Call for Justice* (Raincoast 2004) and *In Flux: Transnational Shifts in Asian Canadian Writing* (NeWest 2011), an essay collection, as well as five books of poems. His third book of poems, *Surrender* (Mercury Press 2001), received the Governor General's Award for Poetry. He has also co-written, with his wife Slavia, a children's book, *Dolphin SOS* (Tradewind Books 2014), awarded the 2014 BC Book Prize for best illustrated children's book. As a Kiyooka scholar, he edited *Pacific Windows: The Collected Poetry of Roy K. Kiyooka* (Talon, 1997), which received the Poetry Award from the Association of Asian American Studies, and Kiyooka's posthumously published work on Tom Thomson, *The Artist and the Moose: A Fable of Forget* (LINEbooks 2009).

Juliana Pivato is a visual artist, improviser and educator. She has training in theatre and degrees in music and visual arts, obtaining her MFA in Studio (Sculpture) from School of the Art Institute of Chicago in 2009. Solo exhibitions include MacLaren Art Centre and Division

Gallery along with group exhibitions in Canada, the United States, Japan and Italy, where her work is featured in a number of private collections. She has been awarded project funding from the Canada Council for the Arts, the Ontario Arts Council, FQRSC and SSHRC. Since 2012 she has been a lecturer in the Department of Arts, Culture and Media at the University of Toronto Scarborough. *Pictura: Essays on the Work of Roy Kiyooka* is her first edited collection.

Tavleen Purewal works on Canadian literature and women and critical race studies in the Doctoral Program of the Department of English at University of Toronto. Her dissertation explores Black Canadian writing and the inscriptions of land, Indigenous lands, and of encounters with Indigenous subjects in order to uncover the entangled affects between Black diasporic and Indigenous realities on Turtle Island. She has written and presented on Dionne Brand, Lee Maracle, Zora Neale Hurston, Leanne Simpson, M NourbeSe Philip, and on pedagogy and pedagogical strategies. Her non-academic work practices community-building with various groups who seep into the academic sphere and inflect her methodologies and interpretive practices. She gains much from her kinships with #blacklivesmatter-TO, Indigenous resistance camps against pipelines and logging in BC, and Fat Panic! Vancouver-Coast Salish Territories.

Felicity Tayler writes about print culture and contemporary art, and has an artistic and curatorial practice. She holds a PhD in Interdisciplinary Humanities from Concordia University, and a Masters in Library and Information Studies from McGill University. She is the author of the bilingual, *Petit Gris/Grey Guide to Artist-Run Publishing and Circulation* (ARCA, 2017); has been published in several anthologies; and in journals including the *Journal of Canadian Art History, International Journal on Digital Libraries, Printmaking Today, Esse art + opinions*, and *C Magazine*.

Sheila Watson (1909–1998) was a writer, editor and professor of English at the University of Alberta (1961–1975). She completed her doctoral studies at the University of Toronto under the direction of Marshall McLuhan. Her dissertation *Wyndham Lewis and Expressionism* was completed in 1965. She is best known for her novel, *The Double Hook* (1959). It was celebrated as a literary classic and all 3000 copies of the first print run sold out. In 2015, Guernica Editions published *Sheila Watson: Essays on Her Works*, as part of their Essential Writers Series, edited by Joseph Pivato.

Jason Wiens is a Senior Instructor in the Department of English at the University of Calgary. His teaching and research interests focus on contemporary Canadian literature, with a secondary interest in nineteenth-century British and Canadian literatures. His publications include essays on Margaret Avison, Dionne Brand, George Bowering, Sharon Pollock, Robert Kroetsch, and the Kootenay School of Writing. His work on Kiyooka for this volume is part of a larger project looking at the poetics of the archive in Canadian poetry since the 1960s.

Sergiy Yakovenko completed his PhD in Comparative Literature at the University of Alberta. He also holds a Candidate of Philology degree from the Institute of Literature at the National Academy of Sciences of Ukraine. He currently teaches in the Department of English at MacEwan University. His research interests include Canadian literature, English literature, Slavic literatures, and literary theory. He has published on Sheila Watson, Howard O'Hagan, and Charles G. D. Roberts. He also is an author of two comparative monographs (in Ukrainian) on Polish and Ukrainian prose fiction of the twentieth century and modernist literary criticism.

Acknowledgements

This book would not have been possible without the assistance and support of many. I am grateful to the generous authors who have contributed to this book. I would like to thank the estate of Roy Kiyooka for permission to publish the images in this book and Kiyo Kiyooka, Mariko Kiyooka and Fumiko Kiyooka for their support of this project. I am grateful for the research assistance that I received from librarians and archivists who met my many questions with such kind support. Thank you to University of Toronto Scarborough librarians Frank Tong, Chad Crichton and Sarah Fedko as well as John Shoesmith at the Thomas Fisher Rare Book Library and Simon Rogers, Archivist at the John M. Kelly Library. I would also like to thank Tony Power for responding to my numerous emails about the Roy Kiyooka Fonds in Bennett Library Special Collections at Simon Fraser University. Thank you to Veronica Austen for researching images on my behalf while visiting the collection. Since beginning the project, I made a number of inquiries to many people directly or indirectly involved with Roy Kiyooka's work. Among these there were a number of galleries and museums. I would like to acknowledge the assistance of Brian Meehan at Museum London, Catriona Jeffries, Kristy Waller at Western Front, Kyle Besuschko at Bau Xi, Vancouver, and Shaunna Moore, Archivist at the Morris and Helen Belkin Art Gallery. Thank you all for your help and your interest in the project.

To my friend and mentor, Thérèse Mastroiacovo, I am grateful for your generosity, and for discussing your work with me and allowing me to take a few small liberties in my interpretation. Amanda Boetzkes, your insight and time on topics that were well out of my comfort zone were crucial to my sanity. Thank you Johanne Sloan for your excellent suggestions and encouragement. Thank you to Michael de Courcy for your detailed responses to my many questions and thank you again for the use of your striking photograph of Roy Kiyooka for the cover of this book.

Lastly I must extend my gratitude for the editorial assistance that I received for this project (official and unofficial). To Michael Mirolla at Guernica, thank you for your support of this project. To David Cecchetto, thank you for your crucial check of the introduction. As usual, your comments were perfectly timed. To Emma Pivato, I offer a lifetime of thanks for nudging me along, and this also extends to Joseph Pivato, who offered an ideal quantity of support and gentle advice for this project over the last 2 years. My gratitude to Tymea Sarkozy, Anna Hostman, Dara Weiss, Jess Abramson and Tanya Mars for reminding me to be kind to myself inside the whirlwind of life-work balance. To my partner Marc Couroux, I am so fortunate to have your eyes and thoughts on all things tricky. Thank you for the numerous late-night edits of my introduction and your incredible support throughout this project. Also, you were right. No, really. And to my son Xeno and my daughter Anonyme, thank you for your staggering inspiration.

The following texts were previously published:
Felicity Tayler's "Serial Positions: Roy K. Kiyooka's 'Conceptual Art Trips'" was previously published in the *Journal of Canadian Art History / Annales d'histoire de l'art Canadien*, Vol. 36, No. 1 (2015), pp. 129–153 and is republished here with permission.

"With Roy Kiyooka," was previously published in *White Pelican* 1.1 (Winter 1971).

Image List

Cover:

Roy K. Kiyooka, 13 Cameras/Vancouver meeting, The Blue Mule Studio/ Gallery, Powell St., 1978, Photograph by Michael de Courcy.

Deanna Fong:

"No. 5 North Takahashis Pomes / 8 The Kids in Banff." Image appears courtesy of the Estate of Roy Kiyooka and Simon Fraser University Special Collections. Photo by Deanna Fong."

Felicity Tayler:

1. Wrap-around cover of Roy K. Kiyooka, Transcanada Letters. Talonbooks, 1975, 28 × 22 cm, closed; 28 × 46 cm, open. With permission of Kiyo Kiyooka. (Photo: author)
2. Double-page spread from Roy K. Kiyooka, StoneDGloves. Coach House Press, 1970, n.p., 23 × 34 cm. With permission of Kiyo Kiyooka. (Photo: author)
3. "Opal, Alberta: Early '40s," from Roy K. Kiyooka, Transcanada Letters. Talonbooks, 1975, n.p. With permission of Kiyo Kiyooka. (Photo: author)
4. Pages 2 and 3 of the 18–page photoseries, Long Beach BC to Peggy's Cove Nova Scotia (1971), from Roy K. Kiyooka, Transcanada Letters. Talonbooks, 1975, n.p., 28 × 46 cm. With permission of Kiyo Kiyooka. (Photo: author)

5. Detail from the photoseries, Long Beach BC to Peggy's Cove Nova Scotia (1971), from Roy K. Kiyooka, Transcanada Letters. Talonbooks, 1975. With permission of Kiyo Kiyooka. (Photo: author)

6. "Halifax /Vancouver Exchange," from Roy K. Kiyooka, Transcanada Letters. Talonbooks, 1975, n.p., 28 × 22 cm. With permission of Kiyo Kiyooka. (Photo: author)

Veronica Austen:

1. Image is from Roy K. Kiyooka, "Pacific Windows." *Capilano Review* 2–3, Fall 1990, np. Image reproduced with permission of Kiyo Kiyooka. (Photo: author)

2. Image is from Roy K. Kiyooka, "Pacific Windows." *Capilano Review* 2–3, Fall 1990, np. Image reproduced with permission of Kiyo Kiyooka. (Photo: author)

Endnotes

1   This interview, conducted by Sheila Watson, appeared in the inaugural issue of *White Pelican* 1.1 (Winter 1971).

2   The Glossary of Poetic Terms defines ekphrasis as a vivid description of a scene or, more commonly, a work of art.

3   A paradox that refers to an individual travelling back in time, and killing his/her grandfather before their mother or father are conceived, preventing the time traveller from being born.

4   Sheila Watson conducted her PhD research at U of T on the work of Wyndham Lewis, an English writer, painter and critic. Marshall McLuhan was her supervisor. This sensitivity to interdisciplinary practice is evident in the questions that were asked. These questions were later edited into title headings for each section of the text. As such, she entirely erased herself from the interview as a presence. This information was confirmed in an email exchange on September 26, 2016, between the Essential Writer Series editor and Douglas Barbour, co-editor of White Pelican.

5   "Laughter: Five Conversations with Roy Kiyooka," *artscanada,* 1975, is quoted frequently in this text. The article, edited by Gerry Gilbert, includes five separate, edited conversations between Kiyooka and five colleagues and friends: Alvin Balkind, (Gladys) Maria Hindmarch, Taki Bluesinger, Jock Hearn and Carole Itter. The article was edited by Gerry Gilbert.

6   I use the term filtration to describe the way in which mediation of content shifts the variable of legibility between disciplinary forms.

7   Recordings are housed in the Roy Kiyooka Fonds, Special Collections, Simon Fraser University. Although much of this material is not accessible, some has been digitized by Deanna Fong for *SpokenWeb*, a web-based archive of digitized audio recordings. See: https://spokenweb.ca/

8   Both the National Gallery of Canada and Morris and Helen Belkin Art Gallery at the University of British Columbia have *artscanada / afloat* in their collections.

9   In the online archive of *The Capilano Review*, in the Spring 1974, 1.5 issue, Gerry Gilbert, the editor of *B.C. Monthly* is listed as being reachable at "Canadas National Magazine, Box 8884, Station H, Vancouver 5. "Boycott the Postal Code." (https://www.thecapilanoreview.ca/issues/issue-1–5/).

10   *BC Monthly*, January, 1974, Vol. 2, Issue 1.

11   The caption in *BC Monthly* reads: "This issue of The British Columbia Monthly (Volume 2, Number 1) is edited by Roy Kiyooka and is part of his exhibition of these photographs at the BFA Faculty show, UBC Fine Arts Gallery, Vancouver, January 1974."

12   Michael de Courcy, who collaborated with Kiyooka on *13 Cameras / Vancouver* (1979) offers some perspective on the "intermedia-style artist-collaboration" projects that were so common in Vancouver in the 1960s and 70s: "it can be a challenge to sort out the genesis of such projects. The traditional notion of single authorship for a work-of-art was often suspended (challenged) in favour of the notion of collaborative art-working/making with an all-for-one and one-for-all attitude." He also states that "an acknowledgement of the lack-of-definition regarding specific authorship and intention in projects such as *artscanada / afloat* and also *13 Cameras / Vancouver* provides important context to our understanding of these works" (de Courcy, n.p.).

13   At the time of this publication, a version of *artscanada / afloat* was accessible in a digital republication of *BC Monthly* 1:1 1974 hosted by *Independent Voices*, https://voices.revealdigital.com/

14   On the Western Front webpage, Filliou's *Teaching & Learning as Performing Arts, Part II* (1979) is listed as: a) *Video Dinner*, b) *Four-*

Dimensional Space Time Continuum, c) *Recycling*, d) *Sky Analysis*, e) *Bedtime Her/His Story*; footnotes.

2. *Travelling Light—It's a Dance Really.*

3. *Video Breakfasting Together, If you Wish.*

4. *Footnote to Footnote A, Video Breakfasting with Roy Kiyooka.*

In the Morris and Helen Belkin catalogue it is listed as 5 videos totaling a little over 60 minutes, with Filliou's *Video Breakfasting Together, if you wish* ... and Kiyooka's response listed as the last two videos in the series. It is produced by Kate Craig with "guest appearances by Glenn Lewis, Taki Bluesinger, Marianne Filliou, Marcelline Filliou, Roy Kiyooka" (Filliou et al, 91).

15 *Robert Filliou: From political to poetical economy* (1995) the Morris and Helen Belkin Art Gallery catalogue that accompanied an exhibition of Filliou's video works, describes *Teaching & Learning as Performing Arts, Part II* as a supplement and update to Filliou's 1970 book, *Teaching & Learning as Performing Arts* (Filliou et al, 91).

16 For this and additional works by Robert Filliou filmed at Western Front, please refer to https://front.bc.ca/events/teaching-and-learning-as-performing-arts-part-ii/.

17 These works among others were uploaded to the VIMEO video-sharing platform in 2012 by the Western Front Archive. At the time of this publication, the video was readily accessible on the Western Front Website as an embedded Vimeo link: https://front.bc.ca/events/teaching-and-learning-as-performing-arts-part-ii/.

18 In an email exchange between myself and Western Front's archivist on May 12, 2017, it was clarified that not much information is available for Kiyooka's video beyond a contract and some edits for a catalogue write-up that is not in the file.

19 Issei is the term for an individual born in Japan who has immigrated to North America. Nisei is the term for an individual born in the US or Canada with parents who were born in Japan and immigrated to the US or Canada.

20 Kiyooka addressed his family's treatment by the RCMP in his letter, ("Dear Lucy Fumi, published in West Coast Line, 24:3, Winter, 1990, p 125–6, Print. A summary of the labour jobs Kiyooka performed

prior to his career as artist and teacher can be found in "With Roy Kiyooka," the last chapter of this book, under the section: CAN YOU LIVE OFF ART AND OTHER MATTERS.

21 *Hello Fellow Artists,* Optica, Montreal, 2002.

22 A brief description of the work for context: In *Hello Fellow Artists,* we view Wegman's video playing on a monitor by way of a video recording of the monitor made by Mastroiacovo. Wegman's hand holds a stick as he states: "Wow what a neat stick. Boy is it crooked. Well that's nothing you oughta see my finger." Replaced by a bent finger we hear: "Wow neat finger. Boy is that crooked. Well that's nothing you oughta see my stick." Mastroiacovo inserts herself by tilting the handicam, rendering a now crooked monitor and voicing "Wow" in unison with Wegman who repeats the performance. Tilting the handicam again, on Wegman's third iteration, her unison "wow" is followed by the handicam falling and a Mastroiacovo's "shoot!" ending the segment.

23 This excerpt from "October's Piebald Skies & Other Lacunae," is taken from the original, self-published chapbook that Kiyooka distributed among friends and colleagues. A revised version of the poem with considerable changes appears in *Pacific Windows,* Roy Miki, ed. 1997.

24 Additional works reflecting Kiyooka's movement between media and degrees of participation, though not readily accessible in existing catalogues, are among those listed in Canadian gallery exhibitions including: Walter Philips Gallery, Banff; Scarborough College (now UTSC) gallery which is now known as the Doris McCarthy Gallery. Catriona Jeffries also represented the artist (by way of the estate of Roy kiyooka) for a few years beginning in 1996 (Jeffries, n.p.).

25 Although the term sediment (sedimentation) is of geological origin, it is employed here as metaphor. Tavleen Purewal uses the term throughout her text to describe the complexity of factors (implicit rules in language, taken-for-granted institutional structures, social conditioning) that can underpin dynamics, relations or actions.

26 Published by Talonbooks in 1975 and republished by NeWest Press in 2005.

27 The exhibition, Accidental Tourist, was at the Walter Phillips Gallery in Banff, Alberta, 2003–2004.

28 Daphné Marlatt and Roy Kiyooka lived together from 1974 to 1982.

29 Many of Kiyooka's letters were published in two separate volumes three decades apart: *Transcanada Letters* (1975/2005) and *Pacific Rim Letters* (2005). However, a bulk of his unpublished letters are housed in Simon Fraser University Library's Special Collections.

30 404 recordings made between 1963 and 1991 are archived in Simon Fraser University Library's Special Collections.

31 Frye's conclusion for *The Literary History of Canada* (1965) offers a narrative of the economic, political and historical issues that underline what he describes as "Canadian sensibility." His "garrison mentality" theory, read by many critics as suggesting a context of ambivalence towards *Indigenous populations* is a frequent reference for discussions on the development of Canadian literature in the 1950s and 60s.

32 Sedimentation: please see endnote 24.

33 Please see endnote 20 for the definitions of these terms.

34 This chapter builds upon, and is in dialogue with, my recent chapter on the Kiyooka archive in *Un/Archiving the Literary Event: CanLit across Media* (McGill-Queens, 2018). My contribution to that volume examines the practice of sound recording from an ontological standpoint, asking what auditory media can tell us about live situations and acts of recording as events in their own right.

35 As Roy Miki explains in "Unravelling Roy Kiyooka: A Re-assessment Amidst Shifting Boundaries" (*Arsenal Pulp Press*, 2002), this relation is one of simultaneous inclusion and exclusion. The majority depends upon the illusory construction of an other that it imagines as outside of it, a position which it needs to affirm its own boundaries and sense of coherency. Miki talks about Kiyooka's liminal Japanese Canadian identity as "athwarted"—in Kiyooka's words, to grow up "athwarted" by mainstream white culture means that "[y]ou are of it and, and you are not of it, and you know that very clearly" (qtd. Miki 72). The position of being neither inside nor outside is, in this sense, a "double-edged" phenomenon: it at once exposes the ideologically constructed boundaries that delineate the centre, but also the gaps, fissures and contradictions that must be disavowed and contained in order to maintain the centre's coherency.

36 A tape recording of this talk was presented 17 May 1961 at a conference of the Group for Research on Everyday Life convened by Henri Lefebvre in the Center of Sociological Studies of the CNRS. Debord was interested in the way that the technology of the tape recorder could intervene in the structured space of the conference by drawing attention to its normally invisible social conventions. In his words, "It is thus desirable to demonstrate, by a slight alteration of the usual procedures, that everyday life is right here. These words are being communicated by way of a tape recorder, not, of course, in order to illustrate the integration of technology into this everyday life on the margin of the technological world, but in order to seize the simplest opportunity to break with the appearance of pseudo-collaboration, of artificial dialogue, established between the lecturer 'in person' and his spectator" (1).

37 Exhibition organized by the Vancouver Art Gallery.—Itinerary: 21 Nov.-16 Dec. 1975, Vancouver Art Gallery; Jan. 1976, University of Calgary; 20 Feb.-28 Mar. 1976, Art Gallery of Windsor; Apr. 1976, Robert McLaughlin Art Gallery (Oshawa).

38 There is substantial crossover between the content of the *artscanada* piece and *Laughter*, and both contain versions of Gerry Gilbert's introduction to the material, which suggests that these two artifacts are instantiations of the same project.

39 See, for example, Scott WATSON and Dieter ROELSTRAETE, eds., *Intertidal: Vancouver Art and Artists* (Vancouver: Morris and Helen Belkin Gallery; Antwerp: Museum van Hedendaagse Kunst Antwerpen, 2005) or Reid SHIER, "Vancouver," in *Art Cities of the Future: 21st Century Avant-Gardes* (London: Phaidon, 2013), 297–319.

40 Roy Kiyooka is credited with the design of the book alongside his publisher, David Robinson. Like Coach House Books in Toronto, Talonbooks was known for its unusually close engagement with writers and artists in matters of book design.

41 Eve Meltzer's term, "aesthetics of information" describes a variant of conceptualism in which the rational processes implied by a systems-based approach are disrupted by the fluidity of emotional states and embodied forms, this will be further elaborated below with regards to *Transcanada Letters*. Eve MELTZER, *Systems We Have Loved: Conceptual*

Art, Affect, and the Anti-Humanist Turn (Chicago: University Of Chicago Press, 2013), 8–25.

42   The exhibition *Roy K. Kiyooka: 25 Years* was organized by the Vancouver Art Gallery, showing there from 21 November—16 December 1975; January 1976 at t he University of Calgary; 20 February—28 March 1975 at the Art Gallery of Windsor; and April 1976 at the Robert McLaughlin Art Gallery (Oshawa).

43   For a reading of Newman's painting as an "ideograph of Creation," See Hal FOSTER et al., *Art Since 1900: Modernism, Antimodernism, Postmodernism*, 2nd ed., vol. 2 (London: Thames and Hudson, 2014), 403. John O'Brian explores the significance of Newman further in his discussion of Kiyooka's *Hoarfrost* series; see John O'BRIAN, "White Paint, Hoarfrost, and the Cold Shoulder of Neglect," in *Roy Kiyooka* (Vancouver: Artspeak, Or Gallery, 1991), 19–25.

44   See, for instance, Roy MIKI, ed., "Coruscations, Plangencies and the Sybillant: After Words to Roy Kiyooka's Pacific Windows," in *Pacific Windows* (Vancouver: Talonbooks, 1997), 315–16.

45   I was not able to confirm the date of this event, but Itter remembers it took place before the 1963 Poetry Conference. Telephone interview with Carole Itter, 10 July 2014.

46   A press release lists Roy Kiyooka as part of the organizing committee for the 5th Festival of Contemporary Arts (1965), *The Medium is the Message*. Collection of the Morris and Helen Belkin Art Gallery Archives, Belkin Art Gallery Fonds, 13.4–5.12. Accessed 14 Oct. 2014, http://vancouverartinthesixties.com/archive/19.

47   Sontag ends her 1964 essay, "Against Interpretation," with this phrase. My reading of Sontag is further indebted to the work of Craig J. Peariso, "The "Counterculture' in Quotation Marks: Sontag and Marcuse on the Work of Revolution," in *The Scandal of Susan Sontag* (New York: Columbia University Press, 2009), 155, 169 n. 19.

48   Quoted here is the phrase used in Patrizia Di Bello and Shamoon Zamir's introduction to *The Photobook From Talbot to Ruscha and Beyond*, 6. See also Matthew S. WITTKOVSKY's discussion of Ruscha's appropriation of the "subgenres of literature such as the paperback" in *Light Years*, 18. Johanna DRUCKER goes so far as to lament

this tendency as an art historical "cliché" in *The Century of Artists' Books,* II.

49   Jim Brown and David Robinson have explicitly linked the founding of *Talon* magazine and Talonbooks to the aesthetic and social environment surrounding Intermedia and the Vancouver Art Gallery. Both are interviewed in Kathleen SCHERF, "A Legacy of Canadian Cultural Tradition and the Small Press: The Case of Talonbooks," *Studies in Canadian Literature* 25:1 (2000): 131–49.

50   I was unable to access a production docket that would confirm details such as print run, price per unit, or distribution points. Correspondence between Karl Seigler (Talonbooks) and Roy Kiyooka regarding royalties for *Transcanada Letters* show that 384 copies were sold in 1976, and sales steadily declined in subsequent years. Roy Kiyooka Fonds, MSC 32.7.3 Kiyooka Correspondence, Talonbooks. Contemporary Literature Collection, Simon Fraser University, Vancouver, B.C.

51   Roy KIYOOKA, *Transcanada Letters,* ed. Smaro Kamboureli (Waterloo, ON: New West Press, 2005), 370–77. Scott Toguri McFarland notes a similar shift in aesthetics when *StoneDGloves* was anthologized in *Pacific Windows,* see "Un-Ravelling StoneDGloves' and the Haunt of Hibakusha," in *All Amazed For Roy Kiyooka,* eds. John O'Brian, Naomi Sawada, and Scott Watson (Vancouver: Arsenal Pulp Press, 2002), 119.

52   A list of "publications" in the exhibition catalogue accompanying *Transcanada Letters* includes his contribution of images and text to art magazines such as *artscanada* or *Studio International* as well as literary magazines such as *BC Monthly* or *Imago. Roy K. Kiyooka: 25 Years* (Vancouver Art Gallery, 1975).

53   Kiyooka represented Canada at Expo '70; it was while he installed the large-scale industrial sculpture, *Abu Ben Adam's Vinyl Dream,* that he took the series of photographs for *StoneDGloves.* The title is shared between the bookwork and a series of photographs circulating as a travelling show organized by the National Gallery of Canada's Extension Services from August 1970 to January 1972. The photographs ranged from 30 × 40 in. to 60 × 40 in. and were installed on the floor, walls, and ceilings of a gallery as an environment. The bookwork

replaced the standard monographic catalogue that usually accompanied an exhibition organized by the National Gallery of Canada.

54 The dedication page of *Transcanada Letters*, states that is was "begun as a book for the G.S.W.S. in Halifax N.S. Sept. 71." The acronym, which stands for the *Georgia Straight Writing Series*, attests to conflicted ties in the period between writers associated with *Tish* magazine and the newspaper. In 1970, the *Supplement* began issuing books as the Georgia Straight Writing Series (GSWS). Following a split from the *Georgia Straight* in 1972 (which also formed *The Grape* and the "York Street Commune"), the GSWS continued to publish under the imprint Vancouver Community Press.

55 See for instance, Jörg HEISER and Ellen SEIFERMANN, *Romantic Conceptualism* (Wien: Kerber, 2007).

56 *Long Beach BC to Peggy's Cove Nova Scotia*, 1971 (567 silver gelatin prints, 41.5 × 551.25 in. overall) is part of the collection of the Vancouver Art Gallery; however, Kiyooka's decision to reproduce and circulate the work as an integral part of *Transcanada Letters* signals that as a serial medium, the photographic prints exist across multiple places at once: in the institutional gallery space and the mass culture form of the book.

57 Due to changes in travel plans, the exchanges between cities took place at the same time. This meant that contrary to Kiyooka's intentions for the artists to be exposed to each other and to their conflicting forms of conceptualism, the participants were not able to meet in person. Telephone interview with Carole Itter, 10 July 2014.

58 Vancouver visitors included: Cheryl Druick (now Sourkes), Don Druick, Zoe Druick (their young child), Gathie Falk, Carole Fisher (now Itter), Gerry Gilbert, Garry Lee-Nova, Glenn Lewis, Michael Morris, Vincent Trasov, Dallas Sellman, and Dave Rimmer, alongside other Halifax participants. Halifax residents in the group are Bruce Parsons, Toby MacLennan, Alistair MacLennan, Peter Zimmer, Anita Martin, David Martin, Ellison Robertson, Ian Murray, Doug Waterman, and Charlotte Townsend.

59 Glenn Lewis presented a performance at the New Food Restaurant in SoHo, 19 March 1972. A photo-essay chronicling the trip to Halifax

and New York is published as "National News" in *FILE* 1 (April 1972): 6–7.

60   See Fred Wah's description of proprioceptive writing in Fred WAH, "Introduction," in *Net Work Selected Writing*, ed. Daphne Marlatt (Vancouver: Talonbooks, 1980), 15–19.

61   Sheryl Conkelton in "Roy Kiyooka: '... the Sad and Glad Tidings of the Floating World ...'" discusses "Pacific Windows" briefly amidst her survey of Kiyooka's photographic expression. Scott Toguri MacFarlane in "'Kiyooka' and the Desert of Living in General" discusses "Pacific Windows" similarly in passing as part of his discussion of the spectral aspects of Kiyooka's poetry.

62   As Roy Miki, the editor of *Pacific Windows*, explains "Space limits did not allow for the inclusion of this accomplished work—but the text, which so richly informs the whole of *Pacific Windows*, became the inevitable moment to close this collection" ("Afterword" 314).

63   A slash mark will indicate a page break.

64   In a published conversation with Jock Hearn, Kiyooka announces his philosophy of art: "If it doesn't in some way astonish you in what it reveals of and through itself, then you haven't made a painting. You have simply copied some tracing that you are already familiar with in your mind" (Gilbert 15).

65   The full passage from the original version of "October's Piebald Skies & Other Lacunae" as it appears in excerpt in "A Celebration of Roy Kiyooka" reads, "... don't ask <u>me</u> how it really felt to be <u>finger-printed</u> and duly registered as an <u>enemy alien</u> . ask—if you can locate him, that, dumbfound, yellow kid . ask his <u>mother</u>" (n. pag.); the revised version in *Pacific Windows* alters the punctuation and concludes with "Ask his imperturbable mother" (281), but I confess I prefer the starkness of the original conclusion.

66   Miki frames this coming together as "open[ing] the spaces 'in between' where the principle of transience and chance is regained" ("Afterword" 316).

67   Although Miki does reference Wah's ideas about the hyphen, he does not overtly connect his choice of the descriptor "pivot" to Wah's descriptions of the swinging door.

68   These images are recognizable as part of Kiyooka's series *Powell Street Promenade* (1978–80). See Ian Rae's *From Cohen to Carson: The Poet's Novel in Canda* for a brief description and analysis of this photographic series (27).

69   The face is readable as Kiyooka's or as one of his brothers, but since the image is somewhat abstracted, I hesitate to identify a subject.

70   Elizabeth S. Anker and Rita Felski's *Critique and Postcritique* includes a number of essays that shape a critical archive for the development of "postcritique," itself a response to the emergent sense that "the intellectual or political payoff of interrogating, demystifiying, and defamiliarizing is no longer quite so self-evident" (Anker and Felski 1). Heather Love, for example, locates Eve Kosofsky Sedgwick's "reparative reading" as having "had the greatest impact in the field," and as a precursor to "Sharon Marcus's just reading, Stephen Best and Sharon Marcus's surface reading, Cannon Schmitt's literal reading, and Timothy Bewes's reading with the grain" (69 n5). Defining postcritique in the negative, Christopher Castiglia triangulates Paul Ricoeur's hermeneutics of suspicion, Sedgwick's paranoid reading, and Best and Marcus's symptomatic reading to articulate that which postcritique defines itself against: "the assumption that texts conceal beneath their surface an abstract agency, sinister and ubiquitous, to be unearthed by the astute and usually indignant critics" (211).

71   I read a resonance between Harney and Moten's pairing of abolition and construction and Castiglia's contribution to *Critique and Postcritique*, which argues for a critical *"hopefulness,"* defined as a "combination of critique and imaginative idealism" (216). Castiglia's project, in part, seeks to reorient the "disposition" of critique, from "mistrust, indignation, ungenerosity, and self-congratulation" (214). As he asserts, "critique and hopefulness are not mutually exclusive. They are profoundly intertwined in any genuinely activist impulse" (216–217).

72   The town of Forget, Saskatchewan is a real place; however, as Miki notes, it is "named after Amédée E. Forget, the first Lieutenant Governor of Saskatchewan, 1905–1910" ("Afterword" 165). On a first reading, Kiyooka's choice for the narrator's hometown operates as a pointed gesture to the centralist nationalism of the centennial period, which

posits Ontario as the root of Canadian culture while ignoring or "for-getting" the rest of the country. Miki's note, however, extends this gesture into the text's very form or language: "how are we, as readers, to pronounce ... *Forget*: as the English *forget* or as the French *forget*[?]" (165). That is, in its playful oscillation between English and French, the individual sign "Forget" recapitulates the text's concern with major and minor, or centre and periphery.

73   In a later text, and writing again about Kiyooka's term "athwarted," Miki draws a connection to Fred Wah's notion of the "hyphen": "The site of this poetics ["Half-Breed Poetics"] for me, and many other multi-racial and multi-cultural writers, is the hyphen, that marked (or unmarked) space that both binds and divides" (Wah, *Faking It* 72; see also Miki, "Unravelling" 72).

74   While Kamboureli doesn't explicitly note the connection, I read a sunk-en reference to Len Findlay's famous exhortation to "Always Indi-genize!" in her gesture to the protagonist's work of sabotage. In his essay, published in 2000, Findlay seeks to mobilize the term "con-spiracy," divesting it of valences that index "silence, secrecy, violence, and hate" (373). Rather, "conspiracy" designates an "Indigenously led, strategic interdisciplinarity" (371) that operates as a tactical subversion of the dominant Eurocentrism of the Canadian academy. Kamboureli names the protagonist "saboteur" precisely in response to his decision to sign "his name (in Cree) on the bottom of the line of the official Document that gave him back his freedom" (Kiyooka, *Artist* 102; qtd. in Kamboureli 26).

75   I want to dwell briefly on the appearance of "appropriation" in *The Artist and the Moose*, in part because the text's unique history of pro-duction throws into relief the literary, cultural, and social debates that, in my reading, inform the emergence of a politically conscious "poetics of appropriation" in the past twenty-five years. As mentioned, Kiyooka rewrote *The Artist and the Moose* intermittently throughout his life. Particularly in the late-1980s and early 1990s, "appropriation" becomes a central topic of discussion in Canadian literary studies. In 1988, at the Third International Women's Book Fair in Montreal, Lee Maracle addressed non-Indigenous writers and academics, urging them to

"move over"; grievances over the appropriation of racialized voices and the concomitant marginalization of Indigenous and writers of colour led to the formation of the Racial Minority Writers' Committee in 1990, as well as conferences such as "The Appropriate Voice" (1992) and "Writing Thru Race" (1994), among others. In light of this shift in public discourse towards the end of Kiyooka's life, it is possible to read the "appropriation" called for by Ol' Moose as a particularly pointed response to the dominant, white Canadian literary culture's diminishing or outright silencing of racialized writers.

76   Miki opens his "Afterword" to *The Artist and the Moose* with a playful comparison of the "rhythmical linkage" and "structural symmetry" in the letters that make up the names "Tom Thomson" and "Roy Kiyooka" (135). He muses: "Could he, Roy Kiyooka, be another version of the emblematic artist, Tom Thomson?" (136). It's clear that Kiyooka himself welcomes this kind of winking gesture. In light of *StoneDGloves*, one such moment of playful equivalence between Thomson/Kiyooka can be located in the claim, attributed to "Iris Earwig," that "Tom could find beauty in an old glove lying beside the road" (68).

77   The full text of the nursery rhyme reads:
Hey, diddle, diddle,
The cat and the fiddle,
The cow jumped over the moon;
The little dog laughed
To see such sport,
And the dish ran away with the spoon.

Without reading too deeply, it might be worthwhile to consider the rhyme's imagination of the emotional or affective lives of the non-human characters it represents, alongside the myriad non-human characters that appear and act upon the protagonist's quest in *The Artist and the Moose*.

78   Kiyooka's protagonist often quotes in the sections of the novel that are presented as pages from his "*Notebook.*" In some cases, these quotations come with citations; for example, the paragraph immediately preceding the quotation about Socrates is cited as "*(Schweitzer, 1925)* (Legend, Myth, and Magic in the Image of the Artist *20–21)*" (30). The

uncited passage appears to be a slightly altered version of a statement from Rudolf Arnhein's *Visual Thinking* (1969), 239.

79   This quotation is elsewhere attributed to David Milne, although a number of sources show that Milne's original statement is that Canadians "like our *heavens* made to order" (see, for example, Brown 445 and Thompson and Seager 163). This switch constitutes a major, pointed divergence from the original, one that again places emphasis on the role of the "hero" in Kiyooka's narrative.

80   In a compendium titled "Celebration of Roy Kiyooka," published shortly after his death, Daphne Marlatt remembers "love" as a central component of Kiyooka's various arts practices and links it, intriguingly, to the "common": "against the dominant drift in our culture towards specialization and disintegration, he consistently offered an art that animates what we share in common, and a responsiveness to it that is a form of love" (14).

81   For another example of Kiyooka's complex treatment of non-human characters, we can look to the "tiny bird" that resides in the protagonist's "inner ear" (19). This tiny bird, we learn, "empowered [the protagonist] to peruse the Texts without succumbing to / their authorial Colonial Tropes" (19). How are we to understand or think the tiny bird? Is it a non-human character, a literal bird that nests in the human protagonist's ear, and thus a symbol of the often unseen yet intimate relations between human/non-human? Is the tiny bird a manifestation of the protagonist's internal psyche or unconscious? Or, does the tiny bird function as a physical marker of otherness? Is it precisely this otherness that allows the protagonist to recognize and resist "Authorial Colonial Tropes"?

82   "Remembering Roy Kiyooka: 1926–1994," Story Archive, The Bulletin: A Journal of Japanese Canadian Community, History, and Culture. 7 Feb 2014.

83   Scott Toguri McFarlane, in his "Un-ravelling *StoneDGloves* and the Haunt of the Hibakusha" details the venues at which the exhibition was hosted. Mostly presented in universities, *StoneDGloves* toured Canada between 1970 and 1972, and then premiered in Kyoto, Japan "as part of the Japanese Artists in the Americas exhibition at the National Museum of Modern Art" (McFarlane, note 1).

84 Stephen Morton observes a similar dichotomy of representation in *StoneDGloves*, but he contextualizes his analysis in the terms of the counterpublic, wherein the artist inhabits a withdrawn (subaltern) space that also forms part of the resistance; in "Multiculturalism and the Formation of a Diasporic Counterpublic in Roy K. Kiyooka's *StoneDGloves*" (Canadian Literature no. 201 (Summer, 2009): 89–109), 200.

85 Smaro Kamboureli, "Introduction." *Critical Collaborations: Indigeneity, Diaspora, and Ecology in Canadian Literary Studies*; Roy Miki "Interface: Roy Kiyooka's Writing, A Commentary/Interview."

86 86 E. Brian Titley, "Forget, Amédée-Emmanuel," *Dictionary of Canadian Biography*.

87 I switch to "Relation" only momentarily to evoke Edouard Glissant's work, *The Poetics of Relation*, for its ground-breaking theorization of relation as the mode and object of study. Other terminological overlaps include "ethical bonds" (Butler) and "epistemologies of respect" (Lai).

88 Kamboureli (ed), *Pacific Rim Letters*, 26; letter to Victor Levy-Beaulieu.

89 Malissa Phung, "Are People of Colour Settlers Too?" (*Cultivating Canada: Reconciliation through the Lens of Cultural Diversity*), 294.

90 See: Malissa Phung, "Are People of Colour Settlers Too?" and Lee Maracle, "Oratory on Oratory"; Maracle's inverse perspective is one of implicating white settlers as diasporans—a whole shift in semantics and methodology that does similar work to Phung and Lawrence and Dua that discusses settlers and diasporans as participants within a settler-colonial system.

91 Eve Sedgwick, "Tales of the Avunculate: Queer Tutelage in *The Importance of Being Earnest*," (*Tendences*, Durham & London: Duke University Press, 1993), 60.

92 See: Lee Edelman, "Queer Theory: Unstating Desire" and Sara Ensor, "Spinster Ecology: Rachel Carson, Sarah Orne Jewett, and Nonreproductive Futurity."

93 A further analysis might take into account the possibility that all these women are white. What is the place, then, for white women in racialized and male-centred kinships? How do they differ in the depiction of whiteness from Tom Aplomb?

94 To explore the discordance between the two epistemologies, see also:

Katherine McKittrick, "Worn Out"; Nandita Sharma, "Strategic Anti-Essentialism: Decolonizing Decolonization." Jared Sexton, "The Vel of Slavery: Tracking the Figure of the Unsovereign."

95　This essay was presented at the 31ˢᵗ Annual Conference of the Canadian Literary Society of Japan, in Sapporo, Japan, on June 15, 2013.

96　The significance of this lineage is apparent in Kiyooka's decision to use a "Portrait of my Mother and Grandfather" as the frontispiece for *Transcanada Letters*.

97　All three works are in *Pacific Windows*. Page numbers for citations from these works refer to this book.

98　I say "adult" here because in 1930 Kiyooka as a child, was taken to Japan by his mother, Kiyo Kiyooka. His "relatives were all astonished that [he] could speak both Japanese and English" (Cited in Kamboureli, "Roy Kenzie Kiyooka—A Chronology," in *Pacific Rim Letters* 150).

99　My thanks for Takaomi Eda and Syuzo Fujimoto for providing information that helped me understand both the locale and the circumstances of Kiyooka's poem.

100　It is important to note that although scholarship on *Mothertalk* as well as Marlatt's introduction indicate that Masutani did the recordings, Kiyooka's stated at a reading of the text at the Kooteney School in 1992 that he did the recordings himself, before Masutani's intervention. Whether this is a detail that got lost in the complex collaborative production of *Mothertalk*, or the recordings and the interviews were somewhat combined in Kiyooka's manuscripts, the final version is a "cumulative" text that continues to challenge forms of recollection (Saul *Writing* 83).

101　As mentioned in the introduction of *Mothertalk*, Roy Kiyooka's daughters requested that Marlatt edit Kiyooka's unfinished manuscript after his death in 1994. It was one of Roy Kiyooka's daughters, Fumiko Kiyooka, who suggested that Marlatt incorporates his poems in *Mothertalk*.

102　In their essay "The Many tongues of *Mothertalk: Life Stories of Mary Kiyoshi Kiyooka,*" Susana Egan and Gabrielle Helms examine the text in the context of "serial collaboration," paying attention to the many interwoven authorial voices and choices of *Mothertalk,* and emphasizing both Kiyooka's, his mother's, and Daphne Marlatt's roles in the production of the text.

103 In *Errata,* George Bowering coins the term 'biotext' in his discussion of the autobiographical writing of Michael Ondaatje. The term becomes popular with Fred Wah's use of the term in describing *Diamond Grill* as 'biotext' or 'biofiction.'

104 *StoneDGloves* was originally published in 1970 by Coach House Press. It was revised and included in *Pacific Windows: Collected Poems of Roy K. Kiyooka*, published in 1997 and edited by Roy Miki. All excerpts of *StoneDGloves* in this chapter refer to the version printed in *Pacific Windows.*

105 Because poetry, rather than photographs, is the main focus of the current essay, for references I use *StoneDGloves'* reprint within Kiyooka's *Pacific Windows* collection. As McFarlane testifies, although this edition has fewer photos than the Coach House Press catalogue, the poetry is corrected and completed with the verses missing from the previous edition (119).

106 Kiyooka passed away in 1994, so I occasionally refer to the poems published in *Pacific Windows* as having that date, even though the collection was published in 1997. However, given my argument in this paper, we might see the poems, through Miki's editing, as having an afterlife of sorts.

107 Digitization of the Kiyooka audio, already underway, would allow me to provide a link to the audio file, but to my knowledge this file, while digitized, is not yet available in any digital collection.

108 Joseph Pivato transcribed this interview from the original publication in 2017. During that time he contacted Douglas Barbour in Edmonton. He was informed that the interview had actually been conducted by Sheila Watson in 1970.

109 John Cage was an American composer, theorist and writer. He was one of the first composers to employ indeterminate methods in his concert and electroacoustic music. He came to prominence in the 1950s and 1960s and taught at Black Mountain College, N.C. where the Black Mountain poets were active.

110 bpNichol and Bill Bissett were experimental poets in Vancouver and
    Toronto from the 1960s to 1980s.

111 Kiyooka went to Halifax to teach at the Nova Scotia College of Art
    and Design from 1971–72, after this interview was conducted and
    published.

112 Sir George Williams University in Montreal was the site of a 14–day
    student sit-in that resulted in the destruction of computer equipment in
    the main building on Feb. 11, 1969. Sir George Williams University is
    now Concordia University.

MIX
Paper from
responsible sources
FSC® C100212

Printed in March 2020
by Gauvin Press,
Gatineau, Québec